CULTURAL, STRUCTURAL AND STRATEGIC CHANGE IN MANAGEMENT BUYOUTS

Also by Dean F. Berry
THE POLITICS OF PERSONNEL RESEARCH

Cultural, Structural and Strategic Change in Management Buyouts

Sebastian Green
Professor of Management
University College, Cork
Ireland

and

Dean F. Berry
Senior Vice-President, The MAC Group and
Visiting Professor, The London Business School

Foreword by Michael C. Jensen
Edsel Bryant Ford Professor of Business Administration
Harvard Business School

St. Martin's Press   New York

First published in the United States of America in 1991

Printed in Hong Kong

ISBN 0-312-04615-4

Library of Congress Cataloging-in-Publication Data
Green, Sebastian.
Cultural, structural, and strategic change in management buyouts/
Sebastian Green and Dean F. Berry.
p. cm.
Includes bibliographical references.
ISBN 0-312-04615-4
1. Management buyouts—Great Britain—Case studies.
2. Organizational change—Great Britain—Case studies.
3. Organizational effectiveness—Case studies. I. Berry, Dean F.
II. Title.
HD2746.5.G745 1991
658.1'6—dc20   89-70328
                                                          CIP

Contents

List of Tables

List of Figures

Foreword

The 1980s witnessed major changes in the structure and governance of corporations, first in the United States and then in Great Britain and the Continent. Management buyouts in which managers, often in conjunction with an outside financial and governance partner, take a division or an entire company private have been an important part of this organisational restructuring. Financial and operating data studied by many scholars indicate these organisational changes are, on average, associated with large increases in productivity, cash flow and value, and that the gains do not come at the expense of employees or outstanding bondholders. Palepu (1990) provides a good review of much of this evidence. In the three years after a buyout, cash flow increases by over 90 per cent, capital expenditures fall by 20 per cent relative to the industry, nominal equity value triples, and market adjusted value increases over 90 per cent.

In *Cultural, Structural and Strategic Change in Management Buyouts* Sebastian Green and Dean Berry add considerably to our knowledge of MBOs. Based on discussions with forty managers in ten companies in the period 1985 through 1987, their detailed case histories of six UK management buyouts taking place in the period 1981–3 are illuminating. The cases illustrate many problems of large corporate organisations and the role of MBOs in resolving these problems and achieving organisational change. This work is a refreshing addition to the literature because it pushes behind the primarily financial orientation of prior studies to reveal the social, cultural, behavioural and strategic changes associated with the success of MBOs. Baker and Wruck's (1990) detailed documentation of the contractual and organisational changes accompanying the successful management buyout of O. M. Scott from ITT in 1986 is a rare companion to the Green/Berry analysis. This type of detailed study of the organisational implications of MBOs is required in order for us to tell whether the financial gains reflect real increases in productivity and efficiency, or whether they simply reflect wealth transfers from taxpayers, old bondholders, employees or other contracting parties.

The Green and Berry analysis adds considerably to the growing evidence that the typical large corporate organisation is counter-productive. Their results are consistent with the hypothesis that the corporate headquarters of these organisations reduce efficiency by

(1) stifling initiative through rigid policies that overly constrain the ability of local managers to respond to changes in their business environment, and (2) implementing performance measurement and reward systems that sap motivation and direct the effort of divisional managers to unproductive activities. The result is a substantial increase in the agency costs of the corporate organisation, and a reduction in corporate efficiency, shareholder value, and aggregate living standards.

All of the buyouts studied by Green and Berry were completed in a recessionary period, and all of the parent companies had been experiencing difficulties. Five of the six MBO companies were sold within the first five years, three after experiencing troubles of one kind or another. The ventures were highly profitable for the participants – five of the six deals resulted in large increases in equity value, one appeared to break even, and none declined in value. These results are particularly interesting because all these companies were 'bought out because the parent companies could not make the business work to their satisfaction'. These facts are consistent with the notion that the MBO form of organisation is efficient for industries experiencing decline (and therefore where exit is necessary).

Each of the MBOs had suffered poor performance as a division under the more centralised and constraining influence of corporate headquarters. Green and Berry confirm the importance of decentralised decision-making that occurs with the purchase of freedom from the parent as well as the role played by increased managerial ownership and high debt levels. The authors conclude that the buyouts and resulting separation from the political and social pressures of the parent's corporate environment produce high-commitment organisations that demonstrate major improvements in their social, cultural and behavioural environment. Green and Berry also highlight the difficulties associated with managing these MBO enterprises over time and the pressures that arise from management as well as outside equity holders to realise some of their substantial gains.

The period of major organisational change and experimentation in the United States is in remission. Begining in mid-1989, US financial regulations shifted substantially to inhibit the use of high leverage. This shift was fuelled partly by the controversy over the losses by thrifts (mostly in real estate), a general concern about and antagonism toward leverage, and the intense desire of many chief executives of large American corporations to eliminate the threat from the market for corporate control. The resulting restrictions on banks, thrifts and insurance companies has brought about a credit crisis in which, to a large extent, credit is no longer allocated on the basis of price and risk. The high-yield (junk bond) market has been thrown into disarray, capital has become extremely difficult for small- and medium-size companies to obtain, and credit lines and other lending arrangements have been cancelled or severely reduced.

The flourishing US market in private reorganisations of companies in financial distress (what I have called the privatisation of bankruptcy) has been significantly inhibited by new bank regulations on highly leveraged transactions (HLTs), court decisions and tax laws that impose penalties on private reorganisations outside of bankruptcy court. Drexel Burnham Lambert, a major player in this reorganisation market, and a thorn in the side of the business establishment, has been bankrupted. These factors, coupled with federal tax increases and reduced spending (prior to the Gulf war) have played an important role in bringing on a US recession. These policies have not only reduced the optimal debt-to-equity ratio for all firms, including MBOs, but have also made it difficult for firms to readjust their capital structures to the new environment, a task that had become relatively easy to accomplish prior to the change in regulatory climate. In the current climate highly leveraged organisations that get into difficulty will enter bankruptcy at a much higher rate. Bankruptcy of these organisations formerly was a rare event even though it was not rare for them to become distressed. The experience of UK organisations wil be a useful control sample in determining whether the US MBOs were highly sensitive to slow-downs in business conditions or whether the anti-leverage US regulatory policies (nominally designed to protect against problems in the banking and financial system) became a self-fulfilling prophecy.

I compliment the authors of this study for their very useful analysis of the non-financial aspects of MBO organisations. Many, if not most, of the changes and gains generated by MBOs can be implemented within the traditional corporation. Thus there is much in this book that will interest every business person devoted to improving organisational performance. It takes one more step to dispelling much of the misinformation that the press, public and policy-makers believe is true about MBOs. It is clear, however, that to complete our knowledge of this phenomenon we must develop an understanding of the politics of finance, the ways in which the political sector influences and constrains corporate financial policy and organisations.

MICHAEL C. JENSEN

References

Baker, George P., and Karen H. Wruck (1990) 'Organizational changes and value creation in leveraged buyouts: the case of the O. M. Scott & Sons Company', *Journal of Financial Economics*.
Palepu, Krishna (1990) 'Consequences of leveraged buyouts', *Journal of Financial Economics*.

Preface

This book is about management buyouts (MBOs) and more. It is not about how to do them but about why they occur and what happens afterwards. This book is also about the significance which MBOs hold for managing corporate enterprise in the UK and perhaps elsewhere. Our study is, in effect, a miniature study both of the failings of the large corporate organisations from which some MBOs emerge, and of the inherent advantages and disadvantages of private ownership and new financial structures.

Our interest in buyouts, and the research on which this book is based, dates back to the early 1980s. This was a time of recession, rationalisation and corporate restructuring. Divestment, spin-off, management and other buyouts, suggested that for many UK public corporations, all was not well with corporate strategy and executive decision taking. The initial sucesses of MBOs in both the UK and the US appeared to suggest that a new entrepreneurial organisation structure was emerging to address aspects of this malaise. We wondered why a change in ownership and capital structure should of itself lead to significant shareholder gains, especially when acquisition synergies or new management could not be invoked as the reason. We asked ourselves: why in the case of management buyout through corporate divestment, should one company's dog become a manager's dream? Two lines of argument seemed plausible: financial alchemy, or ownership and capital structures inducing real increases in economic performance?

The financial alchemy argument suggests that MBOs add nothing significant of real value but involve redistribution of benefits between organisational stakeholders and between taxpayers. If inside information, the ability to manipulate the value of the company to steal from public shareholders or other stakeholders, or tax advantages of debt, account for much of the increase in shareholder value obtained through a MBO, then no real economic value is created: merely tax gains, paper profits and unethical wealth transfers. The notion of entrepreneurial professional managers risking their all to become owner-managers becomes myth, window-dressing for reality. The MBO – and the new fads in finance which, especially in the US, it has helped foster – junk bonds, mezzanine debt, interest rate caps and power investing – would have become just this decade's opportunistic structure for financial engineering, enriching not the country's productive wealth but the partners of financial houses and complicit managers.

The other argument says that MBOs are a new type of organisation structure leading to fundamental changes in the way managers manage, and hence to real value increases. Sound theoretical reasons exist for believing that ownership may lead managers to be more efficiency conscious, more innovative, and to pull together as a team focused on organisational rather than private goals. In addition, concentration of outside shareholders, often having board representation, may improve external monitoring and financial advice. Finally, high levels of debt, and the need to reduce it, may encourage operating efficiencies in working capital and higher-valued use of assets, at the same time as curtailing unproductive reinvestment of free cash flows. The resolution to the central issue of whether MBOs create real economic value has implications far beyond its own particular circumstances. Small facts speak to large issues and if in fact, owner-managers of highly leveraged, private companies can successfully implement new strategies to deliver better shareholder results (or can better harmonize performance with shareholder expectations) then this suggests inherent deficiencies in the mid-twentieth century model of the large, diversified, public corporation that the MBO phenomenon is, in part, redressing.

In order to shed light on these issues, we decided to investigate the changes brought about by a MBO. In view of the complexity of these changes and our need to illuminate management process, rather than just financial performance outcomes, we opted for longitudinal, qualitative research. By following the progress of ten MBOs over a six year period, we have attempted to glimpse through the eyes of those most involved – owner-managers, corporate investors and parent company managers – what happened and why. We have found that it is the freeing up of organisation structure, culture and strategic decision-making processes and the disciplinary effect of debt on managers' behaviour that account for results obtained. We argue that the experience of many of the divested buyouts we looked at is an indictment of the ways some corporate headquarters' management exercise control over their subsidiaries. A recurring theme from our research was the perception of autocratic, frequently paternalistic and patronising, corpocrats, controlling rather than motivating subsidiary management. We argue that the 'deadweight hand of corporate control' is a serious indictment of US and UK companies' failure to adjust in their managerial practices and scale to the competitive market place of today.

Another finding was the forced use of outmoded procedures geared to the needs of a corporate whole with little regard for the relevance, appropriateness or demotivating consequences to subsidiary management. The potential added value from the corporate centre was rarely achieved in the cases we looked at. The managerial inefficiencies of large corporate holding companies helped to destroy shareholder value, while the energy released by the new MBO structure helped to create it. Clearing the weeds from the stem of a plant facilitates growth; private ownership may facilitate as much as it incentivises beneficial changes. We found numerous positive ownership effects: the alignment of owners' and managers' objectives, the pulling power of true teamwork and social relationships built on a clear mutuality of interest, enhanced managerial freedom and responsibility, greater vigilance and commitment, clear feedback and reward systems reinforcing effort and achievement, and greater transparency of skills and efforts in achieving success and failure. Our data also confirmed that as regards debt, its positive role has been focusing managers' attention on squeezing every last inch of waste out of the business; its negative role, constraining market development strategies. In high leverage situations, the primary objective is improving efficiency while maintaining or marginally improving market share into the future. Once efficiency is achieved and leverage reduced, the next phase of revenue enhancement or market development can be embarked upon. This may require or coincide with a different ownership structure to that of the MBO.

MBOs have recently attracted some adverse publicity, following the highly publicised financial failures/restructurings of some highly leveraged management buyouts. We believe that this has focused attention on the outliers rather than on the main population, thereby tarring the whole buyout phenomenon with the idiosyncratic excesses of a few shaky deals. Certainly, an MBO is not a panacea for all corporate ills. Not all of our MBOs were successful and many of the owner-managers in them committed follies as great as, or greater than, those perpetrated by managers in the corporations divesting them. Nevertheless, from what we have observed, and despite the hazards of moving from the particular to the general, it is our contention that MBOs encourage 'self-induced corporate restructuring' (in terms of managerial behaviour and processes). They also enhance the prospects and motivation for eventual corporate renewal and growth even though they may have to go through a further metamorphosis to bring this to fruition. Finally, there are indeed general management lessons to be learned from MBOs for the better governance of, and decision-taking in, corporate enterprises in the UK and elsewhere.

SEBASTIAN GREEN
DEAN F. BERRY

Acknowledgements

Many people have contributed to this book. First and foremost are the owner-managers of the companies we investigated. Without exception, they gave freely of their time and perhaps, more importantly, spoke openly, frankly and with much thought about their experiences and the issues raised by a MBO. Robin Tavener at Stone International, Keith Hirst at Metsec, Philip Jeffrey at Jacoa, Tom Moore at March Concrete, David Simons at John Collier and Mervyn de'Ath and Terry Casey at Trend Control deserve special thanks.

Various organisations have also contributed in terms of providing research resources and stimulus. The Centre for Business Strategy at the London Business School provided all of the initial funding for the empirical research and the lion's share thereafter. Victoria University of Wellington, New Zealand and The MAC Group (UK) Ltd. have provided ongoing research resources and moral support. Thanks John Rolander. Ed Goldstein challenged us intellectually and in detail clarifying our heads and beliefs simultaneously.

Colleagues, in particular John McGee, John Roberts, Charles Baden Fuller and Rob Grant at CBS gave support and acted as a sounding board for the early development of ideas and research methodology. Mathew Bishop, Research Fellow at CBS, assisted in interviewing executives at March Concrete and Trend Control and contributed to writing the case histories of these two companies. Needless to say, we alone are responsible for the ideas expressed in the book.

We are also indebted to Jane Roberts, who typed up interviews, to Rosie Davis and Mary O'Doyle who provided administrative support and to the MAC group support staff: Jaspa, Fay, Nikki and Christine. Special mention must be made of the extreme patience of our publishers, and of the excellence of the unstinting editorial support provided by Keith Povey. Finally, thanks to Colette, Aran, Dylan and Holly and the knowing others whom we deprived of our attentions to complete the book; progeny, erstwhile cuddlers, clients, colleagues and friends.

SEBASTIAN GREEN
DEAN F. BERRY

For our parents and for Richard

1 The Magic in Management Buyouts

> The widespread waste and inefficiency of the public corporation and its inability to adapt to changing economic circumstances have generated a wave of organizational innovation over the last 15 years – innovation driven by the rebirth of 'active investors' (Jensen, 1989:63).

1 INTRODUCTION

Very occasionally, new ideas, concepts or forms, evolve from the normal business landscape to capture the spirit of fundamental change that is underfoot. Management buyouts – firms in which the executive managers have acquired a significant ownership stake in the business they were formerly managing – are one such phenomenon. They have risen from the ashes of corporate conglomeratisation to symbolise the rebirth of the new values of enterprise, whether real or imagined, not only in post-Thatcherite Britain but in America and on the Continent as well.

The social significance of management buyouts (MBOs) derives from individual ownership and private enterprise. These are powerful symbols connoting a wide range of positive attributes: independence, freedom, self-reliance, security, and revealed merit. More importantly, however, MBOs combine ownership of the firm's assets with control of those assets,[1] a principle long compromised by capitalism, yet nonetheless continuously affirmed as essential for effective economic organisation. Since the time of the Industrial Revolution and before, people have argued, both theoretically and practically, the harmful consequences of ignoring this principle. Adam Smith (1776) for example, wrote that the managers of other people's money cannot 'well be expected to watch over it with the same anxious vigilance with which the partners of a private copartnery frequently watch over their own [so that] negligence and profusion, therefore, must always prevail more or less, in the management of the affairs of such a company'.

Ironically, it was the very success of the economic system favoured

1

by Adam Smith which created the conditions for the separation of ownership from control. Companies which began their existence as an entrepreneurial effort, supported usually with the private capital of a limited number of people, prospered and quickly outgrew their limited capital base. The owners increasingly turned to public financial markets to raise further capital and make their own more liquid. As a consequence, the ownership of the firm became dispersed among a wide range of investors having no managerial responsibility.[2] Management, on the other hand, became increasingly professional and separated from ownership (Trostel and Nichols 1982:48).

The 1980s have, however, seen an important hiccough to this process of separation of ownership and control. Disappointing results from two decades of diversified mergers and acquisitions have revealed the flaw in the assumption that 'Big is Beautiful' for its own resource power; or that conglomerate acquisitions always add real value to shareholders. The world recession and the harsher trading conditions of the late 1970s and early 1980s have seen many companies forced to divest past acquisitions. A recent study by Michael Porter (1987) at Harvard showed that 53 per cent to 74 per cent of acquisitions made in the period 1950 to 1980 were later divested. It seems doubtful that this study or its forerunners will lessen the drive from managers of public companies to continue to acquire to the detriment of the shareholders of the acquiring company.

Divestment has provided the spur for managers to obtain an equity stake in their business and thus remarry ownership with control through the medium of the MBO. (When, as is usual, MBOs are financed primarily by borrowed money such that the capital structure of the new company consists mostly of debt, they are also referred to as management-led Leveraged Buyouts, or LBOs.)[3] The growth in buyouts serves as an interesting counterpoint to the perceived concern with the effects of acquisition.

The success of buyouts (i.e. lower rates of failure than start-ups, buy-ins or acquisition; 10 years of growth in the number and size of MBOs; worldwide growth in MBO activity, etc.) allied to the need for outside equity (and significant debt), has also paved the way for the institutional providers of capital to become owners and, in many cases, active directors:

Everyone has a stake in LBOs. The investment bank arranges the deals and makes short-term bridging loans to fund them . . . Commercial banks lend most of the cost of LBOs (usually 60% and more). Insurance companies, mutual funds, pension funds and thrifts buy the junk bonds. Finally all invest equity in numerous LBO funds. (*The Economist*, 5 November 1988)

The importance of institutional investments and managerial involvement is underlined just by the magnitude of the sums involved.

In the US, for example, specialist firms like Kohlberg, Kravis, Roberts (KKR) – who engineered the $25 billion buyout of RJR Nabisco – as well as old-line, blue chip merchant banks like Morgan Stanley, have helped create a phenomenon which, according to Charles Schultze, former Chairman of the Council of Economic Advisers, is 'beginning to be macro-economically significant' (quoted in *Fortune* 2 January 1989). Morgan Stanley and Merril Lynch have $3.1 billion in funds committed for buyouts (*Business Week* 20 June 1988 p. 117), KKR have a $5.6 billion LBO fund for equity participation in buyouts, the base onto which at least $35 billion of bank and subordinated debt can be placed (*Fortune* 4 July 1988:53); and a recent Federal Reserve survey found that LBO finance accounted for 9.9 per cent of all commercial loans at large banks (*Fortune* 2 January 1989).

The major ultimate impact of MBOs and LBOs might well be on a realignment of the managerial and financial structure of firms in western economies. To some this closer integration might raise the spectre of J. P. Morgan and robber-baron capitalism. To us it speaks of a greater strategic fusion between finance and management and raises important questions about the social structure of capital and ownership and the managerial behaviours that follow.

Buyouts, in particular the management variety, constitute a new type of business organisation (albeit transitional), the success or failure of which is a comment on more than itself. Small facts speak to large issues and our interest in them is driven by a desire to understand the strengths and weaknesses of this new corporate form relative to the possible corporate failings of the organisations that spawn buyouts. If subsidiaries prove to be unprofitable within a large organisation structure but are perfectly viable on their own after a MBO, or if a change from a publicly owned organisation to management based ownership enhances efficiency and shareholder wealth, then these phenomena raise questions about (1) the circumstances in which large corporate structures subtract more value than they add; (2) the role and added value of the corporate centre; (3) highly leveraged capital structures and their implications for traditional wisdoms on appropriate ratios of debt to equity; and (4) ultimately whether more managerial ownership and control could be a primary ingredient for business renewal and regeneration.

These are important issues for the future of shareholder democracy. Yet debate has for the most part skirted over them. Numerous MBO 'issues' have taken attention in the public press and research away from the fundamental principles involved. Normally, the process of turning managers into owners and hugely increasing the new companies proportion of debt over equity (leverage) has created two powerful new forces *vis-à-vis* 'normal' corporate organisation and practice. After 10 years of MBO success it is time to try to account for and explain the drivers of this success and to measure those findings against the outcomes of professionally managed, publicly held corporations.

At a philosophical level of economics, the core arguments relating to the incentive effects both of ownership and leverage are, in large part, those advanced by Berle and Means in 1932. They derive from the observable phenomenon that the objectives of management may, in a number of situations, differ from those of the shareholder.[4] As Rappaport (1986) states:

> Responsibility for administering companies or 'control' is vested in the hands of professional managers and thereby has been separated from 'ownership'. Since the ownership of shares in large corporations tends to be diffuse, individual shareholders are said to have neither influence on, or interest in, corporate governance issues such as the election of board members. Therefore boards are largely responsive to management which, in turn, can ignore shareholders and run the company as they see fit.

If, in fact, new owner-managers of private companies can deliver better shareholder results (or can better harmonize performance with shareholder expectations) such an outcome is powerful and needs examining. In general, however the public's attention has been obscured by two sets of MBO issues:

1. Long-term economic viability: worries about the creation of overly risky financial structures. The current hike in interest rates and the well publicised failure of some LBOs has increased concern that the MBO is just this decade's opportunistic structure for financial engineering, enriching not the country's productive wealth but the partners of financial houses. Every decade

generates new financial instruments, fads in finance (junk bonds, mezzanine debt and 'power investing'), new riches and new specialists. It is not surprising, therefore, that people ask whether the MBO is just an exercise in financial acrobatics.

2. Valid ethical concerns about such issues as fiduciary duties of managers; immense personal and/or corporate changes in wealth or market values when the MBO is taken public; and trading on inside information. These matters, however, are about buyout deals; not about the structural or managerial behaviour which accounts for firm results over time.

Interesting as these issues and contentions are, they do divert attention from what we consider to be the underlying matter of economic concern. Do private owner/managers behave differently post-MBO than they previously did as professional managers? Has this structural change led to behaviours that increase economic values for shareholders? If the answers to the first two questions are positive, what fundamentally accounts for the results? On those rare occasions when these questions have been addressed views have, with certain notable exceptions,[5] for the most part been based on armchair speculation, on received wisdoms or on the perceptions of everyone except those who are most intimately connected with MBOs: the managers themselves.

This book attempts to fill this gap by addressing these specific questions directly and by doing so primarily through the eyes of owner-managers. It is not a book on 'how to do an MBO' – of which there are plenty – nor is it about the different sorts of buyouts that exist. It is about what happens to managers and managerial processes as a result of a buyout, and why. Through the medium of the case history, it looks at the corporate culture, structure and strategy of subsidiaries prior to a buyout and about the changes to them which occur thereafter as a result, in particular, of the ownership and control changes.

Before presenting the case studies which constitute the major part of this book, some preliminary comment is required. In Section 2 of this chapter, we consider the postwar organisational history of US and UK firms that led to the wave of MBOs/LBOs in the 1970s and 1980s. Given two decades of growth, acquisitions and SBU (Strategic Business Unit) managed public corporations, we offer two theoretical concepts (relatedness and shareholder value) to explain why MBOs/LBOs were logical answers to that twenty years of business history.

In Section 3, we look briefly at the nature of the MBO phenomenon in the UK and how it differs from the US experience; Section 4 considers the impact of ownership and debt on managerial behaviour and process; and Section 5 outlines the research methodology adopted.

2 BUSINESS AND ORGANISATIONAL HISTORY (1960–75) AS A PRELUDE TO THE RECENT RISE OF MBO/LBOs

After the postwar growth years of the 1960s and early 1970s (and the success of the multibusiness conglomerate) most large corporations faced periods of economic recession and increasing international competition during the 1970s. In order to focus managerial effort 'beyond divisionalisation', many corporate managements turned to a more sophisticated analysis and management of their portfolio of companies. Investment and resource allocation decisions were facilitated by arraying individual businesses according to such criteria as the attractiveness of their markets and their ability to grow in those markets. Corporate executives also employed the organisational focusing device of the SBU as the structural corollary to portfolio strategy techniques. In that way, they could look at the cash flow characteristics of these units as a way to analyse the potential creation of market values. Divisions became groupings of SBUs, departing radically from the previous divisional/profit-centre organisational concepts of Alfred Sloan and Peter Drucker. While the SBU was promulgated originally as an aid to strategy *formulation* in the complex, multiproduct organisations, it became a *mode of simplifying implementation* by breaking up the inherent organisational complexity of diversified conglomerates or multibusiness firms into more manageable pieces.

These US corporate and organisational planning conventions were incorporated into UK businesses previously run as holding companies (Channon, 1973). With their imperial history of investing throughout the Empire, British firms were frequently financially driven from the centre, yet seemingly run by genuinely decentralised, local managers.

In these organisations business plans and budget proposals came upward for financial approval: capital rationing became the group's decision; management the individual companies prerogative. This was culturally parallel to the British military veneration of the regiment as the principal fighting unit. The centre didn't fight, the company (regiment) did. The centre concerned itself with strategic resource provisioning and deployment. During the 1970s the centre became known as 'corporate' and groups of companies became divisions as the American form of divisionalisation became popularly imitated in form if not practice. The individual companies' boards were maintained (largely, it seems to us, to preserve the status of directors) and the chairman of 'the group' turned 'his' strategic attention to the City to compose (or recompose) his portfolio. His managerial duties were usually limited to evaluating the portfolio or making judgements about 'stand-alone' capital expenditure proposals. Corporate strategy was therefore focused almost exclusively on financial evaluation and planning or divestment and acquisition activities.

In the US, as SBUs began to ascend in importance, managers' allegiances shifted from the firm to the SBU. In the UK, allegiance was already at the company level due to years of operating the firm as a holding company. The move to structural divisionalisation was largely based on the philosophy of 'each tub on its own bottom'. In both the US and UK cases, the local managers' primary focus in evaluating and recommending strategic alternatives was the prospect for the individual SBU/company. The centre relied on company or SBU financial performance measures for evaluating capital projects and managerial performance. That reliance further contributed to local managements' political desire to isolate their own SBUs or companies for evaluation and reward purposes (Gouillart and Wortzel, 1987). Twenty years of this kind of organisational and management tension left US and UK firms ill prepared to integrate acquisitions, a second feature of that period.

Acquisitions

As firms grew and diversified in the 'go-go years' of the late 1960s and 1970s, acquisitions or 'deals' were increasingly justified by investment or merchant bankers on the basis of 'synergies'; 2 plus 2 was meant to create a merged 5. It seemed to many observers (i.e., Bettis, 1983) that these linkages were often weak or non-existent. Whatever the strength of the case (and either way bankers got their fees) very few acquisitions were successfully enough integrated to capture these 'synergies'. The problem was that few diversified conglomerates possessed the requisite management skills. In fact, managers of the acquired companies were frequently let go after the acquisitions were completed! Implementing a strategy to exploit synergies (either from acquisition or across existing businesses) requires a long time horizon and the relentless dedication of the chief executive. He or she must devote significant resources to convincing their markets and their organisations of the value of a more integrated approach to management. This is extraordinarily hard to do if:

1. The primary focus of the CEO is on quarterly earnings' growth.
2. The loyalty and rewards for business managers are in their own, local patch.
3. Corporate Centre evaluates and rewards (through capital allocations, promotion, and pay) the stand-alone behaviour of local SBUs or companies.

As US and UK firms looked for competitive advantage, the experience of overseas companies, particularly in Japan and Germany was instructive. In industries such as chemicals and pharmaceuticals, electronics, automotive, and telecommunications, for example, strong functional experts in their corporate centres actually managed the interdependancies *across* SBUs by what Porter (1978) preferred to call 'horizontal strategy' – presumably to differentiate the *real* managerial opportunities from the conceptual 'synergies' promoted by the banks. Interestingly, one researcher (Cable, 1984) has argued that in Germany the close liaison, characterised by bank shareholdings, board representation and the supply of financial expertise between industrial companies and their banks, resembles a 'quasi-internal capital market'. These integrated decision-taking relationships more closely resemble those in MBOs than in the traditional UK corporate formula pattern of a holding company with external financing and a weak central staff.

Porter observed that most acquisitions failed because they failed to capture a source of competitive advantage entailing *horizontal* (across) management unit activities. The managerial history of most firms was in *vertical* (up and down) management. As examples, witness firms in the US and UK who were overly SBU-ed or managed to 'stand alone' during the 1960s and 1970s. Economic values could be created, he argued, from managing *across* the multibusiness company with commonly shared assets such as shared customer bases, functions, management expertise or financial structures (Porter, 1985).

Applying this horizontal logic to mergers or acquisitions to create value, the acquirer must argue at least that:

1. The skills learned in one business can successfully be applied to another, and,
2. That the existing management of the acquirer can operationally capture the horizontal or relatedness opportunities presented by the new assets of the acquired.

In practice, numerous studies have shown that: 'On average, shareholders of buying companies earn little, if anything, from mergers. What is important to emphasise is that the *aggregate* net change in the [market] value of the buyer plus seller is positive. This suggests that the [stock] market believes that the combination will create value. Most, if not all, of the value created appears to be captured by sellers' (Rappaport, 1986).

These arguments about 'relatedness', acquisitions and any other forms of adding economic value to shareholders explain why companies wish to sell various units they see as underperforming businesses and, equally, why existing managements wish to buy those businesses which they see as undervalued. Part of the answer lies in the connection between how the stockmarket actually values businesses, their performance and acquisitions versus how senior corporate managers *believe* their performance has been evaluated by stockmarket investors.

A financial theory of business strategy

The notion that major business choices (plans, strategies, acquisitions) should be judged by the value they produce to shareholders is itself neither novel nor controversial. The problem is how to measure it. A recent survey of CEOs by Welch and Pantalone (1987) found that only 20 per cent held stock price maximisation as their ultimate goal; the other 80 per cent indicated that a variety of measures of financial performance such as earnings per share, return on equity, net income, cash flow and sales growth were more important to them.

During the 1970s both conglomerates and large, multibusiness companies believed that increased *earnings per share* (EPS) was what the financial markets wished to see and would reward with a higher share price rating. But throughout this period of double-digit earnings-per-share growth, falling productivity and inflation actually created small or even negative returns to shareholders. The empirical fact that earnings per share is an unreliable predictor of the value created for the shareholder is exemplified in Tables 1.7, 1.8 and 1.9 (see p. 46.) Numerous studies (Rappaport, 1981; and others) showed that investors discount earnings figures and projections for numerous reasons:

1. Accrual based accounting numbers do not provide a dependable or consistent picture of either the current or future performance of the organisation. Earnings numbers can be calculated using quite different but acceptable accounting methods, especially in regard to: inventories, depreciation, and in acceptable acquisition accounting practices.
2. There is an *unreliable* relationship between earnings growth and *total* shareholder returns – even over a ten year period.
3. The financial risk of using debt must be added to the business risk of operations to know what rate of return shareholders will require on their equity. In turn this must be related to the cost of obtaining and using the capital to judge whether positive economic values or returns will be created from a corporate investment. *Earnings figures do not incorporate any consideration of such risk*. But common sense would urge most shareholders to want a higher total return from a business investment than from relatively riskless treasury bills or government securities which are clear investment alternatives. They do, and they impute a risk adjustment to managements' earnings figures.
4. In order to create economic value for shareholders, sustained investments in working capital and fixed assets are usually needed. These are *excluded* from earnings calculations thereby initially overstating the free cash flow from an investment for the period under consideration. In subsequent periods there is an offsetting understatement.
5. Earnings calculations ignore the time value of money whereas *economic* value is created by discounting the anticipated values of future cash flows over the time period in which they will be realised.

Yet so deep was the commitment to increasing earnings per share as the driver of corporate strategy, that investments and acquisitions were approved throughout the 1970s that did not even return their true cost of capital. Even where they did, attempts to promote EPS by actively acquiring other publicly traded companies frequently did not pay off for stockholders. The latter may be able to diversify their portfolios more cheaply than companies who have to pay inflated premiums for shares in acquisition targets. Moreover, 'stockholders acting on their own can purchase just the right amount of stock to diversify their portfolios optionally' (Welch and Pantalone, 1987:78).

Finally, it is also demonstrable that many, if not most companies, actually rewarded their executives for increasing earnings per share – regardless of the effect on the shareholder via dividends and share price appreciation. Misguided acquisitions and investments were made throughout the 1970s which increased the scale, diversity and complexity of the management task in large public corporations, while not rewarding their shareholder investors.

The resulting structure and performance of such US and UK companies did not go unnoticed by arbitrageurs and later by hostile raiders. They had their analysts value separately the individual pieces that made up the corporate whole and compared that against the market value. In many cases the prices that potential buyers were willing to pay for the individual pieces of a corporation *exceeded* the market value of the corporation (share price × the number of shares outstanding). This became known as 'the conglomerate discount'. Alternatively, takeover specialists ignored the phantom money of earnings and focused on cash flow, either to repay the debt and service the junk bonds used to finance a takeover or because cash flow (especially 'free' or undedicated cash flow per share) is considered by many to be a better measure of successful operations than EPS. Consequently, corporate raids, hostile takeovers, asset stripping, downsizing, spin-offs, carve-outs and leveraged or management buyouts became common (Gouillart and Wortzel, 1987). And the other side of the coin, as *The Economist* 29 October 1988 suggested, is that LBOs/MBOs 'signal the demise of the advantage the large conglomerates have had for decades through their access to capital through the stockmarket and their right to building empires of diverse companies'.

Let us now bring the strands of the argument together.

1. LBOs/MBOs are only one of a series of options to corporate managements where the contribution of that piece of the corporate portfolio is judged to be lowering the total market value of the whole or vice versa (i.e. where the potential market value of that piece is inadequately reflected in or undervalued by the market value of the whole).

2. Such a situation has arisen because of:

   a. Mismanagement of the past or a failure to capture the 'relatedness' value of subsidiaries. The ability of corporations to respond internally has been limited by their management history; by overly SBU'd or stand-alone organisation structures with few skills or opportunities to practice relatedness management; reward systems based on faulty accounting standards (ROI, earnings-per-share) relative to the creation of economic value; and problems of managing ever larger, more complex and diverse business structures.

   b. An originally unsound acquisition; either because of an over-valuation at the time of acquisition or an inability to capture its value through better integrated corporate or business management of the acquired company (i.e. heavy overhead burdens, poorly structured financing, excessive inventories, inefficiency, failure to invest, inadequate adjustment to competition in the product markets, etc).

3. The rise in takeovers (the market for corporate control) increasingly threatens corporations whose pieces destroy shareholder value or whose capital structures and financial strategies fail to maximise shareholder wealth.

4. LBOs/MBOs attest to the flaw in the view that by multi-divisionalisation, multibusiness firms can easily overcome the inherent inefficiencies of information, incentives and resource allocation under conditions of growth in scale that have been suggested by authors such as Williamson 1975; Sloan 1964, Drucker 1946.

5. Where the sharemarket values the total worth of divisions as independent entities higher than they do the corporate whole, there must be a strong possibility that: either the corporate headquarters adds negative value; or that the relationships between divisions are not exploited effectively; or that the corporate centre prevents divisions from maximising their full potential.

In summary, we see the emergence of the LBO/MBO phenomenon and the way it has seemed to gain substantial momentum in the 1980s, as a reflection of: the mismanagement of corporate assets, including acquisitions; the failure of many large public corporations to create adequate structures, incentives and managerial behaviour for delivering economic value; the arrival of a large and liquid market of financial assets for corporate restructuring; and intensified competition – on a global scale – for control of corporate assets. This managerial and financial framework sets the occasion for a buyout. An example, comparing a company well-known for managing the relatedness amongst its divisions, American Express, with a British two-division company, makes the point. Here (see Table 1.9) the market awards a premium to American Express as a whole because of their proven ability to, say, sell a bank-by-mail product from its International Banking division to the German holders of its American Express credit cards based in the data base of another division (Travel Related Services). British company A is discounted in the market because of its apparent inability to exploit relationships across the two divisions. Projecting and discounting the cash flows from the two divisions indicates that the market would rate each division higher on its own; thereby setting the occasion for a raid, a break-up or an MBO.[6]

At the micro level, the LBO/MBO occurs because at least two parties place differing values on the specific entity involved. Corporate management acknowledges their historic inability to create shareholder value from the entity; the units management believe they can create shareholder value for its new owners unfettered by the constraints of the old situation, now refinanced and motivated to do so. In our previous example, the management of one of the divisions of company A may believe they can deliver enhanced shareholder values from the future cash flow of their division's assets. The corporate management of company A might believe themselves vulnerable to a raid or feel that they would be better off deploying the cash raised from a divestment either in other divisions or in a new, easier-to-integrate-and-manage asset. If this explanation establishes an outline theory as to why the occasion of an LBO/MBO arises, two interesting questions are raised:

1. How to account for and explain – if and when it occurs – the successful later performance of LBOs/MBOs. What are the new forces, not present previously, which allow the better creation of shareholder value in the LBO/MBO? and,
2. What, in the old situation prevented this from happening? If the LBO/MBO movement continues to grow and develop, are there

inherent deficiencies in the mid-twentieth century model of the large, diversified, public corporation that the LBO/MBO phenomenon is addressing? And, if so, what can we learn more broadly from a detailed behavioural examination of the processes of British MBOs that would help us establish better management paradigms for the more successful future of business management and economic capitalism?

In order to start this search let us next turn to the relatively recent experience of British buyouts.

3   THE MBO PHENOMENON IN THE UK

Although MBOs have been around for a long time, it was really the end of the 1970s which saw their emergence as an important socioeconomic force with important implications for managers, organisations and the economy. Such has been their success as a mechanism both for facilitating ownership change and as an acceptable financing form, that by 1987 the numbers of UK buyouts rose to 300 deals worth £2.82 billion. The October 1987 stock market crash had almost no effect on MBO initiatives. In the first nine months of 1988, 210 deals were recorded worth £2.33 billion. In the US, the rate of LBO activity was $39 billion for the first nine months of 1988 versus $38 billion for the whole of 1987. Tables 1.1 and 1.2 show the rapid build-up in the numbers and size of UK buyouts over this period.

In both the UK and US markets, the amount of finance available for MBOs/LBOs has steadily grown. In fact, by late 1988, buyout teams were in a strong position to negotiate deals in their favour as

Table 1.1   Number of buyouts in the UK, 1967–87

	1967–78	1979	1980	1981	1982	1983	1984	1985	1986	1987	1988	1989*
MBOs	79	52	107	124	170	205	210	229	248	335	400	300
Total value (£m)	N/A	26	50	114	265	315	415	1150	1438	3250	5000	5410

Notes: Figures for 1989 provide an estimate of the total deals for Jan–Sept, 1989.

Sources: Centre for Management Buy Out Research, University of Nottingham, 1988; and Peat Marwick McLintock, quoted in *Financial Times*, 11 November 1989.

Table 1.2 Larger UK management buyouts 1981–8 (total funding in £m)

	Under £25m	£25–50m	£50–100m	£100–250m	£250m+
1981	Famous Names (8) Wiltminster (10) Gleneagles (13) Ansafone (14)				
1982	Isis (8) Stanley Gibbons (9) Stone (18) Amalg Foods (21)	First Leisure (44)	NFC (54)		
1983	SPP Group (9) E and Am ins (10) Tgernakute (12) Victaulic (15)	Hugin (26) Timpson (42) Collier (47)			
1984	Evans Halshaw (10) Westbury (18) DRI (22) Paragon (24)	Wordplex (28) Simplex (29)	Target (50)		
1985	Brymon Airways (9) Bison (10) Willis Faber (10) Tibbet & Britten (10) Essanelle (11) A J Archer (12) Record Ridgway (13) Secur Homes (13) Royco (13) Ellerman Lines (15) V Thornycroft (19) Wades (19) Bradstock Ins (20)		St Regis (52) Haden (60) Caradon (66) Mallinson–Denny (93) Mecca Leisure (98)		Lawson Mardon (280)
1986	Exacta (10) Leyland Bus (10)	Haleworth (25) GBE International (25)	Unipart (52) TIP Europe (60)	VSEL (100) Premier Brands (102)	

Table 1.2 Continued

	Under £25m	£25–50m	£50–100m	£100–250m	£250m+
	KDG Instruments (11)	Evans Healthcare (27)	Parker Pen (74)		
	Jeyes Hygiene (11)	UK Paper (38)	United Machinery (86)		
	Maccess I (11)	City Merchant Dev (40)			
	Trend (12)	Norwest Holst (45)			
	Furmanile (12)				
	Gomme (12)				
	European Ind Ser (12)				
	Partco (13)				
	Intercraft Designs (15)				
	Cundell Corrugated (15)				
	Nestor BNA (15)				
	Computing Devices (19)				
	Technitron (21)				
	Berketex (22)				
1987	RFS Industries (10)	Istel (26)	BTA (50)	Wickes (120)	Hays (255)
	Venture Plant (12)	United News Shops (29)	Fairey Eng (51)	Int Leisure (156)	MFI/Hygena (718)
	Porth Dec Products (12)	Clares Equipment (29)	Pontins (58)	Compass (160)	
	Holiday Dyes (12)	Crown House Eng (36)	Assoc Fresh Foods (68)	ASW (181)	
	Janson Green (13)	Rentco (43)	Moores Furniture (80)	Humberclyde Inv (205)	
	Clairmont (14)				
	AVO (15)				
	Serco (15)				
	Gold Crown Foods (15)				
	Aqualisa Products (16)				
	Aynesley China (18)				
1988	Kirklees Chemicals (10)	Sheffield F'masters (26)	Glass Glover (61)	Crowther's Clothing (103)	Bricom Inds (405)
	Burlington Int (10)	Mono Pumps (29)	York Trailer (61)	Oval (120)	Reedpack (631)
	Radstone Tech (10)	Harveys Furnishings (32)	Lewis' (74)	Argus Press (207)	
	Celebrity CP (10)	Ward White Footwear (36)	Invegordon (24)	Virgin (248)	
	National Express (10)	Dwek (39)			
	Motor World (11)	VF Int (39)			
	Reestar (13)	Goldsmiths (43)			

	1989 to date				
AMG Inds (15)	Busways (10)	Elizabeth Shaw (25)	British Syphon (53)	London Clubs (120)	Allders (260)
Peerless (18)	Citylab (10)	AEC (28)	Crockfords (53)	MW Marshall (175)	Magnet (665)
Lowndes Lambert (19)	Range Valley (1)	Beacon (29)	United Carriers (55)	Charles Church (203)	Gateway (2,375)
Maccess II (20)	Abacus (11)	Trinity (31)	Kenwood (62)		
Washington New Town (21)	Seckers Silks (11)	FFL (31)	Square Grip (65)		
ABI Caravans (20)	Haigh Castle (12)	Court Cavendish (35)	Ryan (70)		
	Hill Leigh (13)	Fenchurch Corrugated (36)			
	Ratcliffs (13)	MBS (38)			
	Tallent Eng (13)	Dowty Mining (45)			
	Valor Stoves (14)	Tyzack (48)			
	Country Casuals (14)	Illingworth Morris (49)			
	BREL (14)				
	May Gurney (15)				
	British Air Ferries (15)				
	Geest CD (17)				
	Britannia Data Mgt (18)				
	Mercado (18)				
	Oyez (20)				
	Harland & Wolff (21)				
	Hamleys (21)				
	Themes Int. (22)				
	Barbour Campbell (22)				
	Rubatex (22)				

Source: Peat Marwick McLintock, 1 October 1988 *Financial Times*, 11 October 1989.

Note: PMM have acted as reporting accountants in 47/125 of the above cases involving total funds of some £2.1 billion. Larger management buyouts are taken as those with total funding of over £10 million in 1988 values. UK MBOs are strictly so defined and exclude, for example, management buy-ins, leveraged refinancings and UK financed offshore MBOs.

competition brought commercial (clearing) banks, pension funds, insurance companies, development capital groups and venture capitalists into a recognised and intensely rivalrous market. The chief executive of Electra Investment Trust was quoted (*Financial Times*, 13 October, 1988) as saying: 'The buy out market has become as competitive as merchant banking in the 60s, syndicated loans in the 70s and equities in the 80s.'

It is clear that MBO financing has become an established financial market activity where management is able to compete with trade buyers; it is also an accepted method for companies wishing to sell. A recent fillip has been given by UK public companies going private as an attractive option in the aftermath of the market crash in October 1987 (i.e. the Virgin group, see Table 1.3). But the MBO movement in the UK seems not so much driven by financial techniques and markets; rather, it is a successful form of divestment and asset

Table 1.3 Public share market transactions (including buy-backs, refinancing and MBOs), 1985–8.

		£ million
1985	Haden	50
1986	Gomme	12
	Raybeck/Berkertex	22
1987	International Leisure Group	156
	Lee International	198
	Wickes	114
	Microlease	5
1988	Dwek	34
	Glass Glover	55
	Harris Queensway	450
	Virgin	248
	Invergordon	94
	British Syphon	50
	Blue Arrow	670
	Lonrho	1106
	British and Commonwealth	745
	Prestwich	43
	Chrysalis	30
	Unigate	655
	Chloride	129

Source: Bankers Trust, 1988.

management to which financial suppliers have reacted. The evidence seems directionally clear.

1. While buyouts have grown and matured beyond the 1970s period of restructuring, where poorly performing subsidiaries were sold at below net asset values just to raise returns on the (then) lower asset base of the parent, the necessity for all companies to raise shareholder value has become widely accepted. Aided by a large pool of liquid and mobile capital, corporate raiders have re-established the capital market constituency as a major if not primary force in top management's thinking. Given the size of the RJR Nabisco deal ($23 billion) no public company is safe just because it is big. A worldwide market for corporate control now exists. The MBO is one valid investment mechanism for actualising this market development.

2. MBO failures, particularly in the UK have been rare; organisations like 3i expect one in three of its start-ups to fail as compared to one in ten of its MBOs. In the US, Revco and currently in the UK, Westward Communications Plc, and Lee International, Plc seem to be cases where unduly optimistic growth and profit projections were built into the financial structuring to pay down debt. In Lee International the deal was structured by Citicorp very much along US lines. The UK MBO market, however, seems structured somewhat more patiently (longer time horizons to achieve targets) and is more conservatively financed. Typical debt to equity ratios have been 3 or 4:1 as compared with 9:1 in the US – driving the US buyouts to more rapid asset disposals (see Figure 1.1 on p. 30). In the UK, there have also been a number of refinancings/rescheduling of payments precipitated by the almost doubling of interest rates between May 1988 and August 1989. This hits buyouts particularly hard as it raises debt payments and lowers sales revenues. MFI and Lowndes Queensway are two such companies forced to refinance and reschedule debt (see *The Economist* 18 August 1989:59) with the latter company eventually going into receivership. In the US, given the increasing size of the deals – e.g. RJR Nabisco – there has been a dramatic increase in the use of junk bond financing and a consequent dilution of real equity. The result has been Government hearings, a reappraisal by Banks, Pension Funds, Insurance Companies (who become real risk sharers) and a more jittery

financial market place *vis-à-vis* the financing packages for LBOs. There may indeed be a real source of genuine public concern that the growing use of junk bonds to finance LBOs undermines the financial confidence of investors particularly in a rising interest rate market.

Reasons for UK MBOs

Sellers' Reasons
The larger MBOs tend to come through divestment, privatisation or sales from receivership, and the smaller ones from owners of private companies wishing to retire from the business. Some of the early buyouts arose as an alternative to closure. Generally speaking, however, when it is receivership that creates the opportunity for a buyout, it is not the part that ends up as a buyout which has been responsible for the financial collapse.

Table 1.4 Sources of buyouts

	1981 (%)	1982 (%)	1983 (%)	1984 (%)	1985 (%)	1986 (%)
Divestment – UK parent	53.7	47.4	74.7	62.5	65.5	59.7
Divestment – foreign	12.2	7.8	9.1	12.8	9.5	11.7
Family – private	14.6	21.1	5.1	6.0	16.6	9.7
Receivership	19.5	21.1	9.1	10.7	1.4	2.1
Other*	0.0	2.6	2.0	8.0	6.5	16.8
Sample base	41	38	99	153	239	238

*Privatisation/going private plus overseas divestment.
Source: Centre For Management Buy Out Research, University of Nottingham.

Table 1.4 shows that the largest single category of MBOs by number is divestment. 'Very broadly, it is estimated that as much as three quarters of recorded deals in the UK result from divestments by domestically or foreign-owned parent companies'. (*Financial Times*, 13 October 1988) As mentioned in the introduction, a major impetus to divestment was the recession at the end of the 1970s which prompted many companies to devote their limited resources of management to those areas where they believed themselves strongest in the market. 'Stick to the Knitting' and 'Back to Basics' became rallying calls for the growing spirit of disenchantment with the conglomerate mergers of the 1960s and 1970s and the holding company mentality.

Divestment MBOs tend to arise for one of three reasons: poor performance of a subsidiary; strategic withdrawal from a non-core business; or poor performance/excessive gearing of a group which then sells profitable subsidiaries in order to raise cash to prop up an ailing centre. In the UK, most of these divestment buyouts are instigated, in the first instance, by the parent companies wanting to sell, rather than by the senior management wanting to buy. (Since the Haden buyout in 1985, however, there has been some evidence of the MBO as defence against hostile takeovers.) This has tended to eclipse a discussion of buyers' reasons for wanting to buy in those cases. As the financial market support for buyouts has matured during the 1980s, it appears that the initiative for the sale/disposal has shifted in many cases from the seller to the buyer. The source of initiative is probably less important than the fact of *willingness* to buy and *willingness* to sell. In striking the deal both parties must feel that they can create values for their shareholders.

Buyers' reasons

Often it is assumed that an MBO is such a gift to managers that it is inconceivable that they would turn the opportunity down, or (although this is less prevalent today) that the MBO is a last ditch attempt by a group of washed-up executives to salvage their careers. Hence the frequently heard comment that the incumbent managers have to become entrepreneurs overnight, that they must 'make the transition to entrepreneurs or they, and the buyouts, will become small, ugly failures' (*Management Today*, August 1984).

Neither view seems correct to us, although there is a grain of truth in the former. While it may be true that an MBO invariably presents a once-in-a-lifetime chance for salaried managers to obtain a substantial capital gain, the owner-managers we have spoken to at the outset of an MBO have tended to view the pot of gold at the end of the rainbow as more than a little problematic.

Our own research indicates a variety of defensive, opportunistic and visionary reasons behind the decision to go for an MBO; a subject to which we return, in depth, later.

Defensive

Managers may be likely to lose their jobs or be subjected to unacceptable conditions of employment by new owners. While they may find it difficult to gain employment elsewhere, the image of a group of washed-up executives doing a buyout to preserve their jobs appears almost wholly apocryphal. The financial institutions funding buyouts do not favour ailing companies as buyout candidates. They will only back them if they have confidence in the team's ability to run the company successfully post-buyout or, if necessary, turn it around. Perhaps the major concern of external backers is that the buyout team and, in particular, its leader have the requisite skills to manage the company effectively. If gaps exist, then outside talent can always be brought in.

As far as comments about managers having to become entrepreneurial are concerned, is it not just as likely that buyouts are the result rather than the cause of entrepreneurial behaviour? As Robin Tavener, ex-CEO of Stone International suggested: 'Is there a case that entrepreneurial managers will tend to move to an ownership situation rather than stay in a professional management environment?' The fact that managers have to raise the money for their equity stake through second mortgages or personal loans attests to the entrepreneurial ingredient, even when defensive reasons prevail. If performance lives up to expectations, all the players win rich rewards. If it doesn't, the insistence of many outside investors that individual team members put up personal funds causes owner-managers significant discomfort should the company fail. Defensive reasons for mounting buyouts should not be equated with risk aversion or with incompetence.

Opportunist

Managers may be in a position to purchase their company at a discount due to: preferential treatment, superior bargaining power, privileged information *vis-à-vis* other purchasers, would-be purchasers not wanting to take on disgruntled managers, or undervalued share prices. This has led some writers to raise questions of a conflict of interest, of managers manipulating financial results to obtain an artificially low price for their company. In the US, there have been calls for mandatory auctions in any situation where a MBO is mooted.

Our own research, however, reveals nothing structurally surprising in any 'discounts' that have been obtained, rather good economic reasons for them being jointly agreed. Incumbent managements usually leave it to their financial institutional backers to determine the maximum price at which the deal can be funded and then to negotiate this with the parent company. Hard bargaining from the management is usually confined to discussions with the institutions about the proportion of equity that they will retain after the buy out. If anything, it is the financial advisers who have a conflict of interest. Financers in buyouts make their money in three ways:

1. The management fee – paid to an LBO/MBO financial sponsor for figuring out how to collect and invest the funds; usually around 1.5 per cent of the fund most recently raised.
2. The transaction fees – paid not only to the financing/sponsoring house but to commercial bankers, investment bankers, lawyers and accountants for doing the deal.
3. The 'carry' – the equity ownership put up to finance the purchase which is redeemed on the eventual sale of the shares.

This raises a number of questions:

1. Is an LBO/MBO being set up to earn transaction fees for the investment bank?
2. If an investment bank is a principal (investor) and a fee paid adviser, does the bank have a conflict of interest in its advisory function?
3. If a bank earns multiple fees from underwriting junk bonds, is an investor in an LBO/MBO fund and is also an adviser; does it have a conflict when a company which competes with another firm the bank advises is bought by the LBO/MBO fund?
4. Can advisers who are investors validly offer letters of 'fairness' to boards of companies for whom they bid?

In general, it seems to us that financial houses face serious conflicts of interest in all their business (mergers and acquisitions and even lending) and have not acquitted themselves well; as recent court cases, jail sentences (in the US) and settlements attest. But it would seem that the process of a financial house taking an equity stake does have the substantial benefit of their now wanting substantially the same thing as new owner managers – the creation of shareholder value. As owners, and therefore fee *payers*, they should want good advisory services. Whether they can behave equitably is another matter, for certainly they are not impartial.

On the management side, while there were large discounts to assets in many of the early MBOs, and while it is still commonplace for the management to pay at or near book value for an MBO, discounts are fast becoming a thing of the past.

The buyer's market of the early 1980s for unwanted subsidiaries or whole companies has become a seller's one. Most of the larger MBOs can now be expected to be contested by third party purchasers; frequently at the behest of outside directors who, at a minimum, wish to be seen to be getting their shareholders the best value. The title of a recent *Harvard Business Review* article: 'No More Cozy Management Buy Outs', is a legal and moral argument largely overtaken by market events. Competition from financial institutions for new deals has also pushed prices up. The result is that typical P/E (price/earnings ratios) for MBO deals of between 6 and 8 have now risen to 10 and in some cases above 12. The latter ratio can impose a considerable burden when high debt levels have to be serviced without recourse to the cross-subsidisation possible when a subsidiary is owned by a multibusiness company.

Given the inherent difficulties in valuing a business, it is not surprising to find differences – not so much on the basis of inside information – but on the basis of who owns it and what they plan to do with the ownership. On the whole, passive investors seem to value a business lower than active owners with a vision.

Visionary
Managers going for an MBO invariably believe that they can run a business better without head office control and without having to subscribe to the corporate structure and culture of a distant, yet dominant and perhaps domineering, parent company. The visionary element explains why there is often a divergence of opinion as to the long-term viability of the subsidiary. Given that both have recourse to much the same information, why else would the managers want to buy when the parent company wants to sell? Most of our buyout managers blamed the corporate overhang rather than any fundamental economic weakness in the business for the failings of their enterprise prior to the MBO.

It may well be that the terminology is itself partly responsible for underplaying the visionary nature of managers who would go for a MBO. What is really happening is a 'buy in' by senior managers who have faith in the business they are running. Often they have owned their business, not in a material but in an emotional sense, far more than their corporate overlords. 'Buyout' suggests exclusion, rupture and getting rid of an unwanted appendage; whereas 'buy in' suggests joining up, inclusion, and participation in an exciting venture. From the perspective of the parent companies, the term 'buyout' may be appropriate, but for the team members, it is a 'buy-in'. The case of the Jacoa MBO, recounted later, is a good example of how the material facts of ownership can be the result of entrepreneurial behaviour rather than the cause of it.

Whatever the reasons, however, for managers wanting to buy, it has now become a fact of life that going for a MBO is the norm rather than the exception when a sale of a part of a corporate company is being mooted. It has become part and parcel of the thinking of corporate salaried managers: 'I recently asked a main board director of a large listed company what he felt when the management team said they wanted to do a buy out rather than just be sold off. He said it's a fact of life. Every time you try to sell a division or subsidiary, the manager asks whether there is any chance that he can buy it. It's now the norm' (Robert Smith, managing director of Charterhouse Development Capital Ltd, quoted in *Euromoney*, 1987: 22.)

Capital structure

Changes in tax, financial and economic environments during the decade in which the MBO phenomenon has been gaining momentum, have meant that MBOs have themselves undergone many changes in the relatively short time-span since their arrival on the corporate scene. Nevertheless, two key features remain. The first concerns the financial arrangements whereby managers are able to obtain part ownership in their company.

In any but the smallest MBOs, the managers can only afford to put up a fraction of the total purchase price. Therefore, the difference between what they can afford to pay and the purchase price has to be financed largely by outside debt. In the larger MBOs a consortium of financial institutions put up quasi equity capital such as convertible preference shares and subscribe various layers of debt secured on the assets of the business.

This leads to 'abnormally' high levels of gearing. It is important to point out that the distinction between debt and equity in MBOs is muddied by equity conversion rights attached to the various classes of debt.[7] Whereas the debt to equity ratio is not normally above the still high level of 2:1 in MBOs, if we are looking at the leverage on the pure capital base (i.e. excluding preference share capital from equity but including it as debt), then the ratio can rise to 10:1.

The second feature concerns the size of the deal and distinguishes the MBO from the purely financial LBO typical of US buyouts of billion dollar plus public companies. Beyond a certain point, dictated by management's ability to afford sufficient equity capital themselves, management's ownership stake falls to a level where it is no different to a stock option scheme. In the larger US LBOs management's stake is generally less than 10 per cent. However, in both UK and US MBOs, management frequently obtain a majority stake and generally not less that 25 per cent of the fully diluted equity. Wright and Coyne (1985) and Hanney (1986) found that in about three-quarters of cases in the UK, management have a majority equity stake, and are often the single largest equity holders. Kaplan's (1988) study of 76, US, MBOs showed managers raising their equity stake from a mean of 9 per cent pre-buyout to 31 per cent post-buyout. It may be, however, that MBOs constitute a smaller proportion of LBOs in the US than they do in the UK, primarily because the size of deals has typically been so much larger in the US than in the UK. It is also because in the US the history of MBOs is one of Wall St money chasing managers whereas in the UK, it has been managers looking for financial support to achieve independence. Although the financial arrangements vary markedly among different buyouts, a rough guide to the difference is shown in Table 1.5 which compares and contrasts a 'typical' MBO and LBO. Whereas the LBO, as its name implies, is essentially a financial mechanism, the MBO is essentially a managerial phenomenon allied to a distinctive financial structure. The impact of the capital structure in MBOs is nonetheless critically important. First, it tends to favour certain sorts of companies. While MBOs occur in all spheres of business life – there is virtually no sector, whether manufacturing, high tech, service, or financial, where the management cannot raise the finance for a buyout – some circumstances are more propitious for MBOs than others. Companies in mature industries with assets which can be converted into current cash flows to service and reduce debt, where development capital is not required, where tax regimes are favourable to debt rather than equity, where tax breaks[8] for depreciation allowances exist, and where there are stable, high cash flows, are all cited as ideal.

Second, there is the worry that leverage ratios are being driven above what is financially prudent by financial institutions with growing funds earmarked for LBO investments. 'When expectant money starts to drive the hunt for deals, speculative absurdity is seldom far away. . . . LBO lending has all the charm of Latin American in the

Table 1.5 Typical financial structures of the larger buyouts compared (on start up before equity rachets)

	US LBO US$ 100m (%)	UK MBO US$ 25m (%)	Subscriber
Pure equity			
(ordinary shares)	1	15	Management*
(preferred ordinary shares)	9	15	Venture capitalist
Quasi equity			
(preference shares)	10	30	Venture capitalist & institute backers
Total	20	60	
Primary/senior debt	60	40	Institutional backers
(or sale and leaseback)			Bank
Subordinate debt			
mezzanine: junk bonds			
@ fixed premium rate)	20	–	
Total	100	100	
*Management ownership			
of pure equity	10	50	
of total equity	1	25	
IRR required by venture			
capitalist on equity	(25 to) 40% p.a.		
Exit	5 to 7 years		

1970s'. (*The Economist*, 29 October 1988.) Fortunately, however, new financial instruments, such as interest rate 'caps' which limit hikes in variable interest rates on debt, have so far limited the financial risks involved.

Third, the high gearing encourages cash flow management and a managerial focus on the immediate post-buyout period. As we shall see in some of the cases that are presented in this book, the high gearing seems to constrain management choices to cost reduction rather than revenue enhancing strategies, because it increases the risk of new product development or new marketing strategies. For this reason, some commentators, especially in the US, have criticised buyouts for substituting debt capital and pre-empting capital otherwise destined for more innovative start-up companies.

The situation is not clear. Simply looking at Table 1.6 indicates UK MBOs have occurred across a wide range of industries and services,

Table 1.6   Management buyouts by industry

	Number	Value		Average size*
		£m	%	£m
Manufacturing:				
Engineering	26	841	18	32
High technology	8	126	3	16
Wood	5	134	3	27
Paper	3	370	8	123
Chemicals	2	83	2	41
Textiles	1	12	–	12
Total	45	1566	34	35
Retail and distribution	16	1266	27	36
Construction and property	7	162	3	23
Insurance	6	115	2	19
MELT	6	526	11	88
Banking and finance	5	367	8	73
Transport	5	342	7	68
Food and agriculture	5	214	5	43
Business services	5	130	3	26
	100	4687	100	40

*Average size is computed after excluding MFI/Hygena (£718 million).
Source: *Financial Times*, 13 October 1988.

many of which are known both for their entrepreneurship and for their focus on revenues and investments for revenue enhancement. What does seem unassailable is that in the typical MBO, the financial combination of leverage and risk forces the manager's attention to the most efficient use of costs *and* improving the allocation of resources. For example, *Business Week* (20 June 1988 127–28) report the story of 7 UP, post-LBO. The new CEO cut $20 million out of the $34 million overhead budget and launched two new soft drinks, Cherry 7 UP and 7 UP Gold.

Finally, the capital structure encourages a stock market flotation within a three- to five-year time span. This is often needed to allow the management to retire various classes of debt, boost the common equity of the company, reduce their own borrowings, and allow the venture capitalists to exit and themselves to cash out. The following comment, though made about LBOs in the US, is pertinent to MBOs from divestiture in the UK; though to a lesser extent, given the smaller size of the UK animal.

In three to five years, after the acquisition debt has been paid down and the managers have fulfilled their contractual commitments, everyone – managers, investment bankers, lenders and investors – feel powerful pressure to sell the company, either as a whole to another company, or in part to the public. Almost as quickly as it began, the recent rejuvenated team of just a few years earlier will have ended its brief day in the warm sun of private, entrepreneurial ownership (Lowenstein, 1986).

The direct costs of flotation plus the need to divert limited management resources to *both* preparing the requisite voluminous literature and negotiating with the institutions, can distract attention away from the business and exact a heavy price from firm performance. It can be argued that the greatest problems for the achievements of buyouts are, and increasingly will be, here. The culture and behaviour that can be changed (as we demonstrate later) can easily – perhaps too easily   change back again. And this leaves open the question of the sustainability of the change process initiated by LBO/MBOs. In order to understand both the significance and subtlety of the MBO-led change process, we present a conceptual outline of the major factors of change in Figure 1.1 below.

4   OWNERSHIP BEHAVIOUR

A question frequently asked of MBOs is: how is it that one company's dog ends up an owner-manager's dream, especially when this transformation occurs with essentially the same managers at the helm? If it is the personal equity stake that gives managers the incentive to work harder, to be more committed to the business, or to take better decisions, then this has serious implications for an economic system which depends largely on professional managers controlling other people's money. Or if ownership allows managers to be more effective, by giving them the legitimacy to implement their preferred policies and strategies, this is an indictment of the ways these corporate centres influence what their subsidiary managers can do.

In order to summarise the structural and behavioural forces at play in a buyout, and describe what the cause-effect linkages are likely to be, we will present a simplified post-MBO model. The essence of the model is to assert that there are three enabling causes of successful

Figure 1.1 Post-MBO three-factor change model

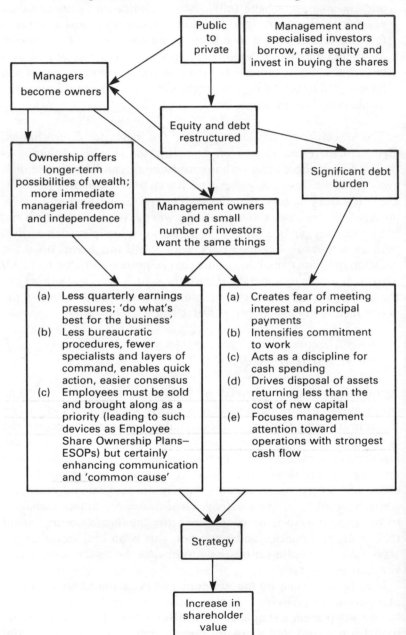

3 ENABLING CAUSES

post-MBO performance: private ownership, managers as owners, and financial restructuring. We view the other elements (debt, wealth incentives, freedom of decision-taking, and the harmonisation of investor/manager interests) as forces released by the enabling causes, and as processes that work by changing managerial behaviour.

We believe, for example, that it is as much, or more, the changes in managers' behaviour that accounts for results obtained rather than tax advantages of debt or the mechanical fillip leverage lends to the equity invested. Rappaport (1986) concludes 'economic theory and evidence say it is misleading – if not flat-out wrong – to conclude that "leveraging up" creates shareholder value'. Michael Jensen of Harvard (1986) argues that investors *discount* the shares of firms that:

- generate cash flows in excess of what is needed to finance the business;
- lack plans for investing excess cash flow in projects that will return more than their costs of capital;
- do not distribute excess cash to shareholders.

While all factors play a part in the final outcomes, *we believe that it is the management, behavioural and process changes which account for more of the resulting performance improvements than have heretofore been suggested.*

Although it would be impossible to rank the effective sources of power in this model and to state precisely all cause and effect connections, several elements stand out.

1. The LBO/MBO model unleashes a powerful set of managerial dynamics. As one LBO investor stated: 'The LBO amplifies fear and opportunism in management'. The MBO/LBO changes the way managers behave and the cultures in which they act.
2. LBO/MBOs have paid off handsomely to investors and owners with average returns of 50 per cent. In the short to medium term (5 years) this is a strong indicator of 'better' management (at least in terms of increasing shareholder value). The results do seem to have implications for the status quo of professionally managed, publicly held corporations, a point to which we return later.
3. For longer-term effects, the economic jury is still out (MBOs and LBOs have been launched and succeeded in a bull market with

low interest rates). But available performance data on MBOs/LBOs suggests increased efficiency of the firms. Kaplan (1988) at the University of Chicago reports that in his study of 76 large, management-led buyouts:

- profits after 2 years are higher than the industry average by 6 per cent;
- inventories are 3 points lower on average, relative to sales;
- capital investment is lower by only one point.

4. A recent McKinsey study of 'restructuring' deals concludes that 84 per cent of the value of the restructuring comes from operating efficiencies realised by the new owners. Where it exists, prior mismanagement of corporate units creates enormous economic opportunities which, inter alia, generate widely different valuation perspectives.

If the broad case for improved management activity or behaviour seems at least superficially persuasive, then we need to know both the cause and effect linkages and the nature of the dynamics set in motion by the MBO/LBO. (This is what we attempt to do in the six cases presented below).

Partial support for our three-factor change model, and the assumptions behind it, is provided by the academic literature on ownership and control (although, as we argue later in this book, the underlying economic paradigm provides a very partial view of the behavioural and cultural complexities involved).

5 THE ACADEMIC HERITAGE: LONG ON ECONOMICS, SHORT ON REAL BEHAVIOUR

A voluminous theoretical and rationalist literature has built up which is pertinent to these behavioural and process issues. Notwithstanding Adam Smith, it was really the work of Berle and Means in the 1930s which sparked off the debate which continues to this day. Berle and Means argued that in the quasi-public corporation, the desire for personal gain cannot be relied upon as an effective incentive to the efficient use of industrial property. This is because without an ownership stake, managers are not entitled to the bulk of profits generated through increased efficiency. Interestingly, their views were for the most part based on armchair speculation ('received wisdoms') for the actual incentives and behaviour of corporate officials received no systematic attention in their work.

Theories of management behaviour; as owners and as professional managers

The ideas of Berle and Means gave rise to two interdependent streams of thought which seek to explain the behaviour of twentieth century, professional managed corporations: managerial theories of the firm and agency theory. The former focuses on the motivations of managers and the extent to which these differ from the entrepreneurial, homo economicus of classical economics (Baumol, 1959; Simon, 1959; Cyert and March, 1963; Williamson, 1964; Marris, 1964). The second reformulates the behavioural assumptions of classical economics, collapsing the notion of the firm into its constituent, stakeholder interests (Coase, 1937; Alchian and Demsetz, 1972; Jensen and Meckling, 1976; Fama, 1980). Both schools expound a model of managerial motivation and behaviour which allows managers to follow goals other than firm profits and profit maximisation.[9]

The formal argument is that if firms are not managed by their owners, and if ownership is dispersed among many shareholders, then managers have a significant element of autonomy in deciding resource allocation within the firm. Because managers maximise desires ('utilities') other than that for profit, they may well maximise personal status, prestige, leisure, respect, political independence, etc., at the expense of firm profits. It is perfectly rational for managers to try to shift some of the costs of their preferences on to others if 'monitoring costs' are greater than the organisational slack created by managerial discretion, or if markets fail to discipline adequately non-profit maximising managers (Williamson, 1964, 1975; Jensen and Meckling, 1976:313).

In other words, given half a chance, professional managers may be expected to look after their own interests rather than those of the owners (assuming, of course, they subscribe to a rational economic calculus). To make matters worse, they may steer clear of innovative or risky projects (although some theorists disagree with this proposition).[10] If the project fails they may lose their jobs whereas if it succeeds the benefits go to the external shareholders (who can better diversify away the risks of failure). 'As the manager's owner- ship stake falls, his incentive to devote significant effort to creative activities such as searching out new profitable ventures, falls' (Jensen and Meckling, 1976:790).

Reversing the arguments, a number of positive attributes of ownership can be adduced. First, collective ownership will reduce the incentive on each manager not to become wholly committed for 'every team member would prefer a team in which no one, not even himself, shirked' (Alchian and Demsetz, 1972: 790). Second, owner-managers may be expected to devote more effort to seeking out innovative projects or different resource allocations. Third, by reducing 'shirking' and risk-averse behaviour, firm per- formance in owner-managed firms will on average (given positive monitoring costs) have higher profit rates than manager-controlled firms.[11]

Applying these ideas to MBOs, suggests that we might expect the newly created owner-managers to relinquish personal goals (status, prestige, leisure, personal respect, etc.), in favour of profit maximisa- tion; to work harder; and to search out more creative and innovative possibilities. If true, the effect is likely to be a marked improvement in firm performance.

Control effects

In addition to these 'self-interest' or agency effects of ownership, there are also control effects.[12] Prior to a MBO, the managers of a subsidiary are subject to control by a corporate head office. The separation of general management from operating management in divisionalised conglomerates, frequently means that subsidiary man- agers are constrained by a corporate culture, strategy and set of procedures geared to the needs of the whole (group) rather than to those of the part (the subsidiary).

Successive studies after Berle and Means have pointed to dicho- tomies between the *theory* of professional managers as agents of shareholders and the *observed behaviour* of corporate managers. These differences, plus the relatively passive behaviour of pro- fessional 'portfolio' shareholders (investors, pension funds) lead to logical questions about whether managers do in fact act in the best interests of shareholders. Managerial practice should be the standard against which to judge the post-MBO performance of new owner-

Figure 1.2 Behavioural elements in shareholder wealth creation

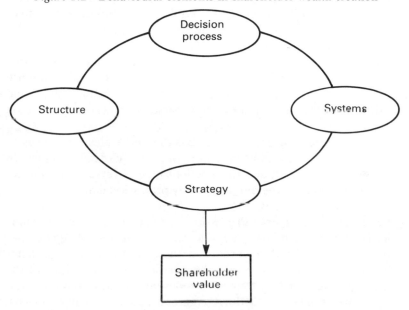

managers. It is here that true comparative shareholder value is created. Such comparisons also offer opportunity for comment on both the theory and the practice of what is the widespread corporatisation of economic life in the West – and increasingly the Far East and newly industrialising economies as well. Assuming a simplified organisational behaviour model as shown in Figure 1.2, the criticisms fall into each element, covering both incentive and control effects.

Decision processes
Rappaport, Jensen and others have stated that since managers are not owners, they do not hold owners' values and therefore do not behave as owners. Managers use the cash flows and assets of the shareholders to maximise sources of personal satisfaction, for example:

● *Empire building.* Because large hierarchical corporations are in-herently political in their decision-taking (that is, personal career and territorial ambitions get mixed with profit maximisation) a number of decisions get made which do not maximise shareholder values but personal, political ones. Questionable acquisitions sometimes fall into this category. Public companies have incentives to expand their firms 'beyond the size that maximises shareholder wealth', states Jensen.

● *Social status.* Perquisites, social values and perceptions sometimes serve as social needs that get optimised in preference to shareholder wealth. Corporate jets, club memberships and other symbols of corporate and personal power are common examples.

● *Time horizons.* The argument here is that the professional investor is perceived to have short time horizons; i.e. quarterly earnings. In spite of empirical studies of benefits to the obverse, this mind set seems to prevail in the minds of many professional managers in the publicly held company.

● *Complacency and risk.* Professional managers are seen by some authors as too patient – a mode conditioned by soft goals, non performance-related rewards and distance from faceless shareholders. Others observe that the personal risks of failure to the managers are higher than the inherent business risks in new investments or cost reductions. Aggressive management of the cost structure may contain little benefit to the professional manager and few penalties if the profit out-turn is unsatisfactory. This is seen to be particularly true for corporate overheads.

● *Accounting numbers.* A great deal of energy is devoted in public firms to looking good in reporting terms and to managing the market price of shares. For example, taking a write-off does not generally look good. But failure to do so mis-states true values and can distort portfolio-based resource allocations to apparently under-performing (in terms of ROI) subsidiaries. In general, managers of public companies seem to pay more attention to Profit and Loss results than to managing the balance sheet – a function reserved for finance directors in their corporate consolidation of business unit results.

Systems

Reward systems
1. Jensen has called LBOs a 'direct indictment of the compensation policies of [professional, corporate] managers'. He argues that professional managers are sometimes underpaid (sharing too little of the values created for shareholders, but mostly that they

Figure 1.3   CEO raises: they just keep rollin' along

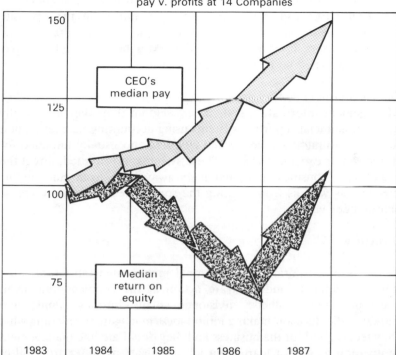

pay v. profits at 14 Companies

Index: 1983 = 100

are mis-paid. Pay and bonuses are tied to deceptive accounting profits rather than the creation of economic value.

2. Repeated compensation surveys in the US consistently show the lack of relationship between CEO pay and the financial perform-ance of the corporate firm. Figure 1.3 appeared in *Fortune* (19 December 1988, p. 58) under the heading 'Where's the risk in CEO rewards'?

The specific criticisms are usually:

a. That base salaries are too large (and therefore inert) as a percentage of total compensation relative to the performance bonus.

b. That too frequently, short-term incentives begin to generate bonuses at low levels of performance; frequently at lower levels than the cost of equity on median ROE's for the industry.

c. That bonus plans allow for wide ranges of discretion to override 'uncontrollable events' that nonetheless affect shareholders.
d. That CEO and senior executive pay moves in the opposite direction to that of lower ranked employees who are the true risk-bearers in terms of reduced working hours, layoffs and pay freezes when performance turns down.

Information and control systems

Management information systems are seldom that: they are usually adapted financial reporting systems using accounting accruals. Their demands, though, are heavy and frequent and usually intended for use at senior executive levels. These systems, it is argued, direct the attention of business unit managers away both from running the business as well as from making the sort of decisions that increase shareholder value.

Structure

Overlays of corporate and divisional management structure often delay, complicate and frustrate action at the business unit level. Functional-line conflicts; divisional versus business aims; and bureaucratic decision-making inhibit local managers from doing what they feel is good for the business and they debilitate line management motivation as well. Clearly, not all organisations suffer from all of these managerial and structural ills – exceptions abound of so-called 'excellent' companies. Yet excellence is a relative concept, defined by reference to the mass of less-than-perfect corporate organisations. The source of many MBOs lies here; in the structural and managerial imperfections of business units mal-administered or poorly designed for competitive survival.

Summary

The conceptual and practical flaws for creating shareholder value in the agency model of professionally-managed, publicly-held corporations are numerous. They lead to sub-optimal strategies and can, and often do, lead to lower shareholder values, thus occasioning the MBO opportunity.

After an MBO, management is freed from many corporate political and organisational constraints. Ownership has given them the right to implement change when they see fit to do so. This in itself may well stimulate the search for better practice. When managers know they can change something without having to go through layer upon layer of corporate bureaucracy, they are more likely to seek out areas for improvement. One commentator has suggested: 'people work best when wearing one hat instead of four, when decision making is unencumbered by layers of executives each in search of a function' (Lowenstein, 1986: 154). Greater management commitment and greater freedom to plan strategy according to the dictates of the individual business may far outweigh any loss from the cut in the umbilical cord. In addition, the removal of excessive head office charges or hidden costs may more than offset the increase in interest charges and in fees from company advisers which arise as a result of a MBO.

Although corporate overseers are replaced by venture capitalists, the control exerted by the latter tends to be hands-off. If things go seriously wrong, then rather than interfere, the venture capitalists prefer to pull out by selling the business over the heads of the incumbent management. When the management holds a majority stake that is pushed through by equity ratchets, management's stake can be reduced to less than 50 per cent if forecasts made at the time of the buyout are not fulfilled.

Control effects are essentially the same as those adduced for the self-interest incentive effects of ownership. The motivation is, however, quite different. A major aim of this book is to explore the relative importance of these two processes in accounting for change, post-buyout. For if ownership *allows* managers to be more effective rather than *incentivises* them to be so, then the catalyst for corporate renewal is organisational – giving managers sufficient freedom to do what they think best within a culture which is geared to the needs of their particular business – rather than personal; finding a better carrot with which to tempt managers.

There is a split amongst corporate commentators as to the beneficial or detrimental aspects of these various ownership and derivative, structural attributes of MBOs. Some argue that MBOs work, not because of any intrinsic processes, but because of extraneous factors such as tax breaks, or recession creating a buyers' market for subsidiaries which can be exploited by unscrupulous management. Others maintain that the incentive effects are largely irrelevant as MBOs from divestiture are largely a disguised form of exit from a dying business. They argue that the short-term viability of MBOs depends on managers exacting otherwise unobtainable concessions from employees; or that the long-term viability of the MBO depends on owner-managers being prepared to accept a lower return on capital than the sellers. Why otherwise would corporate managers be so daft as to sell out to management at a discount? As we have shown earlier, most of these arguments are contradicted by both Kaplan's and Jensen's serious studies. The majority of authors eulogise the positive behavioural aspects of direct ownership and control as the magic in MBOs. The task remains to understand precisely how this magic manifests itself.

5 METHODOLOGY

Separating cause from effect is not easy in MBOs. So much is going on. The change in ownership, the personal ownership stake, an increase in gearing, an increase in the pace of change, hands-on control by a parent being replaced by hands-off control by a venture capitalist, a reduction in size, new advisers and some new senior managers, changing market circumstances, a honeymoon period, and a rescue from difficult if not critical circumstances, all make it difficult to assess in any objective manner the precise and relative impact of any specific change.

The limitations of quantitative research

This problem has plagued quantitative research into the relationship between ownership, control and firm performance. (It is also characteristic of much of the literature on the relationship between organisational structure and performance.) Most such research has adopted what Child (1974) calls a universalistic stance (the presence of certain attributes is of itself conducive to superior performance in most, if not all, circumstances), rather than a contingent one (the attributes favourable to higher performance will alter according to the circumstances under which a company is operating).

Apart from the problem of accounting for and separating off circumstances which may swamp ownership effects, there is the question of the direction of causation. Performance levels constitute an input of information to managers which may cause them to modify policies and action: 'Performance is not simply an end-product, a dependent variable. The fact that the level of performance is found to relate to a feature of organisation does not of itself tell us how much performance is the consequence or the cause of that feature' (Child,

1974: 176). Finally, there are significant definitional problems in making concepts such as ownership and performance susceptible to quantitative statistical analysis.

An alternative approach

In the particularly complex situation of a MBO, we felt, therefore, that applying quantitative techniques was not appropriate. Also we wanted to go beyond mere performance outcomes, to look at the *process* whereby the change in ownership and control affected what managers and their organisations *did* after a MBO. Further, the economic models commonly used to delineate the pre-conditions for an MBO seem deficient in their behavioural assumptions and unable to account fully for what we observed in practice.

We decided to investigate in some depth a small number of buyouts. By talking to more than 40 owner-managers in 10 companies, we were able to glimpse through their eyes what has changed as a result of the buyout. Although one might expect that most managers would be reluctant to admit to, say, not exerting themselves under the old regime, our own research demonstrates just how candid they are in comparing their behaviour before and after the buyout. We have also interviewed a number of interested parties such as venture capitalists, accountants and lawyers as well as parent companies divesting buyouts. We have sought to identify those characteristics of our 10 very different companies which account for their successes and their failures; to see if any patterns emerge across them; and to point out potential problem areas for the long-run viability of this type of business enterprise.

We have probed deeply, revisited the same topic on more than one occasion and crosschecked data wherever possible. However, the essentially subjective nature of partisan views must be recognised at the outset. So too must the bias introduced through interaction with an interested interviewer[13] and reliance on a non-random sample.

The typical objection to relying on perceptions is that people are biased and bound to be self-serving. Such objection tends to be paradigmatic (Burrell and Morgan, 1979). We can not know whether the distortion introduced through subjective bias on the part of interviewees or interviewers is any greater or less than the distortion introduced through false assumptions and methodological limitations in objective methods. Irrespective of their objective veracity, however, we believe that managerial perceptions provide much insight into the process whereby organisational structures intrude into managerial thought and action. Moreover, by focusing on the actor's model rather than the observer's we run less risk of squeezing data into our own model of the world and confirming our own prejudices.

Perhaps most important are the questions raised by the size and composition of our sample relative to generalisations about the large, public corporation. In terms of size, qualitative methodology generally relies on a manageable rather than representative sample. This clearly restricts the potential for generalisation which in cases such as this must always be of a speculative rather than definitive nature. In terms of the composition of our sample, we readily acknowledge that the firms which spawn MBOs may not be representative of all firms. In particular: the pre-MBO corporate environment may be worse than in other companies (otherwise there wouldn't be an MBO); the devisions selected for an MBO have all been screened by their managers and financiers to determine that their value can be enhanced (not true of all unsuccessful divisions in a corporation); the managers of an MBO have been carefully 'selected' by the financial backers (so may be better than the corporate average). Thus any implications that can be drawn from post-MBO success must relate in the first instance to the inefficiencies and inadequacies of the organisations that spawn them rather than to all poorly performing corporate organisations. This does not, however, preclude speculation on the latter or on the failings of large corporations, even if 'the slightest lack of reverence for sacred cows arouses intense resentment among the guardians of the bovine faith' (Lee 1989: xiii).

Research design

A list was compiled from press reports of buyouts which had occurred in the UK since 1980. This list was reduced to 30 buyouts on the basis of three criteria: size (we were interested in the larger buyouts); structure (we wanted buyouts of subsidiaries); and age (buyouts which were more than one year but less than three years old). The latter two criteria were chosen so that owner-managers would be better able to compare their perceptions of being corporate executives with their current status after the initial euphoria of succeeding in the buyout had worn off. Following written communication to each of these companies, access was obtained to 10 buyouts, two of which later withdrew.

Two sets of interviews were carried out, the first during a nine-month period during 1984 and the first part of 1985, the second, mainly during the first part of 1987. The first set of interviews was the more comprehensive due to the need to establish a relationship with the key personnel and to gather background information on each company. All the owner-managers in each buyout were interviewed by the authors and the CEOs were interviewed twice. Forty-three interviews were held with 35 owner-managers. For comparative purposes, an additional 16 interviews were carried out with people nominated by the buyout CEOs. In the main these were people in the divesting parent companies and in the financial institutions supporting the buyout. The aim of the stage two interviews was to revisit as many of the original owner-manager interviewees as possible, to see what changes had occurred during the intervening period. A further 20 interviews were carried out. They were open ended, semi-structured interviews lasting around two hours. All interviews were taped and then transcribed verbatim.

We have also relied extensively on press reports, on published annual accounts information and on documents provided by the companies.

Organisational stories

Space precludes us from presenting all the case histories here. We therefore present six in their entirety and refer to the findings from the other companies and from interested parties in the final chapter.

We refer to the cases as 'stories' in recognition of the fact that the accounts are neither right nor wrong, their worth can only be determined in terms of the insight they add to our understanding of MBOs and any general lessons they yield. We believe that, despite any bias or lack of candour, these managerial perceptions provide a unique window through which to glimpse the various processes, cultural, political and economic, at work in a buyout.

We commence with the story of Stone International, followed by Metsec, Jacoa, Trend Control, March Concrete and John Collier. In the final chapters we draw together the common themes, contrast these with the received wisdoms on buyouts described above and suggest what general lessons can be learned from them.

Notes

1. Ownership of the firm means claims to the assets and cash flows of the firm. These claims can generally be sold without the permission of other individuals who also have property rights in the firm. Control means a degree of autonomous decision-making authority with respect to resource allocation. The separation of ownership and control arises if some claims to a firm are held by individuals who have no direct role in the management of the firm. These owners then have to delegate some decision-making authority to their agents who are managing the firm. The fusion of ownership and control reverses the process of separation and is only complete when one person owns and directly manages the firm.

2. It could be argued that the concentration in the ownership of UK quoted companies over the last decade by pension funds, local authority funds, insurance companies and unit trusts (Wilson Committee Report, 1980) allows these institutions to exert a measure of control. However, 'historically British financial institutions have not been eager openly to involve themselves in management' (Cuthbert and Dobbins, 19 : 291).

3. There are other types of LBOs apart from the MBO variant. The purely financial LBO occurs when a company (or subsidiary) is taken private by an investment group which uses borrowed money to buy out public shareholders (or their corporate agents). There is also the Leveraged Employee Stock ownership plan (LESOP or ESOP) whereby a company borrows money and places it in a trust that invests in the company stock. Annual contributions are subsequently made to the trust which are used to pay down the loan and disburse proportionate amounts of stock to employees. (Often, the shares the trust purchases come from the company's holding of its own stock or from new stock issues. Tax breaks exist for dividends paid on shares to employees, on dividends used to pay off an ESOP loan, and for lenders to ESOPs – a major factor accounting for their success in the US.)

4. The typology of control advanced by Berle and Means (1932) and adopted by much subsequent research, distinguishes five categories of corporate control: (1) privately owned, (2) controlled through the ownership of a majority of the voting stock, (3) controlled through the ownership of a dominant minority of the voting stock, (4) controlled by means of a legal device, (5) management controlled. To a large extent, these categories represent ideal types, for there are a whole host of institutional arrangements whereby salaried managers have a participative equity stake in the enterprises that they manage. And even in those instances when salaried managers become owners of the business they manage, they normally share equity control with financial institutions who take control if things go wrong. The boundary between owner control and manager control may, therefore, be somewhat opaque.

5. For example, the detailed work of Mike Wright and John Coyne at the Centre for Management Buy Out Research at the University of Nottingham, or of Steven Kaplan at the University of Chicago.

6. Throughout this discussion we have avoided the technical arguments about how to *do* the kinds of economic valuations we are discussing. There are widespread software packages for accomplishing this based on equally widespread empirical and theoretical studies. See Fruhan, 1979; Jensen, 1987; and Rappaport, 1986. The latter author has developed the ALCAR valuation software.

7. *The Economist* (1985: 75) argues that in buyouts, subordinate debt is really equity masquerading as debt. In view of the conversion rights frequently attached to the subordinate debt, there is much substance to this claim.

8. Dividends for preferred stock are taxable whereas interest payments on subordinated debt are tax deductible. Without public shareholders, buyouts need not pay dividends so all the company's spare cash can go, tax free, to pay off the debt. In the US a further tax break is provided because in the ownership exchange, asset values are typically written up, thus increasing depreciation allowances over the next few years (see John Thackray, *Management Today*, August 1984: 43; Lowenstein, 1986).

9. In the main, however, managerial theories of the firm do not focus on ownership per se. While affirming that its separation from control creates the managerial organisation, they typically move on to consider how factors other than ownership such as uncertainty, or conflicting objectives, lead to non-profit maximising behaviour. Or they view ownership as just one of a range of factors affecting organisational outcomes. It is agency theory which has singled out ownership for special consideration although some writers, notably Williamson (1964), span both schools of thought.

10. A converse position with respect to the agency costs of the separation of ownership and control has been suggested by Fama. He argues first, that managerial discretion will be curtailed by the market for managers both within and outside the firm and second, that ownership, rather than encouraging innovation, may do the opposite. It may cause managers to be risk-averse because they have a greater concentration of their risk portfolio when not only their human capital but also their financial capital is tied up in the firm. A different line of argument, but with the same conclusion, is given by Demsetz. He argues that owner-managers may also wish to avoid the 'personal costs and the anxieties' that go with managing or learning about new technologies. While absentee shareholders may be expected to want the firm to maximise profits, owner-managers may well decide to trade off risk for a lower return (by using a higher personal discount rate than that prevailing in the market) or they may wish to trade off profits for other benefits such as an easy life: 'Where is it written that the owner-manager of a closely held firm prefers to consume [e.g. leisure] only at home?' (Demsetz, 1983).

11. Evidence suggests that large management-controlled firms are less concerned with profit maximisation or have inferior levels of performance (both in terms of profit rate and growth) than comparable owner-controlled ones (Monsen, Chiu and Cooley, 1986; Radice, 1971; Steer

and Cable, 1978). Other research shows no apparent general relationship between ownership and company profitability (Kamerschen, 1968; Larner, 1970; Child, 1974). Blair and Kaserman (1983) suggest that on balance, however, 'the evidence appears to lean slightly in the direction of supporting a conclusion of relative under-performance by manager-controlled firms'.

12. Some – but not all – of these control effects are a form of agency cost: 'the opportunity cost associated with lost profit opportunities because the organisational structure does not permit managers to take actions on as timely a basis as would be possible if the managers were also the owners' (Weston and Brigham, 1987: 16.) However, if an increment over the organisational structure cost needed to monitor and control managers arises because of poor structural arrangements, then this increment is not an inevitable agency cost. It can be removed by better structural arrangements.

13. Because of this subjectivity, we have resisted the temptation of presenting the perceptions quantitatively in order to give a false semblance of objectivity. There is no good way of measuring objectively different views about complex, multidimensional issues or of measuring the strength of feeling which different people attach to their views. Qualitative data are best interpreted qualitatively – a view long favoured by social anthropologists but often ignored by organisation researchers (Green and Willman, 1987).

Table 1.7 Future EPS growth is not a good guide to current relative P/E ratios (EPS growth by P/E ratio)

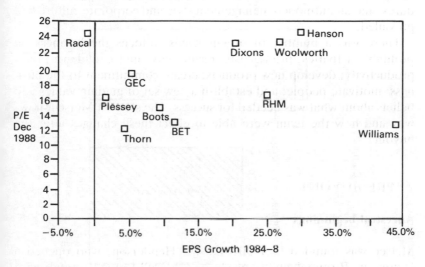

Source: The MAC Group, 1988.

Table 1.8 Nor is historic EPS growth correlated to current relative P/E ratios (EPS growth by P/E ratio)

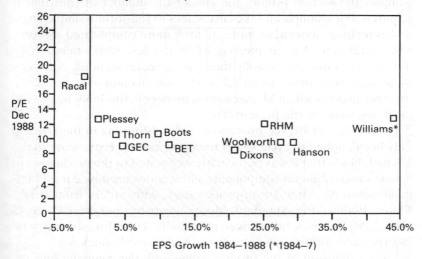

Source: The MAC Group, 1988.

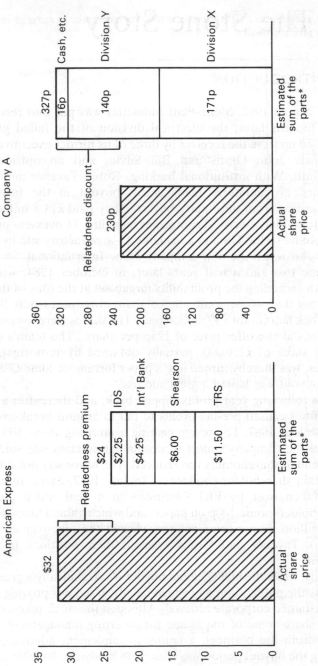

Table 1.9 Relatedness which is effectively exploited can enhance share price

*Based on comparative P/Es and other measures.
Source: The MAC Group, 1988.

2 The Stone Story

1 INTRODUCTION

On 7 March 1982, Stone-Platt Industries was put into receivership. Two months later, the electrical division of the failed group was snapped up from the receiver by three of its former executives, Robin Tavener, John Oratis and Bill Silvie, and an outsider, Peter McGrath. With institutional backing, Robin Tavener and his team clinched an ambitious management buyout in the face of stiff competition from third-party buyers. They paid £14.8 million for all the Stone-Platt electrical companies including 11 overseas operations from India to the US and a valuable 14-acre factory site in Crawley. They christened the new company Stone International.

Some two and a half years later, in October 1984, with profits growth exceeding the profitability targets set at the time of the buyout by more than 40 per cent, the company was successfully floated on the stock market for £37 million plus. The shares were oversubscribed 18 times at the offer price of 125p per share. The team's collective initial stake of £250 000, partially obtained by remortgaging their houses, was thereby turned into a paper fortune of some £7.8 million. The buyout was hailed a great success.

The following year profits slipped back, and thereafter a series of calamities caused pre-tax profits to fall to around break-even in the year to May 1987. To prevent gearing from rising above 100 per cent, one of the company's most successful subsidiaries was sold and the dividend to shareholders was reduced. The move was not sufficient to maintain shareholder confidence. In July 1987, Stone International was taken over by FKI Electricals in a deal which paid Stone shareholders some 100p on paper, and which valued Stone at around £37 million. Some commentators viewed the takeover as a rescue. Messrs Tavener and Oratis retained their positions in the FKI buyout.

Thus, while the management buyout was technically a great success (it was the public company which failed), it did not provide a vehicle for sustained corporate renewal. Although the stock market flotation must share some of the blame for diverting management attention away from the business, a failure to implement adequate controls during the buyout period was seen, with hindsight, to have caused the downfall of the company. Robin Tavener and his team did change the culture of Stone International greatly for the better. They implemented many beneficial changes to management procedures and business practices during the MBO's brief lifetime. It is perhaps ironic that the undoubted positive effects of the buyout were eventually eclipsed by some simple mistakes and by events beyond the control of the company.

We commence with a description of the main events leading up to the buyout.

2 PRE-BUYOUT

Ancestral beginnings

The origins of Stone International's parent company, the Stone-Platt group, date back to 1831. In that year, Josiah Stone established a company in Deptford to supply copper nails to the boat builders of the Thames. The company's activities developed over the years leading eventually to it becoming the world's largest manufacturer of ship propellers, Stone Manganese Marine, and the world's largest supplier of railway air conditioning, J. Stone Deptford. In the late 1950s, the Stone group went on a buying spree with little apparent industrial logic to the sorts of businesses acquired. In 1959, the Stone companies merged with Platt Brothers (Oldham) Ltd, then the world's largest manufacturer of cotton spinning machinery, to form Stone-Platt Industries Ltd (SPI). (Although this was a true merger, there was a bias towards Platt having acquired Stone rather than vice versa.)

During the late 1960s, Stone-Platt increasingly suffered from the problems experienced by a wide range of British manufacturing industry. A large proportion of its activities was in industries which were either declining, or were being increasingly challenged by newly industrialised countries. Added to this was the fact that many of its plants were in need of modernisation. In 1968, as part of a rationalisation and reorganisation plan to stem a significant profit deterioration, the group was broken down into four divisions. The electrical division specialised in the manufacture of air conditioning equipment for railways and mass transit systems throughout the world, and in the manufacture of heating, lighting, and power, electromechanical products. The textile machinery division mainly manufactured machinery for processing continuing filament, natural and man-made fibres. The marine and mechanical division manufactured a range of products for marine energy systems. The pump division manufactured glandless and conventional pumps for power stations, oil and petrochemical industries and for general industrial duties.

In the years subsequent to this reorganisation, the electrical division's performance was somewhat erratic, culminating in a loss in 1973. At the beginning of 1974, in order that greater attention could be devoted to the problems of the electrical division, Robin Tavener was appointed divisional chairman.

Turnaround

Tavener had been brought into Stone-Platt in 1969, at the time of the reorganisation, to be the financial controller of the pump and electrical division. His appointment to divisional chairman in 1974 was his first general management position and he enjoyed it hugely. He set about building a management team with its headquarters at Crawley, the site of the UK manufacturing operations. This team included John Oratis as the new financial controller, together with the existing marketing director, Reg Scott, and the engineering director, Bill Silvie.

During the next eighteen months, there was continuous debate at the Stone-Platt board about whether the division should be closed down. By the end of 1976, however, the imposition of stronger management controls, improvements in the level of location managements, product rationalisation, and improved trading conditions began to show positive results. The strong links forged within the team and the first-hand experience of how to manage a turnaround were later to feature importantly in the buyout.

In 1976, as part of Stone-Platt's stated overall strategy of concentrating on products with growth prospects in the UK and in the USA, two acquisitions were made by the electrical division: Safety Electrical Equipment, the largest supplier of railway air conditioning in North America and Fluidfire Development Ltd, a Wolverhampton based company specialising in fluidised-bed combustion technology. These acquisitions were strengthened in 1979 with the acquisition of two more North American companies, Nycal Company of New Jersey and Johnston Boiler Company of Michigan. The former supplied parts to the commercial transportation industry throughout North America and was complementary to Safety's business; the latter, a world leader in fluidised-bed firetube boilers, was seen as a way of widening exploitation of fluidised bed technology.

By 1978, the electrical division, which had been the least profitable part of the group, was now the most profitable part. About this time, however, things were beginning to go seriously wrong in Stone-Platt as a whole.

Decline and fall

In 1978, the Stone-Platt group was a relatively large, diversified multi-national. It had sales approaching £200 million, in product lines ranging from textile machinery and railway equipment to pumps and marine propellers. Its operations straddled a large number of countries including the UK, the US, Spain and India. Under the stewardship of Edward Smally, Stone-Platt's CEO between 1974 and 1979, the Stone-Platt group had followed a strategy of growth by acquisition.

Some of the acquisitions, however, were dramatically unsuccessful, notably a joint venture with Barry Wehmiller in brewery equipment, the purchase of a French valve manufacturer and the acquisition of Ernest Scragg and Son. These investments and, in the latter two cases subsequent divestment, bit heavily into cash reserves as pre-tax profits dropped from £15.8 million in 1976 to £9.5 million in 1978.

From that point on the Stone-Platt group began a remorseless slide to extinction. The principal reason was a catastrophic decline in the fortunes of the UK textile machinery business, Platt Saco Lowell (PSL). The decline was brought about by world recession, excess capacity and cut-throat international competition. Global output of textile machinery had been falling in real terms since 1975 and British companies had lost market share to imports from West Germany and Switzerland with stiff competition also from Japan, France, Italy and the US. When the extent of the downturn in trading conditions became clear, cost reductions were vigorously pursued. These came too little and too late to offset the serious decline in the order intake for textile machinery.

In just over three years, from the beginning of 1979 to February 1982, PSL recorded pre-interest trading losses of £10 million and an extraordinary loss in excess of £40 million through reorganisation and redundancy costs. In contrast, the rest of the group produced overall profits of £14.5 million.

The crisis in the textile operations led to a major reorganisation of the group in mid-1979. Robin Tavener was taken out of the electrical division and transferred to group headquarters. On 1 January 1980 he was made group chief executive and managing director of the textile division. Shortly, thereafter, John Oratis was also transferred across to group HQ as group finance controller. Reg Scott accepted a short-term assignment to restructure the group's Australian operations. Only Bill Silvie remained as managing director of the electronics and energy systems operations.

Almost immediately, Tavener found himself at odds with the Board over what to do with the textile operations. Lacking the external legitimacy to go against the dominant corporate culture, he was unable to challenge the views of those who, previously, had been so unsuccessful at overseeing the textile division. Until 1980, Stone-Platt was dominated by one family. One member was chairman, another was in the marketing division, another in the finance division. In line with many family-run firms, the management structure was seen as authoritarian and paternalistic. For example, in 1976 the textile divisional chairman formally proposed to the CEO that one of the textile machinery factories in Lancashire be closed. He was refused permission to have this debated at the group board meeting on the grounds that the factory at Accrington was the largest employer in the town and that it would be socially and politically unacceptable to lay of 1300 workers. In such an environment, despite being somewhat of a hero for having turned around the electrical division, Tavener was unable to overrule those who had elevated him to the hot seat.

If 1979 was the beginning of the end for Stone-Platt Industries, it was also the year which marked a change of fortunes in the electrical division. UK operations suffered a loss before interest and tax of £705 000. The reasons were various: an engineering strike in the UK, the strength of sterling, loss of key personnel, and having to help Platt Saco Lowell. (In order to reduce over-capacity in the Platt Saco Lowell plants in Lancashire, the Oldham plant was transferred to the electrical division who then had to make use of the capacity by transferring product into Oldham. This caused serious disruption to the boiler activity in Crawley which had been nominated a transfer product.) Fortunately, these losses were cushioned by profitable trading by overseas subsidiaries.

The electrical division and other profitable Stone-Platt divisions were stripped of cash to prop up the textile division. This was not enough. In April 1980 the Stone-Platt group defaulted on its borrow-ings and was forced to rearrange loans of £40 million under a package arranged by its bankers and coordinated by the Bank of England. Two Lancashire factories were closed down and a third one slimmed down. The pump division, a South African subsidiary, and the propeller business were sold. Again, this was not enough. After losses of £15 million were announced for 1980, mainly due to heavy costs of redundancy and reorganisation of the Lancashire operations, a further rescue package took place in March 1981. City institutions stumped up a capital injection of £10 million and new borrowing facilities of £40 million. At the time, Stone-Platt said that it hoped to break even in 1981.

Later that year Robin Tavener left, followed shortly by John Oratis, in a policy disagreement with the new chairman, Leslie Pincott. Pincott had been brought in by the board at the end of 1980 to help with the rescue. Tavener and Oratis believed that the textile division should be sold at almost any price, partly so that more emphasis could be given to the profitable parts of the business. A buyer had made a tentative offer but Pincott, along with the majority of the board, held that the division should be rescued and not sold off. The disagreement over strategy culminated in Tavener's exit.

By the first quarter of 1982, it was apparent that a significant level of losses had continued as a result of yet further downturn in PSL's order book. The board were now forced to do what Tavener and Oratis had advocated all along: sell off the textile machinery business. The sale required significant write-downs and the group faced attributable losses and provisions of over £20 million in drawing up its 1981 accounts.

Institutional support had been obtained for a further rights issue with the proviso that Stone-Platt demonstrate its willingness to carry out its proposed reconstruction plan. The programme involved the banks supporting Stone-Platt through the summer. In the event, they were not willing to see their security whittled away by asset sales while at the same time having to bear the immediate risk of any further deterioration in Stone-Platt's trading or cash position.

Amidst strong protests from those City institutions which only twelve months previously had participated in the £10 million rights issue bail-out, and notwithstanding protests from Pincott that a further reconstruction would make the Group viable, the clearing banks led by Midland Bank pulled the plug.

The *Financial Times* (19 March 1982) remarked: 'Apart from the problems in the textile machinery business, excessively restrictive covenants imposed by the institutions in return for their support, divided senior management, and loss of control in and over subsidiaries' activities, together conspired to make third time unlucky for what had once been a leading light in the UK engineering industry.'

The decision to call in the receiver sparked off an unprecedented row in the City and in the press as to whether the receivership was warranted. Irrespective of whether a reconstructed Stone-Platt would eventually have prospered, some subsidiaries would still have lacked the resources they required for expansion in the immediate future. Later events were to show that once given its independence, the electrical division could blossom in a way that would have been unlikely had it remained part of the corporate structure of a none-too-well conglomerate. Stone-Platt's organisation and culture had constrained the successful development of the electrical division during the difficult years prior to receivership. Even if the Stone-Platt rescue had succeeded, the electrical division would have been expected to go down a path dictated by group objectives, rather than decide its fate autonomously.

3 THE BUYOUT

Receivership

The main activity of the Stone electrical division was the design, manufacture and supply of passenger comfort systems, air conditioning, lighting, etc., for rail and metro coaches. In the US, Stone supplied similar products for buses and did general refurbishment work for transit authorities. The market was (and still is) characterised by high value contracts granted by transit authorities. As the market leader in air conditioning systems, Stone was invariably asked to tender.

Receivership made such tendering very difficult. The receivers were unwilling to countenance trading unless the cash turnaround was fairly rapid. In view of the long lead times with Stone's production, this ruled out much business. The receivers would not allow Stone to take new orders, or to complete existing ones, unless these could be shipped fairly quickly. Nor would the receivers accept any responsibility for subsequent maintenance or guarantees. This was hardly the framework to encourage people to place orders with Stone.

Stone's management team had to maintain the customer base, if there was to be any chance of survival. They had to reassure customers that the problems of receivership would be resolved. They also had to keep potential purchasers of Stone, some of whom competed with Stone's customers, from seeing confidential information that had been passed to Stone by its customers. There were three big orders in the pipeline: an extension of the Hong Kong metro; a large first-time contract to supply the Seoul metro in South Korea, and replacement equipment for the mainline railways of Iraq. Stone already supplied all the airconditioning for the metro, but Temperature Ltd, a subsidiary of Norcross and Stone's only UK competitor (and already a supplier of air conditioning to the Kowloon–Canton surface railway) tried to muscle in. In Seoul, the Japanese mounted a major offensive and in Iraq, where Stone was the major supplier, the French and Germans were trying to get a toehold.

If Stone had lost these contracts the future would have looked bleak, if not impossible. Fortunately, however, the fact that it was widely known that a management buyout was in the offing (see below) helped maintain customer loyalty. Despite the aggravating circumstances, the senior management were able to keep the company going through the three-month receivership period.

Fortunately, the receivership did no lasting damage to the business. In fact it did some good. The period coincided with a natural, cyclical downturn in orders at the UK production plant at Crawley. Receivership helped forge a new spirit of collective determination; it was a low point from which small improvements engendered a sense of euphoria fuelling motivation to succeed; and finally, it paved the way for acceptance of new management and work practices. The stark facts of receivership and probable job loss following rationalisation were powerful levers unblocking resistance to change.

Motivation for the buyout

> If a buyout is mounted merely as a survival exercise, the managers trying to save their jobs may not have the necessary dedication and enterprise to achieve a level of success comparable to Stone (Robin Tavener).

There were elements of the visionary, the defensive and the opportunistic in the decision to go for a buyout. Robin Tavener was the prime mover in the affair. He had first thought of a buyout in 1975 when he was a year into the turnaround of the electrical division: 'If we were putting all this effort in, wouldn't it be nice to participate in the success?' He asked the chairman of the group whether he might consider a buyout – to which the answer was 'yes', but at the right price. At that time, however, the firm's asset value bore little relation to its earning power and when it was turned around, the management couldn't afford to buy it.

The circumstances leading up to the buyout, the second time round, were rather different. Tavener had been out of work for three months. Nobody wanted to hire a chief executive who was tarred with the brush of corporate failure. So he decided that the best way to get a job and be successful was to build up something himself. He started looking around with Peter McGrath who had been introduced to him by a headhunter who thought that the pair of them would get on well together.

Tavener's wife then asked him in January 1980 why he didn't buy out the electrical division of Stone-Platt. He recollects his reply: 'You must be mad, who will give us the £25 million?' Tavener then talked to McGrath, Oratis, Silvie and Scott and asked them to join him in going for a buyout. They decided that, if successful, Oratis (formerly controller of finance at SPI) would be finance director; Silvie (formerly technical director of Stone and chief executive of Electronic and Energy Systems) would be the engineering director; McGrath would be the operations director; and Reginald Scott (formerly marketing director of the electrical division of SPI), would be marketing director.

John Oratis had confidence in the business and in the team's business ability. They had made money for the group in the past, so there was no reason why they shouldn't now make it for themselves: 'You don't get those sorts of opportunities falling into your lap too many times in your life and if you are lucky enough to be one guy in a million who gets the opportunity, then you are a mug if you don't take it.'

Bill Silvie had been in charge of Stone during the receivership period. He was concerned about his own prospects should the company be taken over by the likes of GEC or Hawker-Siddeley. Also, he did not want to see the company split up:

> It was unlikely that I would have had a job in the new set-up. At my level, you are one of the first to go. Also, being 54, my chances of getting a new job were not good. Now that didn't worry me overly but it made me think . . . I was also very annoyed that there was a possibility that the business would be broken up by the

receiver. Although individual companies within the division might have been just as successful if they had been sold off one at a time, it didn't satisfy us to see that happen. It was very demoralising after having spent years welding the various bits of the company into a global mini conglomerate. Our dissatisfaction was not purely emotional. We have complementary expertise between our locations. We have great strengths in electronics in Spain and we rely on them to prompt developments in other parts of our business. We would have been very sad to lose that balanced expertise.

Peter McGrath's reasons for joining the buyout were his belief that Robin Tavener and he would make a good team. He also felt that the buyout was a wonderful opportunity for himself and the other members of the team to realise their full potential:

> I was convinced that Robin Tavener and I could acquire and develop a business to our considerable mutual benefit and he and I began a joint search shortly after he left Stone-Platt Industries. Our common purpose, as it seemed to me, was to use the skills, energy and experience we felt we both had to make money for ourselves. When Mrs Tavener prompted him to go for a buyout my enthusiasm grew with the widening of our horizons. On being introduced to the other members of the team I became for the first time convinced that we could pull it off.

The final member of the team, Reg Scott, was in retirement. He agreed to come back to work temporarily as marketing director to help the team get the company back on its feet. Because of the temporary nature of his involvement he did not take an equity stake in the new company. Scott felt that the team could run the company better than anyone else. He also thought that Stone deserved better than to be taken over by a remote company:

> It was because with terrible predictability, this awful thing had happened to the company, I didn't feel in any way that I had to be a knight on a white charger and come and rescue it, but I felt, well, here is a business opportunity which might come off. I had known Robin and the other members quite well and I honestly believed that by participating, I would help the team in some way.

Negotiating the deal

When Stone-Platt went into receivership in March 1982, Tavener had to move quickly to come up with a deal which would beat the fairly formidable opposition interested in purchasing the electrical division. With the help of Candover, a financing institution specialising in buyouts, Tavener and Oratis put the buyout proposals together in about ten weeks.

The speed with which they did this gave them a major advantage over other bidders. One very interested company prepared documents which then had to wait a month for the parent company board to meet. There was also a certain amount of brinkmanship: the rumour was that the team might be able to go as high as £10 million, whereas they were quite prepared to go much higher.

The offer made to the receiver was based upon the (anticipated) attraction of a total deal: 'There were no awkward bits left out, we were willing to pay a fair price for the business at its then level of profitability, continue employment at Crawley and do it quickly.' (Robin Tavener)

The strategy worked and for £14.8 million the team purchased the electrical division including a long leasehold property at Crawley in the UK to which a value of £4 million was attributed in the purchase agreement. Thus the business was purchased for approximately £10.8 million, a P/E of 6.0 on the adjusted 1981 pre-tax profits of £3.7 million. This price represented a discount to net assets of over £4.0 million. A further £2.5 million was subscribed for working capital, and additional bank overdraft, performance bond and foreign exchange facilities of £5.0 million were also arranged with the Bank of Scotland. Full details are shown in Table 2.1.

The acumen with which the deal was put together is itself part justification for the rewards that the team have since reaped. As reported in the *Evening Standard* at the time of Stone International's successful flotation in 1984:

> Together they pulled off something of a quiet coup. The buy out which rolled up all the Electrical Division assets into Stone International without being picky was actually clinched at receiver Ernst and Whinney while the Laird Group, which builds railway carriages and systems for Metro-Cammel, still had its investigating accountants on the Crawley site. GEC, Hawker Siddeley and the American Standard Company were all hovering wondering whether to pounce (October 1984).

Table 2.1 The financial structure of the Stone International buyout

1. Share capital	Authorised	Issued	Ownership/subscriber
a) Ordinary shares £1	£1 250 000	£250 000	Buyout Team
b) Cumulative convertible preferred participating ordinary shares £1	£1 750 000	£1 750 000	Globe and Electra 0.7m Candover 0.05m
c) 12% cumulative redeemable preference shares £1	£3 000 000	£3 000 000	Globe and Electra
Total share capital	£6 000 000	£5 000 000	
2. Loan capital			
d) 16% subordinated loan 1989/93		£5 000 000	Globe and Electra
e) Six-year term loan @ 1.75% over LIBOR		£5 000 000	Charterhouse Japhet Kleinwort Benson
f) Short-term 3-month loan @ 1.75% over LIBOR		£3 000 000	British Linen Bank Royal Bank of Scotland
Total loan capital		£13 000 000	
Total funding		£18 000 000	

Notes:
1. The ordinary shares do not participate until year 6.
2. The CPPO in (b) were issued at a premium of £1.33. They carry dividend rights of 10 per cent of subscription value or 5 per cent of pre-tax profits. The conversion terms of the CPPO were such as to give management between 12.5 per cent and 25 per cent of Stone dependent on cumulative profit achievement in the five years to May 1987.
3. e) is repayable in years 2–6. This loan was denominated in dollars.
4. Both the term loan and the short-term loan are secured by way of fixed and floating charges over the assets of Stone.

Source: Internal company information.

4 POST-BUYOUT

Changing the culture

Much of Stone's business involved large and lumpy orders, worth anything from £1 million to £15 million. Fortunately for Stone, the market was not just a price one: a company joke was that marketing couldn't remember when it last got an order on price. The level of commissions and after-sales service were also important and Stone had a good reputation for supporting the product with excellent after-sales service. Owing to worldwide excess capacity, the market was becoming increasingly price sensitive with companies prepared to buy contracts by tendering at unrealistically low prices. The buyout team recognised that Stone had to reduce its cost structure if it hoped to tender at internationally competitive prices while maintaining respectable margins. There was also the matter of the high gearing which had to be reduced to acceptable levels within a two to three year timespan. The major organisational effort after the buyout was, therefore, directed at vigorous cost-cutting.

The need to reduce costs permeated all aspects of the business, starting with the executive directors themselves. An important lesson learned from the experience of Stone-Platt was that headquarters must be monitored explicitly to ensure that it adds value greater than the overhead that it creates. The team pared their central staffs to the bone. Apart from the direct saving in central overhead costs, this gave an important symbolic demonstration to the rest of the company of the importance of reducing costs: 'If the directors are able to do without personal empires, then so can everyone else.' This message was reinforced a few months after the buyout, by the sacking of the presidents of two subsidiaries who had built up management structures felt to be totally inappropriate to the size of the company.

An integral element in pushing through the cost-cutting strategy was increased personal accountability. Prior to the buyout, when a location had a problem, someone would invariably be sent from HQ to do a fire-fighting job. 'If someone fouled up, then the relevant managers just changed jobs: 'Through their mobility, managers were able to avoid the implications of their actions. Now if there is inefficiency, we know who to blame. Also, people in the subsidiary companies have less reason to say, look we are doing what you told us to do.'

Post-buyout, the philosophy was to make sure that each location could cope on its own and to hold them accountable if they do not do so: 'If there is a problem, the supposition is that the managers in that location are not adequate to deal with it. The profit centres are stronger now, but they also carry greater responsibility.'

UK working practices
The primary target for the new culture of efficiency was Crawley. This was the symbolic and economic heartland of Stone International, where the headquarters of the group were located in a building facing the UK factory. Just as in 1973, when the problems of the electrical

division were those of Crawley, so too in 1982, the first thing the team did was to sort out Crawley: 'It soon became apparent that our major problems lay in Crawley, and it was a most horrifying mess.'

The immediate problem was to rebuild stocks and increase production throughput to meet the orders which had begun to flow through immediately after receivership: 'We had a high work load to get our teeth into. It wasn't a situation of sitting back and saying, Christ, we have no orders. A lot of production was already in process and it just needed to be tidied up. The real problems were getting production out'.

The job of reorganising Crawley fell to Peter McGrath. He inherited a factory organised on the basis of three product areas: Stone Chance, Stone Boilers and Stone Transportation. Each had its own separate product manager who reported directly to the MD for the whole of the electrical division. The product managers had a fair amount of autonomy, with their own financial, engineering, marketing and manufacturing staffs. The philosophy had been that product identity should be fostered and that control would be facilitated by cutting things up into discrete entities. Accordingly, the machines for the various product groups were painted different colours and the works staff allocated to one particular product area. The resulting duplication of machines led to high capital intensity, although this was mitigated to some extent by the fact that all the machine tools were of an average age of 20 years and space was not at a premium. A more severe problem was inflexibility in reallocating labour in line with production peaks and troughs. If people had nothing to do, they could not be moved across to other product groups without top-level liaison.

McGrath immediately centralised manufacturing and later engineering, although he left the machine tools where they were when it was sensible. He also removed a number of tiers of management thereby broadening his own span of control. Initially, there was some negative impact on morale from the loss of product identity. Fortunately the workforce soon recovered and accepted working for a common manufacturing facility.

The workforce was reduced from 580 down to 475 in 15 months without any reduction in total output levels. The cuts were mainly in indirect labour: those planning and organising production and ancilliary staff. (Engineering staff were reduced by some 30 per cent but the biggest numerical reduction was in the manufacturing support staff: purchasing, planning, shop planning, stock control, shop control, shipping, works engineers, maintenance, and so on.) No direct production workers were made redundant. Some large new contracts were obtained during the receivership period. Ordinarily these contracts would have required an increase in labour but the increased productivity obviated the need to hire more people.

McGrath achieved the improvements in efficiency by driving people harder:

> If you pay people for effort, after a point, they stop. If people are part of a team, they sweat blood. If you set people targets, they will do it. If you set higher targets, they might complain but they also do it ... the previous manager in this job was a charming and capable chap. But he was not a driver and the man in this job has to be a driver. I go down to the factory floor as a matter of religion and anybody who is seen not working is hauled over the coals.

This more authoritarian management style did not, according to McGrath, dent morale. As later events were to show, however, these changes were not without cost.

Apart from tackling labour efficiency, measures were taken to improve production facilities: a CAD/CAM system, approved in principle prior to the receivership, was installed; considerable investment was made in new CNC machines for cutting metal; a computer-based manufacture control system, Material Resources Programming (MRP), was made fully operational; and inventory control thereby tightened. A value engineering approach was introduced to railway products which, over the next four years, was to achieve cost economies of some 15 to 20 per cent. The immediate effect of all these changes was that Stone started manufacturing on time, something that had rarely happened before.

Finally, a major problem which the buyout team had to deal with at Crawley (and elsewhere in the group) was apathy and sloth in reacting to market problems. For example, after the buyout an order was found which had been on the books since 1976. The order had been taken at fixed prices and although this factor kept the customers on the hook, it did nothing for Stone's profitability. A shake-up of sales and marketing procedures was instigated.

Relations with overseas subsidiaries
In addition to sorting out domestic operations, a great deal of attention was paid to the overseas subsidiaries, especially those in the

USA. The latter were suffering the combined effects of extravagant management procedures and the hiatus caused by the receivership. New management controls and financial procedures were introduced throughout the group. Tavener and Oratis travelled extensively, visiting most of the overseas subsidiaries to restore communications and to review the progress of the management improvements being undertaken.

In the 18 months since the buyout, I have spent one hundred days travelling. I have visited each of the operations on location, doing reviews, assessing acquisitions, and getting involved in their problems. There is nothing better than getting away from HQ, going to a location and having no other problem but their problem for a couple of days. You become fully immersed and begin to understand what their problems are. I did not have that role before. I was effectively promoted into a corporate role and somebody else came and did that. In fact, we have combined the corporate and the management roles now and taken a strata of management away in the process. That is far more rewarding than being in a headquarters structure.

At first, it was thought that a decline in profitability at Safety in the USA was due to competitors gaining a foothold in the market. On closer inspection, it became apparent that it was a case of mismanagement with money being thrown at any problems that came to hand. In just one year, Safety had increased its overheads by some $2 million and that was in a company making $4 million profit. Within a month of the buyout, the chief executive and the production man were released and redundancies instituted. A new president, the former marketing director, was appointed. His first task was to reduce overheads. New marketing and manufacturing directors were promoted from within the company.

Much the same situation was encountered at Johnston Boilers in the USA. The problems were greater than at Safety and Bill Silvie had to spend six months in the USA sorting them out. A new president, Bob Precious, was appointed.

At Nycal, demand for the company's products had fallen. This had led to substantial losses from obsolete and excess inventory and from uncollectable debts. The incumbent management was held accountable for not installing effective management roles. A new president and directors of finance and marketing were appointed from outside the company and a new operations director was appointed from within. New products were sought. Finally a major effort was made to restore the company's reputation which had suffered because of market neglect and association with a former New York City transit official who had been dismissed for corruption.

Corporate control

The relationship between Headquarters and locations was closely reviewed. Prior to the receivership, monthly reporting had escalated, delegation of authority was cancelled, performance reviews abandoned and communication generally ignored. The reduction in the size of HQ improved communication through shorter spans of command. A more balanced structure was put in place which gave:

- group management control over major investment and operating decisions;
- location management autonomy in control of normal day-to-day operations;
- a 'sensible' level of monthly information from locations;
- information to locations on the group's progress; and
- regular on-site meetings to review results and forecasts.

Of particular note was the way marketing was reorganised to reflect the new structure. With the exception of international corporate publicity, marketing was devolved to the locations instead of being orchestrated from the centre. This enabled a dramatic reduction in the number of people at headquarters having a marketing role.

Information needs

The much reduced staff at HQ forced a reappraisal of the sorts of information which could be processed effectively at the centre. Scott introduced a new-style, monthly marketing report from the locations which emphased information really essential to running the business:

> I have said to the locations, all the number crunching is fine but the bit I am interested in is the front-led marketing part and I only want the sort of information that you are using to run the company. If you are not using it, then there is no reason for me to want it. Abbreviated reports, covering much more than marketing now arrive at HQ five days after the end of each month. This allows us

to monitor what is happening much more quickly than previously. The full report comes later with all the numbers. There is a lot less resentment in the locations about filling in unnecessary forms which are merely filed away and never looked at.

Incentives

As part of the cultural somersault aimed at emphasising the mutual dependency of UK and overseas operations, a major incentive scheme was introduced for senior managers. The scheme had two parts. The first was based upon the performance of the individual locations and tied to both the level of return on capital and to the growth of that operation. The second consisted of an equity stake in the company (Electra and Globe released some of their shares to facilitate this): 'Although many of the American managers were tremendously motivated, the old bonus schemes in Stone-Platt were not constructed to increase cooperation. By giving managers a stake in the business, we hoped that this would force them to look beyond sectional interests.'

The boards of management of every operating subsidiary were offered the opportunity to participate in the equity of the firm and the issue was oversubscribed. A number of problems had to be overcome in offering the shares to other countries throughout the world: foreign exchange regulations in Spain, tax in Australia, SEC in America, political considerations in Argentina and exchange controls in India and Pakistan.

Commitment

The circumstances of the buyout affected the buyout team members in various ways but the sum effect was to enhance commitment to tasks. The senior management team became more directly involved in what was going on: 'I am enjoying more what I am doing in this job than previously when I was group controller of finance at head office. The job then was too divorced, the corporate structure with the divisions coming into head office made layers and layers of management barriers. You don't get close to business operations that way.'

The ending of receivership also played a part in motivating the team: 'Pre-buyout we were treated as though we were loss makers because virtually no money came back for reinvestment. Everything just got sucked into the centre. That was demoralising across a very broad front.'

The combination of Stone-Platt's widely publicised demise and interest from friends and colleagues in the buyout raised the stakes for success or failure. The new owner-managers did not consider they had an incentive to work any harder or that ownership caused them to become better managers.

If you enjoy your job then you are going to give everything of yourself irrespective of whether you are working for yourself or for a corporation. Of course it is nice to see that we are better rewarded but I don't think that is a motivating factor.

The basic issue is that because we own a large chunk of the equity, we will earn a big reward in the end. In some ways this can be a demotivating factor because you start thinking do I need to work as hard as I do. It does not stop you, but as the day draws closer when you can see yourself cashing in, you start wondering whether it is time to take it easy and slow down.

The facts of ownership did, however, encourage team members to monitor more closely what each other was doing.

To be objective, I think the buyout has introduced a new element for all of us who have money in it. Previously, I daresay there were times when you sat back and said, well get on with it, because people seemed so involved. But when its your own money it makes you take part. All right it is his responsibility, but it is my money that he is putting in and therefore I have to be more attentive.

Fortunately, this closer attention to what each other was doing did not cause conflict. While there were frequently differences of opinion about priorities, argument was motivated by a desire to see the company successful rather than, as had often previously been the case, by personal considerations.

There are differences but we all somehow feel that we are talking in a common framework and not criticising anyone, just discussing how the business can be run better. The fact that we all have a personal stake in the business could lead to lots of conflict. But so far it has been a very constructive environment and a much nicer one.

Performance

When interviewed in 1984 and 1985, all the team members considered Stone International to be a far more 'effective' company than previously. Financial performance post buyout had improved dramatically as a result of the changes described above and because management had steered the company through a difficult period of time until a natural upturn in market conditions occurred. They did not believe the change was due to any intrinsic magic in the buyout bringing about a transformation in managerial abilities and effectiveness. Robin Tavener summed up the consensus view that: 'It is the people rather than the buyout which has made this company.' Table 2.2 shows the improvement post-buyout.

Table 2.2 Stone International's financial performance before and after the buyout

| | Pre-buyout | | | Post-buyout | | | | |
| | Year ending 31 December | | | 17 months to 26 May | | Year ending 31 May | | |
	1978	1979	1980	1982	1983	1984	1985	1986
Turnover (£m)	36.4	38.2	42.6	84.4	64.3	72.6	78.7	100.4
Profit before interest and tax (PBIT) (£m)	4.6	2.5	3.5	2.9	6.5	7.0	8.8	8.0
Profit before tax (PBT) (£m)					4.7	5.7	7.3	6.1
Net assets (£m)	11.1	14.3	21.0	23.4	23.1	25.3	36.0	48.9
Return on Sales (ROS) (%)	12.6	6.5	8.2	3.4	10.1	9.7	11.2	8.0
Return on Capital Employed (ROCE) (%)	41.5	17.5	16.7	12.4	28.1	31.8	24.4	19.6
Gearing				49.0	42.9	39.9	35.0	42.1

Notes:
1. Net assets data and hence ROCE before and after 1982 are not strictly comparable as they are derived from different data sources. The differences are not sufficiently great, however, to make them unsatisfactory for broad illustrative purposes.
2. The gearing for 1982 represents the post sale and leaseback position.
3. ROS and ROCE use the PBIT figure in the numerator.
Source: Internal company information and Datastream.

Strategic change

While financial performance improved markedly, the business did not undergo any radical changes after the buyout. What changes there were, were in defence of the existing strategy and concerned better implementation rather than a change of tack. The cost reductions and improvement in sales were achieved without change in either the customer or product base. Any changes in the product base were associated with contract specific factors rather than with changes in product technology. Some modern design changes were made but with the exception of CAD/CAM, there were no fundamental changes in technology, nor was it envisaged that there would be. Marketing strategy was geared primarily to retaining existing customers. When new opportunities arose, which happened every few years, a major effort was devoted to gaining new business. But in 1984, the basic customer profile was the same as before the buyout.

With the successful recovery from receivership and the post-buyout reorganisation considered more or less complete, the team felt it time to think about expanding the business. Much of the product range was mature and there was a need to replace those parts which were static or declining. There was a limit to cost reduction: many of the changes that had been implemented, such as getting rid of one or more layers of managerial staff, work rationalisation, the introduction of new work practices, better inventory control, were one-offs. Once accomplished, other ways of generating profits had to be explored.

The team started casting around for companies to which they could apply the same medicine which had regenerated Stone International after the receivership period.

There are areas we haven't touched on. We are on the coach but not on the track, nor in freight. So we have an entrée with the customer and we will be looking for an expanded product range to gain greater access to a market which we have great strengths in. But we all recognise that there is no greater fool than one who moves into a new market area where he has no market knowledge, no production or engineering knowledge (John Oratis, 1984).

The team were very cautious.

This is not like owning 100 per cent of the business, it is not absolutely your own money. Other investors are involved and you still have to make the right investment decision and you have to be careful because you are dealing with other people's money. I suppose my philosophy is that I take greater risks with my own money than with other people's because I have only got to answer to myself if it goes wrong.

There were constraints, however, to Stone's ability to fund its acquisition strategy. While the banks were prepared to grant Stone lending facilities, these were expensive and somewhat more restrictive than other sources of finance. One option was to seek a stock market flotation so that Stone could use its own paper for acquisitions.

5 FLOTATION

There were other factors favouring flotation. At the time of the buyout, it was envisaged that Stone International would seek a listing at the earliest opportunity, considered to be about five years out. The financial success of Stone International led the institutional backers to push for an earlier listing so that they could realise some of their gains.

The team was quite surprised that the stock market would accede to a full listing after only two and a half years of trading. Normally a five-year trading record is required but the pre-receivership period counted towards this. The team were also moved by personal considerations to take the company to the next stage in its corporate life cycle. It was another milestone achieved.

The flotation took up much more of the team's time than had been anticipated. It was a very stressful time for everyone:

> We were told at the start of the flotation that it would more or less involve the board full time for about six months. None of us really believed it. But it turned out to be very much the case. In retrospect, the day-to-day running of the company must have suffered a little and, of course, it cost a lot of money. . . . It was much worse than negotiating the buyout. Perhaps it was because we were the first buyout to go public and our advisers hadn't worked out for themselves the proper way to do it.

The London Stock Exchange flotation happened in October 1984 and was a great success. Thirty-five per cent of Stone International's equity was released for the sale. The shares were oversubscribed roughly 18 times at the issue price of 125p. At this price, the company was valued at around £37 million as compared to the £14.8 million paid to the receiver some two and a half years previously. The issue raised some £13 million for Stone International, comprising £6 million from new shares and £7 million from the institutional share-holders. Robin Tavener and the other members of the buyout team held onto their shares which were now worth some £8 million on paper. The team's stake of 25 per cent was diluted to 21 per cent by the flotation.

Acquisitions

The pace of activity did not let up for the senior management after the flotation. A number of acquisitions were completed in quick succession. Two boiler companies in the West Midlands, W. H. Allen and Danks, were bought out from receivership for £3.3 million. This was financed by the issue of 1 569 382 ordinary shares and from banking facilities. The two companies were put together, the work-force virtually halved, the senior management replaced mainly with in-house people, and the company turned around. Then, in August 1985, a 75 per cent stake in Andrews, a profitable, private company was bought from its family owners for £6 million (The chairman of Andrews, his wife, and the company's managing director retained the remaining 25 per cent.) The deal was financed through a placing at 149p a share to raise £3 million, and by Andrew's acquisition of £2 million worth of Stone's shares and of £1 million worth of unsecured loan stock.

In September 1985, at the end of the first year of trading as a public company, the team sold one third of their shares at approximately 161p a share. (Following the disposal, they held a stake of 4.79 per cent in the group.) They had been prevented from selling any of their shares at the time of the flotation by some of their institutional investors.

> We were slightly trapped into not selling any of our shares. Some of the sponsoring institutions said 'we will undertake not to sell any shares for the next twelve months and you ought to do the same.' So we said 'OK' and then they sold some. It was all very nice having worked five years and being told that you are worth all this money but you couldn't spend any of it. So we all agreed to sell the same proportion of our shares.

Disaster strikes

At the start of 1985, Crawley's order book, always subject to volatility because of the relatively narrow home market, had been unusually low. Hence Stone had cut its margins and tendered for and won an air conditioning contract for the New Jersey Port Authority Trans Hudson (PATH). The order was to be partly sourced through Stone Safety in the US. Because of the need to systems engineer applications to the specific needs of the customer, and because Stone's business was international, these tenders often had to be produced from the branch locations. The branch locations needed a fair degree of autonomy to determine contract terms in the light of customer requirements and anticipated competition.

The team recognised that because of the potential impact of individual contracts on the whole group, there had to be adequate central control to ensure that tenders, while competitive, were realistic. Yet as later events were to show, the following sentiments, uttered in 1984, were to prove prophetic.

> You have to leave this in great trust to the local management but there is always the danger that you only find out what they have done two years later, by which time they have severely dented your profitability. You have to have some system that works very well, which they have some faith and trust in, which you know will hold them in some sort of control but which gives them maximum impact locally. The motto is 'here are the rules', you can deviate from them, but if you do so then tell us.

Hints of trouble emerged at the end of 1985. Interim profits were shown to be down because of UK, and to a lesser extent US, production delays related to the PATH contract and because of a weak order book at Crawley.

Peter McGrath left the following year after suffering a heart attack while on holiday. His management style was at odds with that of the rest of the team and they had agreed by mutual consent to part ways. In the light of problems at Crawley, Robin Tavener wanted to strengthen the board, and to change senior management expertise to match the new pattern of activities that Stone was developing. It turned out, however, to be very difficult to attract the right calibre of person. (By the time Pat Fordham, a new divisional director for the transportation business was appointed and joined the team in January, 1987, the damage had been done.)

The full-year results to May 1986 showed pre-tax profits down from £7.34 million to £6.09 million (and the latter after an exceptional credit of £1.3 million following rationalisation of US pension arrangements). The Crawley transportation division accounted for the major part of the downturn in profits. Despite the problems, a number of sharebrokers at the end of September 1986 were still estimating pre-tax profits for the full 1986/7 year of £8.5 million. Notwithstanding the poorish trading performance, Stone's share price was riding high at 178p on a current P/E ratio of 24 (or of 11 on the expected EPS figure), buoyed by rumours of a possible takeover bid by Hawker Siddeley or Northern Engineering Industries.

Rumours of further problems with the group's trading saw a slide in the share price to around 110p over the next couple of months. In November, in view of uncertainties over Stone's current trading position, the directors announced that the company's first six months of trading to 30 November 1986, had produced a loss before taxation of approximately £2 million.

The principal reason for this was problems at Crawley. The PATH order had been subject to major rectification. The order had suffered from the lack of a project manager and in the end large parts had had to be reworked twice. As Robin Tavener later remarked in an interview with the *Financial Times*: 'We have been shooting ourselves in the foot . . . 'We got the second design so badly wrong we couldn't believe it. The first four units had to be scrapped altogether . . . We were not running Crawley in a professional and systematic manner' (18 May 1987).

In order to catch up lost time, money had to be spent on overtime and subcontracting. This had been expensive and had caused disrupted production processes both in the UK and in the US factories. In addition to the PATH problems, Stone Johnston (based in Michigan) suffered a six-week labour strike which resulted in first half losses of £0.5 million. Ninety per cent of the workforce changed following the strike. The UK boiler industry suffered reduced order intake as a result of uncertainties caused by the oil price fall. Finally, in common with other manufacturers, Stone suffered a major increase in product liability insurance cover in the US.

Nevertheless, it was maintained that the PATH problems were now resolved, that deliveries under this contract would be completed by the end of the year and that production was being restored to normal. The Directors estimated that profits for the second half would be not less than £5 million before taxation, producing an overall profit for the year to May, 1987 of not less than £3 million before taxation.

In a private interview, John Oratis (February 1987) attributed the problems they were experiencing as largely due to the flotation and to the acquisition strategy: 'We're still suffering from the fact that we spent so much management effort on the public issue, and then on looking for acquisitions. We took too much on. I fear we neglected the company as a result of the public issue and its aftermath.'

Divestment

By May 1987, it was apparent that Crawley, now looked likely to incur losses of around £3 million for 1986/7. Net borrowings had reached approximately £30 million (up from £16.4 million at the end of the previous financial year), mainly as a result of poor trading. To improve the balance sheet, it was announced that Stone was selling its 75 per cent share in its recent acquisition, Andrews, for £21 million. This would cut gearing by 30 per cent but it would also cut some £2.2 million profits. As a result, Stone would barely break even for 1986/7 and the dividend to shareholders was to be cut.

Problems with the rest of the Group were also taking longer to put right than anticipated. Stone was still having problems with its US subsidiaries. Safety did not have the right equipment to build the hand-wound custom-built motors which its customers needed. The resulting bottlenecks led to reduced profits. At Stone Johnston, the combination of a 'green' workforce and a flat market resulted in losses of about £1 million. After five years of dealing with problems at Stone Johnston, Robin Tavener and his team finally admitted defeat and started negotiating its disposal to local interests.

Takeover

On 6 June 1987, amidst press rumours of a rescue, it was announced that the directors of Stone International had accepted a takeover offer from FKI Electricals. The offer valued Stone International at £36.6 million, giving two FKI shares for every three Stone ordinary shares. From their issue price of 125p per share, through a peak of 215p, the Stone shares were being valued at just over 103p on paper (for the enlarged equity). Robin Tavener and John Oratis, the only remaining members of the original MBO team (Bill Silvie had retired at the beginning of 1987), were to retain their positions after the takeover. Stone's directors went on record as saying that they believed that the takeover by FKI would enable the company to achieve profitability at a faster rate than otherwise. On 16 July 1987, the offer for Stone went unconditional.

3 The Metsec Story

1 INTRODUCTION

Metsec, a subsidiary of Tube Investments, was bought out by five of its senior executives in July 1981. Taking out personal loans and second mortgages, they paid £150 000 for 60 per cent of the equity, the balance being subscribed by Investors in Industry Plc and Equity Capital for Industry Ltd. The total package price of £500 000 represented a discount to net assets of more than 50 per cent. The company was trading at a small loss after a number of years of poor financial performance.

Four years later, in October 1985, the now profitable company was successfully floated on the USM at an issue price which valued the company at £8.375 million. The reasons for flotation were to raise money to finance the purchase of the company's premises, to permit an employee share option scheme, and to signify a new stage in the development of the company. The proceeds of the sale allowed the directors to repay their personal borrowings incurred at the time of the buyout and realise an additional £125 000 each. After the sale they still retained 44.5 per cent of the company worth just under £4.9 million at market prices (as of 19 February 1986). Thus in just under five years, the buyout team managed to turn around an ailing company and see their investment grow by some 3000 per cent.

A variety of factors were responsible for the turnaround. The threat of closure galvanised enthusiasm and commitment to the painful changes which were necessary to reduce costs; the removal of head office constraints and charges helped foster an organisational structure and culture propitious to the turnaround; and ownership strengthened team spirit among the buyout founders and made them more vigilant in their search for ways to promote the success of the company.

The financial community generally dislikes buyouts of companies which have a record of poor profitability. A buyout is held to be no panacea for a lame duck business. Indeed, many of the financial backers that were approached by the team at the time of the buyout were almost rude about the company's prospects. Yet, despite the maturity of many of its traditional markets, Metsec was far from being a lame duck. The profitable bits had been swamped by

77

loss-making activities; the company had been burdened by parent company management charges and inappropriate corporate procedures; and an outmoded management style and corporate culture had prevailed.

ↄ⟋   There was a number of urgent needs: refocus the business on profitable activities; prune costs; restore customer confidence; raise productivity; develop new products; create commitment to the business; motivate people; and establish a new set of guiding values and beliefs about what was needed for success. The story of Metsec shows why and how the team were able to effect these changes after the buyout.

2 PRE-BUYOUT

Ancestral beginnings

Metsec was founded in 1930 by a Mr Henderson, who opened a factory in Birmingham to produce 'cold roll-formed' metal components. Cold roll-forming is a process whereby coils of metal sheeting are shaped and cut into various sections for use in a variety of industries. Metal strip is passed continuously through a series of rollers which shape the strip into particular section profiles. The more complex the section profile, the greater the number of rolls that is required. For example, it takes five stages to roll-form a simple angle and as many as sixteen, or more, to form more complicated sections. The metal can also be pierced so that holes, slots, raised tags, notches, cut outs, etc., can be made in the metal sections. Although there have been many technical production changes over the years, the basic process which Metsec helped pioneer in the 1930s has stayed much the same to the present day.

Prior to the 1930s, the process of cold roll-forming in the UK had only been applied to cycle wheel rim manufacture. Experience in the US had shown that it was particularly well suited to the production of a wide range of metal components and sections used by car and bus manufacturers. After an auspicious start, with orders from Briggs Motor Bodies, the Standard Motor company and Pressed Steel Fisher, Metsec was taken over in 1932 by Tube Investments who incorporated it into their subsidiary, Accles and Pollock.

Early expansion of the product range took the company into the manufacture of partitioning sections, components for office furniture, rails and slatting for venetian blinds and parts for roller shutter doors. During the Second World War, the company made the frames for Lancaster bombers, the ammunition tracks for Stirling and Halifax bombers and sections of the Lilo rocket launcher.

In order to reduce dependence on automotive components and to fill the gap left by a post-war fall off in government contracts, Frank White, the new managing director, launched a major strategic initiative to gain acceptance of its products in the building materials and construction industry. White had been with TI for a long time, working his way up through the ranks. He knew Metsec's industry very well and was given virtual carte blanche by TI. He was an entrepreneurial leader with a powerful managerial style. This inspired great loyalty and enthusiasm. Under White's leadership, TI Metsec prospered. By 1954, the company was producing around one million square feet of rolled steel sections per week and was planning a major extension of its building products range. It employed 725 people on a 160 000 square feet site in Oldbury in the engineering heart of the West Midlands.

Decline
White did not, however, provide for any management succession. When he retired at the end of the 1950s, he left a gap which TI found hard to fill. Over the next few years, Metsec had a string of TI people as MDs, none of whom stayed more than a couple of years. The turn of the decade marked the first reversal in the company's fortunes. A downturn in the engineering industry and recession in the car industry put the company through a period of difficult trading. Although conditions improved in the early 1960s, increasing competition and maturity in a number of its markets put pressure on profit margins. Attention was focused on costs – on the improvement of office and shop floor efficiency – rather than on the external problems of competition and markets. In 1964, external consultants were brought in to improve office procedures and systems and instigate work measurement of clerical staff. The upshot was a prolonged period of industrial relations problems as management attempted to implement the consultants' recommendations.

The 1970s inaugurated a period of mixed fortunes:

The seventies started well and the management organisation was strengthened and geared up for a major expansion drive.... There were ambitious plans for a new product (infill panels) again aimed at the building industry and a small satellite factory was established at Gloucester. The then 1500 employees represented the peak number in the company's history, but the hopes and plans were soon dashed on the all too familiar economic down-turns of the post war era, and the company faced financial difficulties. In order to overcome these difficulties, exaggerated by quality problems on the new products, the numbers employed and overhead costs were reduced, the Gloucester factory closed down, and a revised management structure was instituted (*Internal Company History of TI Metsec, 1931–1981*).

Metsec went through a number of reorganisations to try to improve operations. At the instigation of TI Group, Metsec's product areas – general roll-forming (GRF), purlins, beams, motor cars, suspended ceilings and coated strips, – were boxed up into independent profit centres. However, problems in apportioning joint costs and the expense of establishing independent facilities led to profit centres being combined to form product centres. The drawback was that attention continued to be focused on production rather than on market requirements. The product groups were reorganised yet again into three market/business areas with supporting service functions to allow independent operation. The first area was building products, which included construction products, lattice beams, purlins and suspended ceilings. The second was buses. The third one was general engineering, which included GRF and motor cars.

GRF had been the original business and it continued to form the nucleus of the company even as various products were spun off internally as satellite businesses. GRF is based on a highly capital-intensive process with the product customised to individual specifications. The customer usually had to bear a proportion of the tooling costs and having paid for these was reluctant to go elsewhere. Thus unlike some of the other, more commodity-type products, customer relations and service were considered very important in this business.

GRF had always been the star performer and the company's major strength. Those who had been in the company longest were in this division. Because of the relatively greater degree of engineering skill, technical excellence and prestigious customer contact required in this business, and because of its linkage to the original business, GRF provided the symbolic heartland of Metsec's corporate culture. The problem was that this impeded the sorts of changes which were needed to accommodate the changing environment.

. . . and fall

In the latter part of the 1970s, GRF started to go seriously into decline. The advent of plastics and other cost-effective substitutes for metal made many GRF products technically obsolescent. Excessive overheads built up in the good years, put the various businesses at a severe competitive disadvantage when trading conditions became more difficult.

There was strong resistance to radical pruning of the business by those whose stood to lose resources from any cutbacks. Despite clear signs that the car business was beyond reclamation, pressure to close it down was resisted by the Metsec management. They were able to obtain TI group backing for their stance by arguing that other TI group business links with Ford and British Leyland would be jeopardised by any cutbacks.

The 1979 recession in the UK manufacturing industry further reduced Metsec's traditional customer base. GRF and, in particular, the car business became a serious cash drain on the whole of the company. Inadequate inventory control, excessive parent company charges, outmoded work procedures, unreliability, management changes and poor customer relations were at the root of the problem. The other divisions also suffered during this period, although the building products business, run by Keith Hirst and his team, suffered less than the other two.

In 1980, a new managing director was brought in from TI group headquarters. A reorganisation was ordered in an attempt to restore the dwindling fortunes of the company. Hirst was made deputy MD and given the additional responsibility of GRF.

TI group

The parent company was itself going through the throes of rationalisation and reorganisation. Excessive diversification and the onset of recession, especially severe in heavy industry where most of TI's acquisition strategy had been targeted, led to severe financial and management problems. In an attempt to 'get back to basics' and refocus on its core business, a strategy of divestment was initiated for non-core, problem businesses.

Although the reorganisation of TI Metsec in 1980 and the proposed closures and sell-offs improved Metsec's cost structure, overheads were still too high to prevent losses in 1980 and the first half of 1981 (see Table 3.2 on p. 91). In strategic terms, the only reason for keeping Metsec in the TI stable was that its motor car division fitted with TI group's important car components business. (TI group had no other businesses in building construction.) When at last it became clear that the motor car division could not be turned around, TI Metsec was put on the divestment/closure list and the motor car division scheduled for closure as soon as the rest of the business could be sold.

The latter proved more difficult than anticipated. In the depressed times of the early 1980s, no one wanted to buy TI Metsec. Heavy-engineering/manufacturing businesses operating in mature markets were not popular. There was a real danger of the whole company being closed down.

3 THE BUYOUT

In the event of closure, TI Metsec's senior management had the option of moving elsewhere in TI. However, because of the problems being experienced throughout TI group, prospects of personal advancement were not good. More importantly, Hirst and his team, comprising Ken Dodd (technical), David Jeavons (manufacturing), James McKinlay (sales) and Steven Tilsley (finance), felt that some TI Metsec products had good potential. Their own division, building products, had been reasonably successful. This was despite having to carry an excessively high central overhead – a severe competitive disadvantage given the highly price sensitive market.

Hirst and his team were a relatively self-contained 'clique' who worked well together, were highly motivated and were willing to stand up for what they believed in. They had a reputation within Metsec for getting things done, even if this meant going against the traditional management style: 'We had an image of independence and there was some resentment against us from others within the company.' This was to have an important bearing on their decision to go for a MBO.

Motivation for the Buyout

Despite the talk of closure, none of the team favoured a buyout for defensive, 'keep my job at all costs' reasons. Keith Hirst did not fancy a corporate job with TI. He wanted to see through the changes he had begun to initiate at Metsec and felt there was a great opportunity to make the company very successful: 'There was a highly motivated team with the management skills that were complimentary, a strong product base and a market that was served by competition that we felt we could beat. Although risk was involved, as a team, we were more than prepared to face the hard work necessary and were highly self-confident we could win'.

David Jeavons felt that 'If this didn't work and the company actually failed, and I found myself out of work tomorrow, then I wouldn't be worried. I know that I am the kind of person who could go out and buy a ladder and clean windows.'

Jim McKinlay had been to see an American company before any talk of a buyout and had been offered a good job. However, he preferred the buyout because 'this gave me an opportunity to amass some disposable wealth, rather than just have income. If I had gone to the States, I would probably have been better paid. But, I wouldn't have accumulated anything.' Ken Dodd felt very committed to the products and thought that: 'if only we could get the numbers right, there was a great opportunity here'.

Steven Tilsley thought that 'when the actual buyout was mooted, the five of us had reached a point where, as individuals we were searching for something. We realised we had a reasonable team and worked well together so that if we made the buyout happen then we could all realise the things we were looking for as individuals.'

Negotiating the deal

Keith Hirst first approached a firm of stockbrokers. They sent him to see David Hagget, a Birmingham lawyer specialising in buyouts. Hirst got on very well with Hagget who was later invited to join the board. In looking to construct a deal giving the maximum chances for survival, they felt it essential that only certain parts of the business be bought out. The remaining parts were to be closed, thereby making redundant some two thirds of TI Metsec's work staff. TI group picked up this liability with the team taking over only the redundancy commitments for the workers kept on.

TI group did not want the adverse publicity that a closure would have created. They also had a genuine desire to see the venture succeed: 'Metsec is located in the heart of TI land. TI has always prided itself on being a benevolent employer and if the company had been sold off or closed down with considerable redundancies, TI's respectability would have been tarnished. With a buyout, TI could at least say that it had saved 180 jobs.'

In looking to enhance the new company's prospects for survival, TI did not want to lumber Metsec with too much debt. Accordingly, they gave the team an interest-free loan of £200 000 with a three-year capital repayment holiday. The purchase price was set at £500 000, representing a discount to net assets of some £457 000. The low price was obtained partly because TI was only willing to offer Metsec a

Table 3.1 The financial structure of the Metsec buyout

1. Share capital	Authorised	Issued	Ownership/subscriber
a) Ordinary shares £1		£150 000	Buyout Team: £32 000 Hirst; £28 750 each: Dodd, Jeavons, McKinlay, Tilsley; £3000 Hall (co.sec.)
b) 12% cumulative convertible preferred participating ordinary shares £1		£100 000	£62 500 Investors in Industry £23 520 Equity Capital for Industry £13 980 Equity Capital Trustees
c) 12% cumulative redeemable preference shares £1		£50 000	£31 250 Investors in Industry £18 750 Equity Capital for industry
Total share capital		£300 000	
2. Loan capital			
d) Long-term, interest-free with 3-year repayment holiday		£200 000	TI group
Total loan capital		£200 000	
Total funding (for purchase price)		£500 000	
e) One year option for a 10-year loan		£250 000	
f) Overdraft facility		£350 000	National Westminster
Total finance available		£1 100 000	

Notes:
1. All Issued shares are allotted and fully paid.
2. The shares shown under (b) were convertible at par and on a one-for-one basis into ordinary shares. On 21 October 1985, all preferred ordinary shares were redesignated as ordinary shares, and all preference shares were redeemed at par, cancelled and redesignated ordinary shares.
3. (e) was not required and was allowed to lapse.

Source: Annual Report and company information.

short lease on its premises. TI intended to sell the site within a couple of years.

The team took out personal loans and second mortgages to fund their portion £150 000) of the equity. The rest was provided by Equity Capital for Industry and Investors in Industry. The finance was raised as shown in Table 3.1. The deal gave the team 60 per cent of the (fully diluted) ordinary share capital of the business.

Agreeing terms for the buyout was a fairly complicated exercise. All the assets, plant, equipment and stock had to be gone through with TI. New terms for creditors and debtors had to be arranged. Without TI backing, creditors had less of a safeguard, and debtors were not part of the deal.

Reassuring suppliers and customers was an urgent priority during this period. Metsec's competitors had told a number of their suppliers and customers that it would be very risky doing business with Metsec without the TI backing. The team had been able to preempt this to some extent by writing round to all suppliers and customers and assuring them that if the buyout went through, they would maintain and indeed improve their levels of service. Some customers whom TI Metsec had let down in the past were also approached, with a view to patching things up now that a new management team was in situ. By and large, the response was extremely positive.

4 POST-BUYOUT

Changing the culture

The immediate priority after the buyout was to reduce costs across all businesses. More effective cost control procedures and better cash flow management were introduced. Inventory control, for example, was improved dramatically from 4 times a year to over 20 times. This was achieved by persuading suppliers to hold stock and by operating on much shorter lead times. At the same time, credit terms were renegotiated: Metsec would not do business unless it obtained 60 days credit, as compared to the 30 days norm before the buyout.

Thoughts of survival, rather than of rich pickings, were the major spur to swingeing cuts in direct and indirect labour. The workforce had been cut from just over 500 to 175 people as a precondition for the buyout. Some of these jobs had been lost because parts of the old business were not taken through the buyout. Most went through reorganisation and rationalisation to avoid duplication and increase productivity: 'With some of the machines, five, six or seven men used to work on a particular line. There was an urgent need to recognise that while such practices were alright in the past, now we were going to do the same job with two or even one person.'

The key to improved productivity was seen to be in changing fundamentally the way the workforce and middle managers related to their tasks and to the priorities of the business. The cut in the umbilical cord to TI group, the hive down in the business, and the need to restore profitability was felt to require a new set of shared understandings, promoted actively and quickly.

Working practices
A change of values concerning working practices was not difficult to engineer. It was common knowledge that without the buyout, the company would probably have closed. The recent redundancies emphasised the sword hanging over the business and the need for change.

> Perhaps the realisation of what we came close to provided the spur. I believe that the workers now associate themselves with the business much more closely. With TI there was always the idea that, well, it is TI, we have been here a long time, we are not doing that badly and they will keep us going. Although it had been apparent that TI was closing businesses down, so that it wasn't the umbrella it had been, it was not as immediate as the present situation.

A new supervisory structure was instituted. People who were positive about the need for change and were willing to question existing practices were promoted into positions of responsibility. A factor promoting receptiveness to change was that only those members of the workforce who were the most productive, or who were willing to accept new practices, were taken through the buyout: 'There was a real sense of being one of the chosen few who had been kept on to see the company restored to its former glory.' The result was much improved industrial relations, and a more relaxed and free dialogue between management and staff.

The new culture of efficiency was reinforced by a general tightening of authority and control. At least one director recognised that he had had to become harder and more aggressive in order that change be a continuing, rather than one-off process. A major worry was how to sustain the momentum achieved at the time of the buyout. The team realised that competitors would inevitably be forced to respond with similar cost reducing initiatives. While it had been relatively easy in the first six to twelve months to make things happen, there was concern that once the honeymoon period was over it would be much harder to sustain the impetus to reduce costs the second or third time around. Nevertheless, the team were successful in obtaining continuing productivity improvements in the years following the buyout.

Customer relations

Attitudes towards customers had been somewhat cavalier in TI Metsec's latter days. In fact, the company's good name had been jeopardised on more than one occasion through orders not being completed on time and customers not alerted in advance. There was a concerted effort to improve customer relations, reinforced by sayings such as 'don't let a customer down, and if you have to, let him know'.

A more positive approach was adopted towards potential business. As one director recalled: 'In the past, when customers rang up the estimation department for a quote, the response was to take the details and then put the telephone down. Now they smell that if there's half a chance of taking an order they start talking about delivery dates, asking when the customer wants the product, and they push far more.' Old systems were overhauled to improve customer relations. For example, quotes used to take upwards of three to four weeks to be processed and sent off. Under the new regime, the easier jobs were turned round in a two- to three-day period.

The buyout itself also helped customer relations:

> Customers now feel that when the management take a decision, it is a personal commitment to the customer, rather than just a corporate decision. They also know that the management will continue to be around at the end of the contract. In TI days this place was like a railway station waiting room, people in and people out, no continuity. It was very important with general roll-forming, particularly to the medium-sized, expanding businesses run by entrepreneurs.

Autonomy

The separation from TI allowed considerable cost savings. For example, Metsec's accounting function had to conform to TI standards. There were well-documented rules laid down and every month, the company had to produce a 65-page report on sales, profit and loss. The report went into enormous detail on such things as overtime work and all the discretionary costs that management had some control over. The report took a long time to produce, and tied up accounting resources for three- or four-day periods at a time.

Another irksome and costly requirement, was that Metsec had to use TI's central computer, a very large IBM machine, located in Walsall. The software packages were written at Walsall and it was very difficult to have them tailored to Metsec's specific needs. TI's software people were generally too busy with 'more important work'. The charges that Metsec had to pay for the privilege of using the Walsall computer (including the cost of their own computer to talk to Walsall plus the people to key in the information) were about £100 000 per year. This was part of the overhead charges payable to TI.

After the buyout, Metsec purchased a digital mini computer for some £15 000 plus about £2000 for software. This provided the management with all the accounting information needed. Perhaps more importantly: 'it allowed us to get some real control into the situation, not just the paper control which appeared to be there in the TI days. That was a massive cost saving. Now the information that is churned out is relevant and accurate and we can make better decisions on this basis. Now we do not generate information unless we need it.'

While the cost savings were substantial, there was a deeper significance. Parent company charges were perceived as onerous and lacking value for money. These charges were replaced after the buyout by interest charges, which were just as onerous but were seen as legitimate. Such perceptions may have far more of an impact than the monetary amounts involved.

Management style
The directors recognised early on in the life of the buyout that they had to spend much more time overseeing operations. This constituted a significant departure from past practice.

> Many people in the organisation will have a wider reponsibility because of the need to introduce overhead exposure and to reduce the degree of specialism that can be afforded. Due account had been taken of this when selecting people for various roles in the new company. The board of directors have also recognised the need for change and the requirement to climb down in the organisation will be given paramount importance (Buyout prospectus, April 1981).

One example of the new hands-on approach was that all directors became responsible for the personnel under them. The company dispensed with the services of a personnel manager.

Commitment
The combination of the buyout, collective ownership and the prospect of survival, encouraged greater commitment to the company.

The first and prime interest is in making sure that Metal Sections is successful. Previously it was to make sure that the particular position one had responsibility for was being carried out successfully. This has led to less rivalry and a less political atmosphere at the top of the company.

Before in meetings, everyone used to point the finger, it was all political battles. Now we sink or swim together and no one can hide behind layers of management.

Being part of a management team and owning a stake in the company makes me far more rational in my decision making. Rather than gearing everything to what I as an individual want, it makes me more objective and more considerate to my colleagues. Until the buyout I saw myself as heading up a team but not being a team player. The biggest change in my thinking is I see myself much more as part of the team.

Decision-making
Decision making was helped by the autonomy afforded by separation from TI. Not having to seek ratification from above speeded up decision making and fostered greater involvement with decisions:

Decisions are obviously much quicker now; before, we would initiate a decision at the management meeting, which then went up to our board, and then up to TI and then gradually back down again. The problem was that at each level you had to convince somebody else that what you thought was right. That is frustrating if you are given a job to do and you have to keep justifying yourself.

There used to be a very top heavy management structure such that it was almost impossible to reach decisions. The whole process was also fraught with politics. You had to go through umpteen administration levels and eventually you might be able to achieve a decision, but the length of time that it took was most debilitating whereas now we can decide things overnight and then act on it.

The impact of these changes was most evident in the areas of investment and marketing. For example, immediately after the buyout, it was decided that manufacturing plant be uprated. Roughly a quarter of a million pounds was spent on newly developed, computer aided design technology. This reduced unit costs and increased flexibility, giving the company a distinct temporary competitive advantage over rivals. The team felt that although this investment would have been possible under the old regime, it would have taken much longer to gain agreement and much longer to have it implemented. The result would have been that competitors would probably have installed their own plant, thereby wiping out the temporary advantage.

It was also easier to introduce new products after the buyout. This was seen as essential in view of the maturity of Metsec's businesses and the difficulty of expanding market share in markets where its position was already dominant.

Performance

The result of all these changes was that performance improved markedly post-buyout. This might have been achieved without a buyout or an ownership change. Nevertheless the fact that TI were prepared to close the company down, that no one else wanted to take it over, and that the turnaround occurred against a background of deep recession in manufacturing industry, suggest that the structure and culture of the buyout played a significant part. Table 3.2 shows Metsec's performance before and after the buyout.

5   USM FLOTATION

When negotiating the buyout, the team had not been able to afford to buy the 13-acre, Oldbury premises from which the company operated. Instead, they had obtained an 18 month lease from the site owners, TI group. One of the major worries for the new owner-managers was that they would have to suffer the upheaval of packing up the works and moving everything to an alternate site.

Table 3.2   Metsec's financial performance before and after the buyout

	Performance[1] pre-buyout							
		Year ending 31 December						6 months to June 30
	1974	1975	1976	1977	1978	1979	1980	1981
Sales (£m)	9.5	8.9	10.4	11.8	13.5	15.3	13.1	5.7
Operating Profit before Interest and Tax (PBIT) (£m)	0.8	0.3	0.4	0.0	0.6	0.1	(0.2)	(0.2)
ROS (%)	8.9	3.3	3.5	0.2	4.4	0.6	(0.1)	(0.4)
ROCE[1] (%)							4.0	(3.7)

	Performance post-buyout			
	18 months to to 31 December	Year ending 31 December		
	1982	1983	1984	1985
Sales (£m)	10.7	8.3	12.4	14.9
PBIT (£m)	0.2	0.3	0.7	1.4
ROS (%)	1.5	3.1	5.5	9.3
ROCE (%)	n.a.	n.a.	39.0	51.7
Gearing[3]	n.a.	n.a.	16.0	0.7

Notes:
1. Trading profit before tax and interest.
2. Operating profit before interest and tax divided by net assets.
3. Total loans divided by net assets.

Source: Company accounts.

TI group intended to sell the site once problems of separating off the provision of services to adjoining property could be sorted out. Fortunately, at the end of the eighteen months, TI found that the time was not right for selling. In order to cover some of its overheads, it offered Metsec a further three-year lease. However, the team knew that eventually, they would have to resolve the situation by buying the site or moving on.

In 1985, following an approach from Keith Hirst, TI said they were prepared to sell the site to Metsec at what seemed a very reasonable price of £800 000. Hirst considered various ways of raising the funds. Floating the company on the USM seemed the most attractive option now that the company was trading profitably. Other factors also favoured flotation. The team wanted to introduce an employee share option scheme; they wanted to reduce their personal indebtedness taken on at the time of the buyout to fund their personal investments in

Metsec; and they wanted to grow the company through acquisitions. Perhaps most important of all, they wanted to signify that the company had come of age: a sort of corporate rite de passage: 'We were concerned about the credibility of the company. It was important that we move from the management buyout thing where everyone patted us on the head and said well done, to a higher profile.'

The buyout team (and other directors) decided to release 15.5 per cent of their shareholding. This left them with an effective controlling stake of 44.5 per cent. The institutional shareholders relinquished 25 per cent of their interest. The share placement price gave Metsec a market capitalisation of £8 375 000. This represented a more than 16-fold appreciation in the value of the company in under five years.

In the aftermath of the flotation, the company experienced a downturn. A downturn in the market and preoccupation with the flotation were held responsible. The team re-evaluated its control procedures and in 1986, reorganised the company. In the same year, after much careful consideration, an acquisition was made in a related products area. By the beginning of 1987, the directors considered Metsec to be back on course and poised for further growth.

6 AFTERTHOUGHTS ON OWNERSHIP

Looking back some months after the flotation, the founders of Metsec Plc expressed mixed feelings about how ownership had affected them. Two Directors suggested that the buyout had caused them to be more vigilant.

> To some extent, we were fortunate in buying a company that had not been terribly well run, had become dissipated, had lost direction, had become fragmented, and had suffered regular changes of management. There was a great deal we could do to improve things. There was organisation slack, there was no motivation, it was really a company that had lost its way. Why didn't we implement many of the improvements before the buyout? Well, it comes back to the difference between being a manager in a company for somebody else and managing it for yourself. I have asked myself long and hard the question and the fact is that it was somebody else's money.
>
> We had no thoughts about flotation at the time of the buyout. It

really didn't come into our thinking at all. Thoughts about money were related to salary rewards. What stimulated people to pull together was the risk of losing what we had put into the buyout rather than thoughts of some tremendous pot of gold at the end of the rainbow.

The material risks and rewards of ownership may have given the team the incentive to be more active in their pursuit of cost economies. However, such behaviour was also motivated by the structural changes accompanying the ownership change.

The buyout was very much about independence, paddling our own canoe, facing the issues, and hopefully, if things worked out, making some money. The buyout made us masters of our own destiny and that's what it is all about. That doesn't mean you become totally despotic and obsessed with control. We're a team and we're trying to develop other teams within the business. We debate things, sometimes at tremendous length until we reach a consensus and then we follow through. I think that with TI, the feeling was that you might be in the business for a year or so and then suddenly you would be called out, interviewed for another job and moved to a completely different business, perhaps in a totally different role. While that was attractive to the individual, it wasn't what the business needed. You need to build a stable team of good people who know the industry, the markets, and who want to grow with the business. We are five years down from the buyout and not one of our senior managers has been poached from us.

This enhanced autonomy, social cohesion and accountability might have been achieved without a MBO. Structural reorganisation within TI giving greater freedom to Hirst and his team, or acquisition by another company might have afforded the owner-managers or another team the stimulus and freedom to introduce much-needed changes. Yet the power of direct ownership for Metsec's management was that it gave them de jure as well as de facto control. It encouraged them to accept responsibility for their own individual actions, as well as a collective interest in what each other was doing. The company's survival was seen to depend on this If performance had not improved, the team would have had to answer to their institutional backers. Yet the gradual improvement in the company's trading operations culminating in the successful floatation gave the team the freedom to pursue their chosen strategy.

Whether Metsec's fortunes will continue to grow as it moves from being a buyout to a plc remains to be seen. Hirst and his team have lost none of their zeal for growing Metsec. Their continued ownership stake and the fact that all the original founders of the buyout are still in situ six years later – something of a rare phenomenon among buyouts – means that the spirit of the buyout lives on as the company enters the next phase of its evolution.

4 The Jacoa Story

1 INTRODUCTION

In 1976 Cdf Chimie, the French state-owned coal board, took over the French paint company, Le Ripolin. The latter was one of the six largest paint manufacturers in the world. The senior executives of Cdf were gradually coming to grips with the acquisition, when they were forced to direct their attention to Ripolin UK, Le Ripolin's 71 per cent owned English subsidiary. The latter's business was the manufacture and retail of Ripolin paint in the UK.

Manufacturing inefficiency, allied to intense retail price competition, were threatening to push Ripolin UK into bankruptcy. The company was on the verge of receivership. In July 1977, Cdf called in Philip Jeffrey, a management consultant, to help them decide what to do with Ripolin UK. His brief was to assess whether the company could be turned around and if not, how closure costs could be minimised. He decided to try to turn around the company. Over the next three and a half years, by strategically refocussing the business on retailing through acquisitions, through the development of management controls and information systems, and perhaps most of all, through charismatic leadership, Jeffrey succeeded in turning a moribund manufacturing company into a successful, vertically integrated DIY retailer and manufacturer of quality paint.

Notwithstanding this success, and possibly largely because of it, relations between Jeffrey and the parent company became strained. Success brings its own problems, something which Jeffrey was to experience more than once during the life of the company. The emphasis on retailing had led to Ripolin UK becoming more and more strategically divergent from Le Ripolin. Also, Le Ripolin appeared to want to run the English subsidiary as a cash cow in order to extract the maximum dividend possible. Jeffrey, however, was a grower not a mower: he wanted to plough everything back so as to maximise growth. The UK market for DIY paint was increasing rapidly and Jeffrey felt that there was good potential for Ripolin UK to improve its market share through significant investment in the retail distribution chain.

The only way out of the impasse was divestment. In October 1980, Le Ripolin announced it was going to sell its holding in Ripolin UK by sealed tender. Jeffrey and his management team decided to tender. They had become increasingly infected by the struggle for survival and were in no mood to let go of the reins. They felt that the turnaround had earned them the right to own and manage the company. A further consideration was that if the company were to be sold to a competitor, the manufacturing plant would be closed down and the shops merged into another identity. Such a fate was felt to undermine all the effort that had gone into the turnaround.

The first step was to buy a shelf company which Jeffrey aptly named Jacoa, formed from the first letter in each of the buyout team's names (Jeffrey, Arundale, Clough, Osorio, Associates). The personification symbolised the importance of management over product. In early 1981, with the help of Barclays Merchant Bank Ltd and Barclays Development Capital Ltd, Jacoa successfully bought out Ripolin UK for £4.8 million (a P/E ratio of nearly 10). The team put up 5 per cent of the money in exchange for 50.4 per cent of the equity. Thus the first UK MBO through privatisation came into existence.

Five years later, Jacoa was subjected to a number of hostile takeover bids in the wake of Jacoa's own failure to negotiate acquisitions. (This failure was considered to have been caused by the control exerted by the financial backers of the MBO.) Against Jeffrey's wishes, the other buyout team members and the financial backers decided to sell out to Jacoa's major competitor, A.G. Stanley. The selling price was £26.5 million. Although the prospect of financial rewards had not been paramount at the time of the buyout, the success of Jacoa proved too much of a temptation to some members of the team. Each £1 invested (in the ordinary stock) at the time of the buyout was being valued at £64 by the takeover bid. Each of the founders would become a millionaire, with Jeffrey's personal stake worth in excess of £6.5 million. Although Jeffrey wanted to carry on running the business as an independent entity, the other founders wanted to realise their wealth and turn to other things. In late 1987, Jacoa became a subsidiary of AG Stanley.

Unlike the other buyouts considered in this book, most of the cultural, strategic and operational changes were initiated prior to the buyout. The buyout was the culmination of a successful turnaround, so that ownership was the outcome, rather than the cause of commitment and entrepreneurial flair. The story of the buyout shows how Jeffrey and his team could never have turned the company around if they themselves had not emotionally 'bought into' the survival of the company. It also shows how the structural and financial aspects of ownership can affect the strategic direction of buyouts.

2 PRE-BUYOUT

Hallowed beginnings

Dr Reip, a Dutchman, discovered 'Reipolin' in 1892. It was the world's first enamel paint. Six years later, a group of City of London merchants acquired the rights to import and distribute this paint in the UK and the Empire. A year later, Ripolin became a registered company in the UK. By 1909, distribution depots had been established in Australia, India, South Africa, Canada and the US.

The paint was marketed in England as the 'Rolls-Royce' of paints. It was considered by the company's management and many specialist decorators to be far superior to any other paint then available. There was very rigid control over the quality of the product from Holland. In turn, the English licensees restricted sales of their product to uses that would fit in with the prestigious image of the paint. People wishing to buy Ripolin had to be 'acceptable', as did the uses to which it was put. Anything that might compromise the prestigious image of Ripolin was shunned.

During the First World War, sales were adversely affected by rumours that the paint was a German product. Heavy advertising by the parent company was needed to persuade people that this was not the case.

By 1932, despite its very up-market status, Ripolin was making little, or no, money. It was the most expensive paint in the UK, being three times the price of other paints. In 1932, there was a sterling/guilder crisis which increased the price differential still further. Dwindling sales threatened the viability of the company. The third generation, family-owned but manager-controlled, company borrowed £20 000 from the French parent company – Le Ripolin – successors to the original Dutch company. The money was needed to start the manufacture of Ripolin paint in the UK. The money was lent in return for 71 per cent of the equity of the UK company. The French were less interested in obtaining control than in avoiding any blemish to the name of Ripolin which might occur through the bankruptcy of a distributor. A factory was built at Southall, from where the paint is still produced under licence from the French to this day.

During the Second World War, the Germans took over the French factory and obtained the formula for the paint. As a patriotic gesture, Ripolin UK gave the formula to the Ministry of Defence Admiralty at Portsmouth. Production of Ripolin was then halted at Southall for the duration of the War because of the shortages in supplies of essential raw materials and because of the company's refusal to tamper with the quality of the product.

In order to maintain production, Ripolin UK bought Temple Varnish company which produced Guardian and Mayfair paint, closed their factory and brought production to the Southall site. No Ripolin was produced between 1939 and 1953 when the shortages finally came to an end.

Decline and fall

Prior to the War, Ripolin was the market leader with 7 per cent of the market. When Ripolin was relaunched after the war, changes in the market for paint led to a dramatic fall in market share. This happened despite the fact that Royal palaces and other prestige locations in England and overseas continued to specify Ripolin.

The market changes occurred through the emergence of a DIY market and with it a popular demand for cheap and easy to use paint. There was no immediate response from Ripolin UK. Management felt that DIY paint was a technically inferior product which would not work and which would not gain a secure foothold in the market. So Ripolin continued to be targeted at craftsmen decorators: less skilled painters would not know how to use Ripolin and so would blame it when things went wrong.

Some retail shops adopted Ripolin, mainly the upmarket shops in Knightsbridge and Chelsea, but most began stocking DIY paint. By the late 1950s, despite much effort on attempting to rebuild the customer base and restore Ripolin to its former glory, the company was in trouble. People had forgotten the name, the craftsman decorator was a thing of the past, and Ripolin had no distribution outlets. Moreover, the company was under-capitalised and short of funds to develop new products.

Ripolin UK's chairman, Edwin Osorio – owner of 12 per cent of the company and third generation of the founding family which had brought Ripolin to the UK – had no choice but to reformulate the paint for the DIY market. Osorio forged technical links with the Americans and poured what resources he could from internally generated funds into developing new products. To ensure an outlet for his paint and being unable to match the advertising capability of the big companies, (and so more easily obtain retail shelf space), Osorio decided to open shops selling Ripolin paint. Starting in 1961, the company began building a chain of 78 small shops. By 1974, these accounted for 70 per cent of sales with the remaining 30 per cent going to the quality professional trade.

However, neither the manufacturing nor the retailing side were particularly successful during the 1960s. The emergence of the multiples who bought trade merchants and passed any volume discount from the manufacturer straight on to the customer at the retail level; the abolition of retail price maintenance; the entry into paint manufacture of the chemical majors; and technical advances in the durability and application of paint, led to a retail price war. Paint prices fell in absolute terms until 1968.

The company somehow managed to keep ticking over although by the early 1970s it was a not-too-well, vertically integrated manufacturer and retailer of paints. Because its retailing activities had been set up more to provide an outlet for the manufacturing business than as a competitive force in the DIY market, it never really came to grips with whether it was producing a product for the DIY market or for the fast contracting quality market. The somewhat half-hearted move into retailing meant that its stores were far too small (average size 700 square feet). The company needed to develop its retail expertise and open larger units if it was to compete with the multiples.

In 1974, Edwin Osorio set into motion a five-year development plan aimed at improving the retailing side of the business. This was the year when OPEC struck and a rise in raw material costs occurred simultaneously with an intensification in high street retail competition. To make matters worse, the company lost some key management which resulted in some errors of timing within the five-year plan. Additional warehousing and computerisation costs came on stream ahead of sales revenue, and the company's profits faltered in 1975, and plunged into major losses in 1976 and the first half of 1977.

From 1975 onwards, Edwin Osorio suffered deteriorating health and was unable to oversee adequately the operation of the company. His closest advisers were members of the old school rather than professional managers. He ruled the company autocratically and despite being a great charmer and a very good motivator of those people who held his confidence, was unwilling to countenance opposing views. His son John Osorio, who was in charge of manufacturing, was a lone voice pointing out that things were falling apart – other dissidents just left. With his ideas in permanent on-going conflict with board members, John Osorio became increasingly isolated from the decision-making process. He acquired the image throughout the company of being obstructive.

At the same time as this was going on, the French parent, Le Ripolin, was also having its own troubles. Having embarked on a series of ill-fated acquisitions in the 1960s, the profitable part (the paint production) could not support the rest. In 1976, Petrofina (Belgium) bid for Le Ripolin. The French Trade Minister then instructed the French state-owned Coal Board, Cdf Chimie, to put in a bid 50 per cent higher. Cdf were successful and in the process acquired Le Ripolin's 71 per cent holding in the UK company.

In March 1977, Barclays Bank informed Cdf that the UK subsidiary's overdraft was £1.5 million whereas realisable assets were only £50 000. Hence it wanted a guarrantee from Cdf (and effectively the French government) to underwrite its debt. Failing this it was going to force the company into receivership. The first thing Cdf did was to buy a further 6 per cent of the UK company from the 24 per cent which was held by the UK shareholders. They did this because under the Napoleonic code, they had to own 76 per cent of a company in order to have total control: 'blockage'.

JLD Associates in Geneva was approached for advice on what should be done with the English subsidiary. The brief was to report on the state of the UK company, see whether it could be turned around, or if this was not feasible, close it down. In particular, the French parent did not want to leave unpaid debts behind if it closed Ripolin UK. Accordingly, it commissioned JLD to find out what the likely losses would be on closure.

Turnaround

The advent of Philip Jeffrey
In July 1977, Philip Jeffrey, a partner in JLD Associates, was brought in as chief executive of Ripolin UK. He found a company which, through ignoring the shift to DIY and the change in the structure of retailing, had experienced severe erosion of its customer base. A continuing belief that a UK without Ripolin paint was unthinkable had buttressed an ill-founded optimism that despite the trading problems, the company would go on forever. In reality the only thing that had kept the company going were the charm and contagious optimism of its former chief executive and his good relations with the absentee parent in France.

Jeffrey's first priority was to find out about the company. There were no management accounts, no information on costs or profits for individual retail outlets and trade centres and no information in sufficiently disaggregated form to see where things were going wrong. The only management information was 'profits', which information appeared six months after the period to which it related. Jeffrey immediately reorganised the company into functional area cost centres: manufacturing, retail, trade and head office services. He then left for six weeks in order to allow the new divisional managers to ascertain the necessary facts and figures. In September there was a mini crisis when Barclays Bank refused to meet the payroll. Jeffrey managed to persuade Barclays to maintain a line of credit despite the fact that the company was insolvent to the extent of £1.2 million. In fact it looked as though Ripolin UK had been insolvent for three years.

Jeffrey estimated that closing down the company would cost between £800 000 and £1.5 million. Apart from the paint factory, all saleable assets had already been disposed of to prop up the ailing company. Fortunately, Cdf were anxious not to be seen to be taking any peremptory action to close down a foreign subsidiary with subsequent loss of jobs. If the company was to continue operations it needed a major capital restructuring, it had to trade differently and it needed a major organisational and cultural change.

Struggle for survival
In the latter half of 1977, Jeffrey and his team faced a number of challenges, just to keep the company afloat. The immediate priority was to get the French to take over the £1.2 million of debt that Barclays was no longer prepared to extend to the company. Cdf was not allowed to invest overseas – the French government had put a block on state-owned industries investing overseas. However, Cdf arranged for the Banque Nationale de Paris in London to take over the debt. (When sometime later Cdf decided that it wanted to close Ripolin UK down, BNP fought strongly not to land its London operations with a £1.2 million debt. The struggle between who was to pick up the debt if the company closed down was one factor leading to the survival of the company.)

Second, the company had to generate more cash internally. This was needed to pay wages, to meet unavoidable liabilities such as landlords threatening to sue, and to stop supplies being blocked as the company was at its maximum credit limits. The French refused to allow the company to increase its borrowings. This was probably a blessing in disguise in that it reinforced the urgency for the company to start generating cash.

In September, Jeffrey told the 332 employees that all he could promise was jobs for a few more weeks. The workforce knew that the company was in trouble – over 100 people had already been made redundant in the six months prior to Jeffrey's arrival. Nevertheless this news came as a terrible shock to many of the employees. One of the pillars of the culture was that Ripolin would go on forever. Jeffrey recalls: 'I was ready to close down the company on September 29th, so I didn't pull my punches. Telling the truth to them for the first time caused much anxiety amongst my fellow directors who feared that everyone would walk out or resign. They had never had their people spoken to in this way and they thought I should make the best of what I had got.'

Because a last-in first-out system of redundancy had been in operation, the average service of the workforce was some 27 years. There was a very top-heavy age structure with the average age of employees being over 50. Many of the workforce were intensely loyal to the product and to the company, and Jeffrey told them that it was just possible that if they could 'produce a lot more cheaply, sell a lot more and keep the cash flow going', that they might be able to stay in business. They were also told that no further redundancies would be made unless the company went under but that the retirement age of 65 would be enforced. This led to 14 retirements.

In October and November the workforce made a fantastic effort: 'Everyone's role changed enormously – possibly for the worse in that the job became less interesting as a production job – everyone helped each other and there were no demarcation disputes.'

Although all the labour was unionised there was no resistance to change. John Osorio, the manufacturing director, was able to implement all the changes that for years he had been prevented from doing. The struggle for survival became infectious. The belief gradually spread throughout the company that if people were willing to change then the company would survive. Productivity improved by 54 per cent virtually overnight, most of which was a result of improved throughput planning.

Proper costing was introduced and the 3500 formulations were reduced to 180. Instead of mixing paints according to indivdual specification and providing very small quantities, a more commodity-like production system was put into operation. This meant that some prestigious contracts had to be dropped even though this entailed loss of status.

Having boosted production, an equivalent effort had to go into improving sales. There were three constraints: inadequate retail outlets (too small and fairly dilapidated); a lack of good managers (many of the talented people had left during the difficult conditions between 1973 and 1977); and no money to do anything. The first of these could not be sorted out in the immediate short term. Nevertheless, whatever could be done to smarten the shops up was done. 'Some were so bad that they had to be given a coat of Ripolin paint by our shop staff.' Prices were aggressively discounted, the product range was extended and shop windows were changed to reflect the new sales policy. All contracts with trade contractors were examined, uneconomic products cut, and prices lowered. Morale in the shops improved dramatically.

A firework was placed under the trade reps. Instead of making two calls a day to 'superior' contractors, they were told to sell to anyone and to make eight calls a day. Whereas the 'average' trade rep in the industry sold some 200 000 litres of paint a year, Ripolin's sold only 47 000 litres. Most had very long service to the company and one was 86 years old. For many of these trade reps the change was very traumatic indeed. Some of them resigned and others were compulsorily retired. But those who stayed gained new accounts and pushed their sales up by between 30 per cent and 47 per cent each month between September and the end of the year. Sales were helped by buoyant demand for paint. Consumer spending was relatively strong in the second half of 1977 as a heat wave in the previous summer had led people to defer painting until the following year. By the end of the year, the first half losses had been eliminated and the company had made a small profit of £18 000.

In December 1977, the first budgets ever produced by the company forecast a trading profit of somewhere between £80 000 to £100 000 for the following year although the company was still technically insolvent. The French were delighted, for if the debt could be brought down to under £1 million then it would not be overly embarassing for them to close it down. But Jeffrey was not prepared to do this:

After all these struggles, I was not going to close it down, especially after all the effort put in by the workforce. The struggle for survival had become infectious, but when I saw the budgets for the next year I began to worry that the infection was getting out of hand. I had come on a short-term assignment and although the company was now making a small profit, it would still take 8 to 12 years in an ever-increasing competitive market to wipe out the debt.

The French parent company eventually responded that as long as the UK company didn't cost them any more money, they would not close it down. The UK subsidiary would have to be self-financing, as indeed it had been since 1932. It would, however, be allowed to reinvest profits, after tax and dividends, as the local management determined.

Jeffrey realised that more cash than could be raised from operations had to be obtained to restructure the organisation, especially the retail end. Through some clever financial manoeuvring, he managed to acquire Reed International's subsidiary, WPM Retail Ltd, for £2.8 million. Although WPM was making losses of approximately £0.7million p.a., its 140 stores provided Ripolin UK with greatly increased retail selling space. This solved previous problems of manufacturing and warehousing overcapacity. The standard product mix was put into the shops and a million litres of Crown paint was replaced with Ripolin paint. Jeffrey obtained bridging finance for six weeks. In the autumn of 1978, the freeholds of WPM were sold off at a healthy profit, and the better sites leased back. Ripolin UK made enough money to pay off the £2.8 million loan and make a profit of £800 000.

By the Autumn of 1978, after the debts had been paid off, Jeffrey for the first time thought that the company was going to survive and prosper. He retired most of the board, and promoted people from within the company. He also poached David Arundale, with whom he had already worked, from ICI. Arundale's remit was to sort out Ripolin UK's financial services. In October 1978, a further acquisition was made. Budget Stores Ltd., which had 21 stores averaging 3000 square feet, was purchased. This acquisition improved the quality of Ripolin's retail sites and gave it an influx of good senior retailing management. The struggle for survival looked to be won. Now it was time to embark on a struggle for independence from the French.

3 DIVESTMENT AND BUYOUT

The French parent, Le Ripolin, was primarily a manufacturer and distributor of a broad spectrum of surface coatings (96 per cent) and decorative paint (4 per cent). It was not involved in retailing. In France, investment in retailing by domestic, state-owned enterprises was politically dangerous on account of the lobbying strength of the small, independent retailer. The French recipe did not offer a realistic prospect of viability for the UK subsidiary. Ripolin UK was becoming a vertically integrated manufacturer/retailer of decorative paint with manufacturing in very much of an ancillary role. Strategically, Ripolin UK was therefore something of an odd-ball in the Ripolin stable. However, the factor which finally triggered the decision to divest was disagreement between Jeffrey and the parent company as to the level of dividend that the latter should extract. Following the turnaround, Cdf increasingly wanted to take cash out of the business, rather than plough it back into developing the retail end.

In 1980, Jeffrey doubled the dividend to £1.20 but the French shareholders wanted £20 a share. Jeffrey felt this went against the spirit of the original brief which allowed for internally generated funds to be reinvested in the business. Then in July, 1980, Le Ripolin did a deal with the English minority shareholders (24 per cent) of Ripolin UK and presented the board of that company with a fait accompli that the dividend would be £20. Jeffrey immediately resigned and David Arundale walked out in sympathy. The French then capitulated and informed Jeffrey that they had decided to sell Ripolin UK if he would stay on.

Motivation for the buyout

Jeffrey and his senior management felt that if Ripolin UK were sold to a third party, it was likely that a competitor would swallow it up and close its manufacturing facility. Such a fate would undermine all the sacrifices they and the workforce had made to rescue the company. They also felt that they could run the company better than anyone else. In deciding to go for a buyout, Jeffrey in particular was less concerned with the potential for personal financial reward than with his commitment to the independence and growth of the business: 'When I took over the firm in 1977, it was worthless. The French shareholders wouldn't give the company a penny and the English shareholders wanted to get out. So I felt, along with the other executive board directors, that because we had turned it around, we should own and control it.'

Ordinary shares which had changed hands in 1977 at £6 and below were, by 1980, being transacted at the equivalent of £86. Although the market for decorative paint was becoming increasingly competitive, none of the team had any doubts about risking their money in the buyout.

> There was never a question of us losing any money, we did not even think about it. We never contemplated it going wrong. There was a lot of team spirit and we all had confidence in the business (Reg Clough).

> It is like driving, you don't think of whether to swerve, you just do it and think about it afterwards. There was no deep logical thought (John Osorio).

Following the intervention of one of the French directors of Le Ripolin, the management were given permission to tender for Ripolin UK. A precondition for this was that they could first raise the finance.

The financial package

When negotiating the financial package for a possible bid, Jeffrey was insistent that the team seek a majority stake. Otherwise the MBO might be vulnerable to a takeover from rival bidders unsuccessful in the tender. Jeffrey's first step was to persuade the English minority shareholders (24 per cent) to back the buyout. They agreed to exchange their Ripolin UK shares for shares in Jacoa – Jeffrey, Arundale, Clough, Osorio, Associates – a shelf company purchased for the purpose of buying out Ripolin UK.

It was a much harder task to persuade potential institutional backers to provide funding for a deal which would give the incumbent management 51 per cent of the equity of Ripolin UK for only 5 per cent of the purchase price.

At first none of the venture capitalists approached would countenance such a deal. Barclays Bank was willing to finance a MBO but was only willing to give the management team 6 per cent of the equity plus share options on another 3 per cent. Jeffrey stuck to his guns. He carried on arguing with Barclays right through to Christmas, knowing that the tender date was not far away in January 1981. To make matters worse, one of the companies participating in the competitive tender was trying to poach members of Jeffrey's management team. Fortunately, everyone stayed firm in their support for a buyout.

Then Jeffrey met Graham Williams of Barclays Development Capital, who was the first person to respond favourably to his proposals. With 10 days to go, Williams came up with a deal whereby Barclays Development Capital would give the buyout team 51 per cent of the voting stock for 5 per cent of the proposed tender purchase offer. Despite a relatively high P/E ratio of 10 (which reduced to 7 after stripping out cash retained in the business), Williams felt that the quality of the management team – principally Jeffrey – warranted the investment.

The tender

Under French law, Le Ripolin was prohibited from giving preferential terms to any party. So the buyout team could not expect favoured status. Nevertheless, there were factors working for the team. Having worked closely with the French parent for some years, they were able to proffer non-financial conditions that accorded with French aspirations. Also, at least one of the directors of the French company felt that, other things being equal, it was only right and fitting that Ripolin UK should pass to its current stewards.

The buyout team warned that competitors might be prepared to pay a higher price because of synergies, rationalisation and because of better access to finance. In the event, these worries proved justified. Jacoa's first tender did not match other bids in terms of price. They were, however, declared joint winners because of the non-financial terms. Jacoa was allowed to tender again on the basis that if they matched the best price offered and maintained the conditions, then they would win the company. The second tender was also turned down but the third was accepted.

In April 1981, Jacoa took over Ripolin UK, paying approximately £4.8 million for the company. Management and employees put up £250 000 and £17 990 respectively of this in return for between 51 per cent and 70 per cent of the equity, the actual amount to depend on the exercise of various conversion rights. Jeffrey put up £150 000 from JLD UK (he had split off from JLD Geneva as part of the deal for his becoming chief executive in the UK for 30.1 per cent of the fully diluted voting stock (see Table 4.1 notes 2 and 4), David Arundale, the Finance Director, was lent £25 000 from the JLD pension fund to subscribe for 5.1 per cent, Reginald Clough, the Retail Director, took out a second mortgage for £25 000 to subscribe for 5.1 per cent,

Table 4.1 The financial structure of the Jacoa buyout

1. Share capital	Authorised	Issued	Ownership
a) Ordinary shares £1	£1 160 422	£267,990	Buyout team 250 000 Employees 17 990
b) Convertible participating preferred ordinary shares £1	£88 334	£88 334	Barclays Development Capital Ltd (BDCL)
c) 12% 1983 redeemable preference shares £1	£350 001	£350 001	BDCL
d) 12% 1986/91 redeemable preference shares £1	£380 203	£380 203	Minority shareholders
e) 6% 1986/91 convertible £ redeemable preference shares	£760 423	£760 423	Minority shareholders
f) 12% Convertible redeemable preference shares £1	£66 665	£66 665	BDCL
Total share capital	£2 801 048	£1 908 616	

2. Loan capital			Source
g) Long term		£1 600 000	Barclays Merchant Bank
h) Temporary		£1 400 000	Barclays Merchant Bank
Total loan capital		£3 000 000	
Total funding		£4 908 616	

Notes:
1. All issued shares are of £1 par value and all preference shares are cumulative.
2. The shares shown under (b) above are convertible into ordinary shares at the rate of one for one. The shares shown under (b) above are convertible into ordinary shares equal to 10 per cent of the issued share capital at the time of conversion. Any of the shares in (e) above which have not been converted by 31 March 1986 shall be redeemed in ten equal instalments starting on that date and six monthly thereafter.
3. 17 990 ordinary shares were issued in July 1981 to employees. The other shares issued during the year were issued in April 1981 in connection with the acquisition of Ripolin Ltd of these shares have subsequently been transferred to employees.
4. The provider of the loan capital has an option, exercisable at any time up to full repayment of the loan, to subscribe at par for ordinary shares equal to 10 per cent, but up to a maximum of 50 000 shares, of the issued share capital at the date on which the option is exercised.
5. 7150 of the shares in (c) and all of (f) were redeemed on 18 December 1981.
6. The loan capital bears interest at 2.5 per cent above the London money market rate and is repayable by ten equal six-monthly instalments commencing 28 October 1983. The loan carries an option to subscribe for ordinary shares. See note 11(iv). The loan is secured by a fixed and floating charge on all assets of the Company.

Source: Company accounts for year ending 26 December 1981 and internal company information.

and John Osorio, the Manufacturing Director and fourth generation of the founding family, put up £50 000 for 10.2 per cent.

The employees put up £17 990 for 4.2 per cent of the fully diluted equity. Barclays Development Capital Ltd put up £83 000 for either 20 per cent or 30 per cent of the equity depending on the exercise of the conversion rights. Graham Williams was appointed as non-executive director to look after BDCL's interests. Barclays Merchant Bank provided most of the long-term capital with an option to subscribe at par for 10 per cent of the equity of Jacoa. The English minority shareholders subscribed for £1.15 million of redeemable preference shares convertible into up to 10 per cent of the equity of Jacoa. The full financial details are given at Table 4.1.

4   POST-BUYOUT

The immediate priorities after the buyout were ensuring a continuation of supplier support and reducing the gearing. Being one of the first buyouts, many people read a buyout as signifying excessive borrowings. The team had to reassure suppliers that the business was safe. They also had to raise cash flow through improved stock turn.

Apart from these measures, life went on much as before. John Osorio summed up the situation as follows: 'In all honesty, I would not like to pinpoint anything that we could not do before that we are now doing. Profits have increased because of processes initiated prior to the buyout. The work staff don't relate any differently to us just because we are the owners, they would have always assumed that we owned shares.'

Strategy

The buyout did not prompt any change in Jacoa's strategic direction although it did affect timing. The high gearing meant that Jeffrey could not implement his chosen strategy – 'Transition' – as fast as he would have liked. Transition was initiated by Jeffrey in 1979, to restructure the retail end of the business. It entailed closing down uneconomic units, typically high cost, low-yielding small stores, and replacing them with larger, cost-effective units.

Transition also involved expanding retail outlets in the South of England where Jacoa was under-represented. Jacoa's main presence was in the North and the Midlands (North 18 per cent North-West 20 per cent West Midlands 21 per cent, North London 23 per cent, South London 18 per cent by sales value at the end of 1981). Modernised stores opened under the 'Decor 8' specialist decorating image.

The new stores were significantly more successful than the old ones. For example, in July 1983 Jeffrey reported that in the first half trading of that year:

> Retail sales increased by 42.5 per cent – 26 per cent coming from new openings and 16.5 per cent from existing stores. As we progressively convert stores to the new 'Decor 8' specialist decorating image, their market share within a locality improves significantly. Sales growth in unconverted stores has been much less buoyant than in converted stores. At the time of going to press, one quarter of your Company's retail trading area has been converted to 'Decor 8'.

The second key thrust to Jeffrey's strategy was cost reduction of (1) the distribution and retailing operations through computerisation and (2) manufacturing operations through further increases in productivity. Cost reduction was not prompted by the existence of organisation slack which could be removed to give an immediate fillip to cash flow and profitability. This had already been done prior to the buyout, counter to the myth that buyouts only succeed through an overdue attention to organisation inefficiency. Rather, cost reduction was a long-term strategy aimed at improving Jacoa's relative competitive position.

In November 1981, new computer facilities were installed in the central services division. These were primarily to facilitate the accounting function. In 1982 Jeffrey embarked on a much more ambitious task as part of his vision to create, by 1986, the fully data-automated, nil paperwork store:

> After 33 months of development work and pilot trials, Jacoa EPOS – electronic point of sale data capture computer systems – is to go live throughout the chain in 1984.
>
> As far as we have been able to ascertain, no retail chain anywhere in the field of general merchandise as opposed to food has yet achieved the concept of the fully data-automated nil paperwork store and we do not underestimate the scale of the task confronting us.
>
> To repeat a cliché, 'Retail is Detail' and it is strategically essential that we develop a sophisticated data base if we are to

achieve our ambition of becoming the best decorating specialist in the world. Unfortunately from the view point of shareholders, the benefits to be derived from EPOS do not fully flow until the total systems package is fully live and operational which will be circa 1985/86. Jacoa EPOS will not be self-financing in 1984 and is another example of how it is sometimes necessary to invest upfront for the future. (1983 Annual Report).

While modernisation of stores and the introduction of EPOS occupied the retailing side of the business, manufacturing continued to look for improved productivity gains. This was notwithstanding manufacturing productivity more than double the UK average, and equal to the best achieved in the USA and Japan. Static final paint prices throughout much of 1982 and 1983, allied to cost price pressures, made improvements in productivity essential if manufacturing profit projections made at the time of the buyout were to be fulfilled. (Weighted price inflation across all products sold in Jacoa's retail outlets was running at 2.8 per cent in the first part of 1983 compared to cost price increases on a like weighted basis running at 8.4 per cent. Litres per man hour rose by 7.5 per cent in 1983 and by 53 per cent between 1982 and 1986. Table 4.2 shows the productivity increases pre-and post-buyout.

Expansion of downstream outlets from 1983 onwards (see below) and the fact that Ripolin paint accounted for some 70 per cent of paint sales in Jacoa stores, meant that demand for Ripolin paint outstripped manufacturing capacity throughout much of the post-buyout period. Rather than invest in new manufacturing plant (a Northern-based paint manufacturing plant was considered) the company decided that they always had the option of operating the existing plant on multiple shifts. Despite showing a positive net present value, additional plant did not present the company with as an attractive an investment opportunity as transforming outlets into the modernised 'Decor 8' stores.

Table 4.2 Productivity per man year (annual average)

	1976	1978	1980	1982	1984	1986
Ripolin litres per factory employee (000s)	58.4	116.2	139.0	143.3	181.4	220.0
UK Average			66.0			75.0

Source: Company data.

The third aspect of Jeffrey's strategy was horizontal integration to achieve synergy and retail expansion. From a very early date, management systems and Head Office support functions were built to cope with a very large number of shops. The plan was to acquire unprofitable stores and then turn them around by applying the Jacoa recipe. Virtually all the retail businesses acquired since 1977 were loss makers at the time of acquisition and then successfully turned around. By 1983, the company had developed considerable expertise in profitably integrating acquisitions.

In March and May 1983, Jacoa acquired 48 retail stores from Leyland Paint and Wallpaper Plc and from Hope and Bond Ltd. Jeffrey had his eye on grander things: a merger which would give nationwide representation. In January 1983, Jeffrey had suggested a merger to Malcolm Stanley, Chairman of A. G. Stanley Plc. A. G. Stanley was Jacoa's principal competitor, and had been one of the outside rival bidders for Ripolin UK in 1981. Stanley was the larger company but Jacoa was the more profitable one. Stanley had some 220 DIY stores trading predominantly in the South of England while Jacoa had some 200 outlets in the Midlands, the North and Scotland. A merger would create the largest home decorating chain by number but not by turnover in the UK.

Malcolm Stanley's initial reaction to the merger suggestion was favourable and after a detailed study, a merger was agreed in principle in September 1983. The following month, Stanley pulled out of the deal owing to what he termed conflict over future trading policy, inherent differences in management style and because Stanley's shops were a larger size – and hence better – than Jacoa's. Jeffrey and his advisers, Barclays Merchant Bank, were confounded by the news. John Standen at BMB was reported as saying that the reasons given by Stanley for pulling out of the deal were not exactly fulsome. 'We thought we had reached agreement on fundamental matters and were very surprised when Stanley pulled out. We tried to talk to them about it but that wasn't to be' *Evening Standard* (28 November 1983). The breakdown in the merger talks was to prove even more significant than Jeffrey realised at the time.

Performance

The result of these various strategic initiatives was to take some time to work through into Jacoa's financial performance. This was partly due to the nature of such investment, and partly due to poor trading conditions in the first couple of years of the buyout. Increasing competition in the DIY market, allied to a fall-off in the growth of consumer expenditure on paint, depressed sales margins at a time when Jacoa was intent on growing its market share. By 1986, however, with EPOS fully operational, the retail conversions almost complete, and an upturn in the market, Jacoa began to reap the gains from its various strategic thrusts.

Table 4.3 shows Jacoa's performance before and after the buyout.

Table 4.3 Ripolin UK/Jacoa's financial performance before and after the buyout

	Pre-buyout				Post-buyout				
				Year ending 31 December					
	1978	*1979*	*1980*	*1981[1]*	*1982*	*1983*	*1984*	*1985*	*1986*
Turnover £m	13.5	17.6	18.9	18.8	20.3	27.9	30.6	32.3	34.8
PBIT[3] £m	0.6	0.6	0.7	1.2	1.1	1.3	0.7	1.1	2.2[2]
Net assets £m	3.0	4.0	4.9	4.3	4.8	5.0	5.1	4.9	5.9
ROS[4]	4.1	3.1	3.5	6.2	5.2	4.7	2.3	3.4	6.3
ROCE[5]	18.8	13.8	13.6	26.7	21.9	26.6	13.7	22.2	37.1
Gearing 1[6]				37.0	30.0	14.1	9.8	6.1	1.7
Gearing 2[7]				63.5	53.7	33.0	28.5	24.2	13.8

Notes:
1. For the first four months of 1981 the company traded as Ripolin UK and thereafter as Jacoa.
2. For purposes of comparability, the 1986 profitability figures have been corrected (downwards by £277 000) for a change in the basis of depreciation used in that year.
3. Trading profit before tax and interest.
4. Actual amounts rather than the rounded up numbers stated in the table have been used to calculate all ratios.
5. Trading profit before interest and tax divided by net assets.
6. Long-term debt divided by capital employed (net assets).
7. Long-term debt plus preference share capital divided by capital employed.

Source: Company accounts.

In view of its heavy investment schedule, it is noteworthy that Jacoa was able to reduce quickly its gearing. This was achieved mainly through a very tight dividend policy (until 1987) and profitable trading. It was not done by reducing fixed assets as is sometimes the case in buyouts where the need to pay off debt requires extensive asset sales and sale and leaseback. While surpluses arising on shop disposals contributed to earnings, these were ploughed back into further shop acquisitions.

5 SELL OUT

The success of Jeffrey's strategy was beginning to show through strongly by 1986. Yet EPOS and the effective management and control systems introduced to deal with all aspects of the business were perceived to have made the job of overseeing the business less challenging. Accordingly, Jeffrey considered that it was essential to grow the business through a sizeable acquisition. An obstacle, however, was the attitude of the institutional backers. They were not very keen on Jacoa diversifying because of the risks involved and because they didn't want to jeopardise the spectacular capital appreciation they had obtained on their investment in Jacoa. Nor did they want to lock in their investment for the time required to apply the Jacoa turnaround recipe to another company. Their caution meant that Jacoa had to adopt strict criteria towards potential acquisitions. This made it very difficult for Jeffrey to succeed in finding and successfully negotiating a takeover. The caution of the banks also had a psychological knock-on effect on the other members of the team. It underlined the fact that the owner-managers were risking the considerable capital gains they had already made on their equity: 'The banks would say, "do you realise that you are risking your own millions in going for a takeover?"'

By failing to negotiate acquisitions, and by being highly successful, Jacoa was itself becoming vulnerable to being taken over. Between November 1986 and the middle of 1987, Jeffrey managed to fight off five takeover bids. One of the most persistent was A. G. Stanley who, in March 1987 offered £16 million, only to have this thrown out by the Jacoa board as inadequate.

When Stanley then raised the offer to a maximum of £26.5 million (depending on the value of Stanley share at the time of purchase), one of the major shareholders on the buyout team decided that he wanted to realise his investment in Jacoa, leave and buy a farm. The other owner-managers, with the exception of Jeffrey, were happy to sell out. The Articles of Association effectively required that Jeffrey agree with the majority decision, which eventually he did with great reluctance. While the merger made strategic sense in terms of creating a specialist, national retail chain serving the home decorating market, the merger spelled the end of Jacoa's independence. At completion, Stanley paid £26.5 million for Jacoa (which was not diminished by the October 1987 crash – with the aid of the takeover, Stanley shares rode the crash remarkably well). It was some consolation to Jeffrey that Stanley intended to retain the production facility at Southall. Jeffrey stepped down as chief executive of Jacoa and along with the other members of the buyout team, departed the company.

6   AFTERTHOUGHTS ON OWNERSHIP

In the immediate post-buyout period, all the buyout team members stressed that their personal ownership stakes had very little effect – ownership being wanted primarily to allow them to carry on at the helm. The wealth-creating aspects of ownership were merely an incidental bonus which could not further motivate a team which was already doing its best. While this was true at the time of the buyout, over the next few years the meaning of ownership changed for the buyout team members (apart from Jeffrey). When the equity stakes became very valuable, this potential wealth could not be ignored. As Jeffrey ruefully admits: 'Success breeds its own problems.'

From the beginning, Jeffrey's dividend policy was very tight, his major priority being to conserve funds for reinvestment. All the development costs for EPOS were written off above the line over three years and depreciation policy was much more conservative than in most other retailers. Although dividends were tripled for the 1986 tax year to a level that made the gross annual dividend greater than the original subscription price for shares, the move was made too late to offset the pent-up demand for some benefit from the appreciation in shareholders' funds.

Moreover, Jeffrey was opposed to a public flotation. The following comments made in the 1983 Annual Report must have worried the institutional backers who typically like to see capital gains realised within a four- to five-year time span.

I am frequently told by potential investors and institutions that Jacoa should obtain a listing for its shares. Your Board has carefully considered this option but believe that it would be more difficult if listed to make the essential sacrifices of short term earnings in favour of future growth as are involved in the development phase of a company's life cycle.

Your Board is already committed to obtaining a listing no later than end 1995 which is *only 12 years away* and will meantime keep the option under review. (Annual Report 1983, my italics).

Possibly, Jeffrey's messianic zeal for Jacoa had something to do with the change of attitude towards ownership. While Jeffrey was looking always to the future, the other owner managers, along with the institutional backers, had shorter time horizons. Principal shareholders in buyouts are effectively locked into their stake, unless there is a public flotation, or a well-developed internal market for transferring shares. The latter is rarely the case in any but the largest buyouts. An obvious point is that if dividends are low, then the only way owners can realise something on their investment is by selling their shares and taking the capital gain. Given the concentration of ownership in buyouts, this can significantly affect the distribution of power, tipping it in favour of the institutional backers or outside predators.

To conclude, in view of the literature on ownership and control (see Chapter 1), it is perhaps ironic that rather than fusing personal and organisational goals, ownership led some of Jacoa's owner managers to go their separate ways. Instead of giving them the incentive to make the business ever more successful and more profitable, ownership encouraged them to leave their jobs rather than do them more assiduously. (The takeover by Stanley was not generally perceived as the best way to maximise shareholder value in Jacoa.) It was perhaps some consolation to Jeffrey that despite losing control of the business, his personal stake of £150 000 became worth in excess of £6.5 million when he was forced to sell out to Stanley. There was also an additional £2.25 million in the pension fund of which he and his wife were sole beneficiaries.

5 The Trend Control Story

1 INTRODUCTION AND SYNOPSIS

In late 1979, two computer whizzkids, Mervyn De'Ath and Terry Casey, met Pierce Molony, a corporate executive with the large Dutch company, Holec. Molony had been charged with finding new businesses in the UK as part of Holec's strategy of boosting international operations. Together they set up a hi-tech new venture, Holec Energy UK, with Molony, Casey and De'Ath as the directors, and Molony as managing director. The company had a notional capital of £100 000 and Casey and De'Ath initially worked from home. After some success in gaining orders, premises in Horsham were acquired and further personnel, in particular Bob Rylatt and Andrew Vickerstaff, were recruited.

Three years later, following mounting losses through an overrun on development expenses and because of the parent company's liquidity problems back in Holland, a buyout was mooted as the only alternative to closure. Holec had lost faith in their English subsidiary's products. The team managed to persuade SUMIT, an investment trust, to back them. Eventually, Molony, De'Ath, Casey, Rylatt and Vickerstaff bought out their company for £75 000. They named the new company Trend Control Systems Ltd. The team took two thirds of the equity and SUMIT one third.

At first, the buyout continued to lose money. Technical problems with the product were exacerbated by a failure to implement adequate information systems. During this period, two of the original buyout team, Molony and Vickerstaff, left the company and Casey became managing director. John Prestwich, from SUMIT, was appointed non-executive chairman. By 1985, the corner had been turned and the company had become marginally profitable.

Inevitably, a developing company such as Trend is cash hungry. Despite a number of capital reorganisations, there was an element of underfunding relative to expansion plans. The small size of the company was a competitive disadvantage when it came to tendering for large contracts. Accordingly, the team started scouting around for a partner.

In November 1986, with profits still low but on an upward trend,

MK Electric acquired 77.6 per cent of Trend for £4.24 million – a capital appreciation of more than 5000 per cent in three years. Casey and De'Ath's initial stakes of around £17 000 became worth around £1 million.

2   ANCESTRAL ORIGINS

The parent company: Holec

Trend Control's former parent company, Holec, was formed by the amalgamation of a number of very old companies holding a combined share of 80–90 per cent of the Dutch electrical market. Initially, Holec stayed a loose amalgam of companies, with a weak corporate structure and no obvious corporate strategy. In the early 1970s, it began to lose money, prompting more centralised direction. The resulting improvement in performance was halted by the 1974 oil price shock. In 1976, the shareholders appointed a new management team, located in Utrecht. It soon became apparent to them that assets were very high, and the approach of the company very insular. A strategy of acquisition and corporate venturing was adopted in an attempt to boost ROI and broaden the company's geographic scope. Holec moved into Germany, France, Belgium, the US, the UK, Nigeria, Indonesia and Australia buying or setting up high-tech companies.

As part of this internationalization strategy, one of their executives, Pierce Molony, was sent over to the UK to see whether more of Holec's existing products could be sold in the UK. His remit was then widened to include sub-assembly manufacture and to recommend new products or acquisitions. Wherever possible, new technology was to be fed back into the parent company.

Holec Energy UK

While searching for possible ventures, Molony was introduced by one of Holec's English consultants to Mervyn De'Ath and Terry Casey. The latter were dissatisfied with their current employment prospects and they discussed an idea for setting up their own company to market energy control systems. They felt that because of the rapid fall in capital costs in electronics, computer systems had excellent prospects for controlling energy usage. Their only problem was that they did not have the money to set the business up.

De'Ath and Casey thought there was tremendous potential for putting together proprietary hardware systems from other manufacturers, writing the appropriate software and then selling the whole system. In their current jobs they were often forced to use in-house hardware which was not best suited to customers' needs.

Molony was greatly impressed with these ideas. Together, the three of them decided to form Holec Energy UK to develop and market an energy management system aimed at reducing energy bills by up to 30 per cent.

Mission
Initially, they decided to focus on boilers. However, the first job was arranged fortuitously because the parent company, Holec, had put a burner into a grass drier and was having trouble with it. Casey and De'Ath were despatched to see if it was a control problem: 'We quickly realised that it was a timer/delay problem. We did a deal with the customer, saying that if he would pay for the hardware, approximately £5000, we would give our time free to set it up and get it working and have a panel maker to construct the cabinets.'

Having sorted out the problem they felt that the market potential was great. There were some 60 grass driers in the UK and no one else was involved in energy controlled systems for them. In the event, however, the initiative proved unsuccessful. Despite offering a payback of between one and two years, their system was implemented in only three or four grass driers. Many of the UK grass driers were going bankrupt because of the rise in energy costs (post-OPEC) and the importation of cheap cattle feed.

De'Ath and Casey refocused their attention on the original aim – controlling boilers. They soon discovered, however, that although savings could be made from boiler control, there was far greater potential in controlling the whole of the building in which the boiler operated. For example, in a thermal building with annual energy costs of, say, £100 000, some £5000 might be saved by controlling the boiler. However, £20 000 might be saved by implementing better controls for the building. Subsequent product development took place entirely within the sphere of building control systems.

The growing availability of suitable component parts and reasonably priced hardware allowed Holec Energy UK to develop a marketable product within six months of the company's formation. In August 1980, De'Ath and Casey held a symposium in Brighton. The outcome was two big contracts: one for Glaxo and one for Hewlett-Packard at Pinewood:

> We had thought that the large companies would have the market tied up but what they were doing was far too crude. Therefore, we went back to Holec and said that we wanted to do full buildings. It was useful having Holec in Holland as our backers as this legitimised our selling. After all, we were only two guys with no track record trying to sell in competition with large, sometimes international companies. But the main thing that enabled us to sell was our enthusiasm. At the end of the day we had to say, it will work because we say it will.

In 1981, Bob Rylatt was brought in to join the team. De'Ath had worked for Bob previously and wanted him to internationalise the business and to replicate their success abroad.

By the end of 1981, Holec Energy UK, in competition with Satchwell, GEC and Transmitton and Johnson (subsidiaries, respectively, of US giants BICC and Honeywell), had captured some 20 per cent of the market. Within 18 months they had come from nowhere to the position of market leader.

Problems

Despite this apparently healthy picture, the team began to encounter severe technical problems with the product during 1981. There was a gap between the specification for sale and what the product actually achieved. Salesmen had oversold the product and problems existed in both hardware and software:

> Our salesmen went out and sold the product while it was still in the development stage. We suddenly became very successful in the public sector. We were getting an order a day – perhaps because public sector bodies had money to spend by the end of the financial year. Instead of taking a year or so as we had expected, we cracked all these customers at once.
>
> The problem was that our finished product would only do about half of what we had told the salesmen it would do, in terms of capacity, not functionality. By the time we had got the software to a level where it would do everything we said it would, we hadn't as much memory left for data storage as we'd expected.
>
> When we got all the engineers together and sat down with all

these jobs to do, we found we would either have to put in three times as many computers as had been allowed for in the quote – which would have cost us a fortune – or we would have to go back to redevelop the product so that we could actually do more with the same computers. The snag was that by then we were hooked. We had the contracts, we had to finish them. There was no way we could just turn the tap off – particularly with the pressure from Holec to meet the sales projections from our original business plan.

De'Ath went off to the US to seek assistance from Hewlett-Packard. Fortunately, they were able to find a way around the problem. Despite some trying times, all the customers stuck with the company. The downside was that the additional costs incurred in sorting out the technical issues caused Holec Energy UK to fall well short of budgetary targets. A loss of £250 000 was incurred in 1981.

The deadweight hand

Holec didn't have the vision to see where we were going. It is very difficult for a large conglomerate to recognise a developing market of this sort. The very structure of how they plan relates to markets that they know. They have a resistance to not-invented-here products. They tend to want in when a product has already been established (Pierce Molony).

With financial performance failing to live up to expectations, an increasingly dissatisfied parent company began to exert pressure on the management of Holec Energy UK to cut back and save costs. De'Ath and Casey felt that the parent company lacked experience in starting up companies, was too distant from the realities facing them, imposed totally inappropriate targets and constraints, and lacked the long-term vision to take the risks necessary for them to expand and grow. Holec Energy UK had to produce detailed, long-term plans. Their performance was measured in strict accounting terms: orders coming in and out; profit; and return on investment. Much of Casey's time was spent on producing these plans, which he considered somewhat inappropriate given the newness of the market they were entering.

Holec's expectation was that having put in the money and the machines, there should be an instant success:

Holec just didn't understand the business. They didn't understand that for a company like this, the trading losses over the first few years are actually development costs. It would have been OK if we were going to set up a factory to make motor cars. They would expect it to cost £50 million for plant, machinery and all the rest of it, and they would call that its capital and be quite happy with it. But if no one else wants to buy that capital, then they have written it off just as surely as they have written off development costs.

There are no capital costs in our business because it is all software and services. Therefore, Holec assumed that we ought to make money on day one. They couldn't grasp the fact that trading losses due to development costs in actually writing the software, or costs experienced in getting further up the learning curve, or marketing costs of getting a higher market share and making it profitable, are all part of the start up costs and should be equated with capital costs.

Holec blew hot and cold with their English subsidiary. One moment they were going to sell the company, the next moment they weren't. In April 1981, Molony was instructed to find a buyer for Holec Energy UK. During the whole of this year, a question mark hung over whether the team would be given the finance to continue developing the product.

3 DIVESTMENT AND BUYOUT

The problems that the team had with the parent were partly due to the financial difficulties the latter was experiencing. During 1981, rising energy prices hit Holec's transformer division so badly that a Fl 12 million grant from the Dutch Government was needed to ensure its survival. The announcement in May 1982 of losses of Fl 66.3 million ($25.5 million) for 1981 led to a drastic reorganisation programme tied to a refinancing package. The latter carried with it the requirement that Holec group substantially reduce its staff.

An agreement with the unions, dating back to 1976, prevented Holec from shedding staff in Holland. It had to turn to its foreign subsidiaries to achieve the required economies. Urgency was increased by a fall in property prices in Holland. This frustrated attempts to improve the case flow position by liquidating assets. Over the following two years, Holec sold some 27 subsidiaries employing 1300 people.

By mid-1982, however, it had become obvious that Holec Energy UK couldn't be sold. The major difficulty in finding an outside buyer for the company was that it was essentially a people business, a feature common to many hi-tech firms . While its products were being developed, the only assets were staff. It was, therefore, highly vulnerable to losses of key personnel. Two major corporations turned Holec Energy UK down because it did not have a strong capital asset base and because as they said: 'We might as well just buy the people.'

A director of Holec group then suggested to Molony that a management buyout might be a good idea. A subsidiary in the US had been sold as one, so the parent company had experience with this sort of transaction. Molony's failure to find a buyer for Holec Energy meant that management ownership was effectively the only option that would secure the future of the company. A buyout had the additional advantage of locking-in key personnel. Indeed, Molony believed that management buyouts had great potential as the appropriate organisational structure for high-tech firms.

Motivation for the buyout

The team's reasons for wanting to go for a buyout were a mixture of the materialistic and the visionary. They recognised that the venture was high-risk but they all had great faith in the product. The risk factor meant that they had to be fairly hard-nosed if they weren't to end up losing everything. Unlike many other buyouts, where an immediate fillip to profitability can be gained by juggling capital assets or by squeezing out organisation slack, the route to the immediate survival of the buyout lay in sorting out the technical problems with the product and increasing sales.

Molony had great faith in the product and in De'Ath and Casey. He saw the buyout as a natural extension of his involvement with them. He had also become somewhat disillusioned with working for a conglomerate and wanted to branch out on his own. Molony saw himself as an entrepreneur whose expertise lay in setting up companies, something he did previously for Inchape in Japan. He enjoyed identifying market openings, gathering expertise to fill management gaps, then negotiating backing from financial institutions. It was his intention to move away from the company on completion of the buyout so that he could set up other companies.

Casey suggested that the two principles underlying the buyout were fear and greed; fear that if the company fell apart it would be fairly painful, and greed in terms of what they might make at the end of the day. Both he and De'Ath both recognised that at the time, the motivation was very mercenary:

> Our experience of working at Eurotherm at the time it went public convinced us that we needed an equity stake. Suddenly, a guy you were out boozing with – your boss who has a stock option – is worth a million. You can work for a company and earn a high income, but the only way of really achieving wealth is through capital accumulation, an equity share. When we went to Holec to start up Holec Energy UK, we didn't manage to get an equity share out of the deal. We tried but they would only grant us a profit share. Had Holec stuck with us, then we would have stuck with them. Nevertheless, the management buyout gave us what we were really looking for, a share in the business. And it is that share which keeps you going, makes you really go in and fight that last fight.

Buttressing the financial optimism of all the members of the team was their shared belief in the product and in themselves as the best people to run the business. They all wanted to be free from the bureaucratic constraints of being part of a large company and nobody felt they would miss being involved in the corporate hierarchy. Casey, for example, said that he had always been something of a rebel. Molony concurred: 'De'Ath and Casey aren't interested in the routine running of the business. They are men of drive and vision who could never work in a conglomerate. Apart from anything else, 90 per cent of corporate time is taken up with politics.'

Negotiating the buyout

Towards the end of 1982, Molony entered a very tricky period of negotiation with the parent company. Senior management there felt that by divesting the UK subsidiary, they would gain additional and much needed cash and remove a significant drain on their resources. Severe doubts about the potential of the UK subsidiary's product, and its ability to overcome technical difficulties, served only to confirm the wisdom of divestment.

Nevertheless, there was some disagreement from middle management within Holec group as to whether Holec Energy UK should be sold. Some people felt that if Pierce Molony wanted to leave Holec group and throw in with the new management buyout, there must be more to it than met the eye. Second, there was resistance to selling a subsidiary which was potentially profitable and a source to the parent company of essential software and technical expertise. The technical brilliance of what De'Ath and his team were accomplishing was recognised and some people at HQ felt that the problems were essentially managerial. They argued that with stricter control and a more cost conscious strategy, Holec Energy UK could become a very valuable asset.

Accordingly, in December 1982 Holec sent over one of their managers to England to sort things out during the Christmas period. He effectively fired Molony and Casey and then tried to get Rylatt and De'Ath to cut back all overheads until sales picked up. They refused. The management buyout seemed to be the only remaining option to ensure the company's survival.

The management team did consider whether it would be better to walk out and start up again. This would avoid their having to become involved in lengthy buyout negotiations and they would not have to pay Holec anything. They had also discovered that in ten months to October 1982, Holec Energy had lost £550 000. However, there were advantages to buying the existing fabric with the problems they knew about, rather than starting from scratch – particularly as they believed that they were close to overcoming the technical difficulties.

Molony found a backer for the buyout in SUMIT, an investment trust. SUMIT were very different from Holec. They were prepared to provide finance because they believed in the product: 'We were from the start very impressed by Mervyn, Terry and Bob. Their enthusiasm and commitment to producing a product in which we also saw the potential, really convinced us that this was a case worth backing.' (Nicholas Talbot Rice, non-executive director at Trend and MD of SUMIT.)

A key element in the buyout package was SUMIT's requirement of a 'painfully' high financial stake from the new owner/managers. They felt this would provide all possible motivation for the team to make the product successful. In fact this incentive was seen by the team as largely redundant. They had other reasons for wanting their products to be successful: their desire to succeed and to show that they could do what they had said they could do. If anything, the personal debt they had taken on to fund the high equity stake was somewhat of a distraction to their concentration on the needs of the business. The team negotiated for some 67.5 per cent of the equity, with a further 5 per cent stake for the other members of staff.

The buyout was eventually completed on 1 March 1983, when a payment of £75 000 was paid to Holec for the company. The new company was christened Trend Control. The financial structure of the deal is shown in Table 5.1.

4 POST-BUYOUT

Trend Control initially suffered a loss of credibility by the severance from Holec. It was no longer part of a £250 million group but a small group of entrepreneurs. Most customers were large companies, or the public sector, who preferred to deal with other large companies. The team also felt that the general perception of buyouts was that many emerged from receivership. An immediate priority, therefore,

Table 5.1   The financial structure of the Trend Control buyout
(A) As of March 1983

1. *Share capital*	*Authorised*	*Issued*	*Subscriber*
a) Ordinary shares £1	£72 500	£71 850; 16 875: Molony, Casey, De'Ath; £8438. Rylatt; £8437, Vickerstaff	
b) Cumulative convertible participating preferred ordinary shares £1	£47 500	£27 500	SUMIT
c) Cumulative redeemable preference shares £1 each	£200 000	£200 00	SUMIT
Total share capital	£320 000	£299 350	
2. *Loan Capital**			
f) Unsecured loan stock 1993		£100 000	SUMIT
Unsecured loan stock 1987/88		£150 000	SUMIT
g) HP		£3427	
Other			
h) Bank loans and overdrafts		£161 828	
Total funding		£557 347	

* This data is given in the accounts to March 1984 so it may diverge marginally from the position existing as of March 1983, the date of the buyout.

Table 5.1 Continued
(B) As of 1 April 1985
First reorganisation 29 March 1985 (to capitalise £300 000 of long-term loan stock)

1. Share capital	Authorised	Issued	Subscriber
a) Ordinary shares £1	£72 500	£71 850; £8437: Prestwich £17 341 Casey £17341 De'Ath £8438 Molony £8906 Rylatt £2437 Vickerstaff†	
b) Cumulative convertible participating preferred ordinary shares £1	£47 500	£27 500	SUMIT
d) Redeemable preference shares of £1	£300 000	£300 000	SUMIT
e) Deferred Shares £1	£200 000	£200 00	SUMIT
Total share capital	£620 000	£599 350	
2. Loan capital			
g) HP creditor		£3427	
Other			
h) Bank loans and overdrafts (secured)		£256 524	
Total funding		£859 301	

† Resigned 16 January 1985

1. The cumulative convertible participating preferred ordinary shares (b) carry the right to a cumulative preferential dividend (net of Advance Corporation Tax) of 9 per cent of the consolidated pre-tax profit of the company and its subsidiaries. These are convertible at any time at the discretion of their holders into an equal number of ordinary shares.
2. The cumulative redeemable preference shares (c) were redeemed in full at par on 29 March 1985, and the proceeds were applied in full to the issue of an equal number of deferred shares of £1 each.
3. The redeemable preference shares (d) carry the right to a preferential gross dividend of 4.33 per cent per annum, rising by way of a sliding scale to 13.33 per cent per annum in 1989 and each subsequent year. They are redeemable at the company's option at any time before 1990. Any such shares not redeemed by 31 March 1990 shall be redeemed by six annual instalments of £50 000 each commencing on that date. The shares are redeemable at the option of their holders in the event of a sale of a controlling interest in the company, a listing of its share capital, or a capital reorganisation.
4. The deferred shares (e) may also be redeemed at the option of their holders in the same events as described in (4), at a price of 25p per share.
5. Both loan stocks (e) and (f) bear interest at a rate equal to the higher of 3.5 per cent over Barclays Bank Base Rate or 12 per cent. The loan stocks were increased by £50 000 on 31 July 1984. All loan stocks were redeemed on 29 March 1985 as part of the reorganisation of the company's capital base.
6. The amounts shown in (h) fall due within one year.

was to impress upon customers that Trend Control was a going concern.

One positive factor working in their favour was that with Holec, there had been a considerable risk that the financial tap would be turned off. After the buyout, the company had secure long- and medium-term finance from an established financial institution. For example, towards the end of the buyout negotiations, the credibilty that came from being part of a large group rapidly diminished as the parent company's financial difficulties became increasingly obvious. A large and important deal that was about to be signed with J. Sainsbury had been threatened by concern over the financial viability of Holec Energy in the light of the parent company's problems.

A leadership change

Despite the good omens, storm clouds began to gather soon after the MBO. Losses for the half-year to August 1983 were substantially more than expected. Again, technical problems were to blame. The team had decided to replace their first control system, which harnessed their own software to Hewlett-Packard hardware, with their own hardware. The new system was phased in soon after the completion of the buyout. Unfortunately, the changeover did not go as well as anticipated. The new product was slightly late into the market place, whilst sales of the older product fell off sharply as people had heard about the new product. This produced a V-shaped transition curve with a low point in September/October 1983. The company experienced severe cash flow problems.

In practice, little could have been done to prevent this from happening, although the fact that it was unexpected exacerbated the problems. If the team had been alerted sooner to the technical problems then they could have accelerated the technical solution rather then trying to rush around and solve each problem on the ground. In his previous work with large companies, Molony had been used to information and analysis being created for him and fed through the system. His failure to build a similar system for himself at Trend, and hence the failure to prepare people (especially SUMIT) for the poor results, undermined his ability to lead the small, developing company.

Casey and De'Ath became increasingly worried about their investment and Casey felt he would be a more effective leader. Whereas as an employee he would probably have done nothing, as an owner he felt obliged to protect his investment. He expressed his concerns to SUMIT who were thinking along similar lines.

When it was suggested to Molony that perhaps Casey was in a better position to lead, Molony readily agreed. He was really more interested in setting up new companies than in steering the fledgeling Trend Control towards its USM listing. Casey became MD and John Prestwich, one of the non-executive directors of SUMIT, joined the board as non-executive Chairman at the end of 1983. Molony sold half of his shares to John Prestwich but retained his position on the board. A few months later, Molony came up with the idea of setting up Trend Ireland to market Trend products in Ireland. In a short period of time it was very successful and Trend Control took 10 per cent of the shareholding for a nominal fee.

Casey introduced a number of changes, including the setting of targets and accountant monitoring of MIELO (materials, installation, expenses, labour and overheads):

> People had become conditioned to failure and we had to change attitudes. An important way of doing this was through the measurement system. We gave targets to the project leader and allowed a financial sum for each element of the project. We then kept a close eye on any variance from these targets. One of the effects of this system was the creation of a certain amount of competition between the project managers on site and the development teams, because if the project manager doesn't have his equipment, then he will scream at the others to provide it.

The management accounting systems were overhauled which led to some friction with Andy Vickerstaff, the financial controller. Vickerstaff had certain differences of opinion with respect to operational procedures and decided to leave at the beginning of 1985. Nevertheless, he retained some of his shares and remained on good terms with his former colleagues.

Although in the year to 31 March 1984 Trend recorded a pre-tax loss of £372 886, things were looking up and Casey, De'Ath and Rylatt felt that the worst was over. The new product had begun to sell well and was performing in line with expectations. In 1984, Trend entered the export market. Bruce Geminsky, a supplier of controls to supermarkets in the USA, became Trend's agent, buying the product from Trend and then selling it. Geminsky had substantial ongoing business, and was able to switch to Trend from an inferior rival product. He generated large amounts of business almost immediately. 'We didn't have to go through a long build up. One day he was selling the old product, the next day Trend's.'

The success enjoyed by Geminsky during the first twelve months led to the establishment in March 1985 of a US-based joint venture company, Trend Control Systems Inc. to market Trend's products in the USA. Casey, Rylatt and De'Ath joined the board of the new company, and, under a reciprocal arrangement Geminsky joined the board of Trend Control Ltd. (In early 1987, after the sale to MK Electric – see below – Trend Control sold its stake in Trend Inc. Geminsky left the board of the UK company, and likewise Casey, De'Ath and Rylatt departed the US company. The sale freed Trend Control Ltd to pursue other US initiatives in areas such as air conditioning, alarms and more general building controls.)

For the year to 31 March 1985, Trend Control showed its first profit since start up of £86 323 (pre-tax). However, the balance sheet was still very weak. This adversely affected customers' perception of Trend who were concerned about after-sales back-up and service. A capital reorganisation was, therefore, agreed to by SUMIT (see also Table 6.1, part B):

> We... gave moral support to customers who questioned the strength of the balance sheets explaining our willingness to stand behind the company as long as it looked sensible from our shareholders' point of view to do so. In the event, there were various capital reorganisations and we finally committed £500 000 of funds on top of our £500 000 equity investment. When it became evident that the structure of £300 000 of loan finance was a weakening influence on the balance sheet and servicing it a heavy cash drain on the company, we were prepared to rearrange the capital. We turned preference shares with a primary coupon into deferred shares producing no income and the loans into redeemable preference shares so that they became part of the equity. We strongly feel that this support for the company was not only warranted but responsible from a development capital institution (Nicholas Talbot Rice, MD of SUMIT).

Profits grew to £126 900 in the year ending March 1986. Perhaps more importantly, Trend achieved second place in the market for building energy control systems in front of such giants as Honeywell and Johnson. (The top five firms share over 70 per cent of the UK market.)

Strategic change

More importantly, Trend Control was making its presence increasingly felt in the market for total building control systems.

> The major companies – like Honeywell, Johnson, Satchwell – have tended to continue producing very standard, traditional controls, without moving into total building control. For Trend, the major motivation was the changing nature of the market, and in particular, the likely switch to the new technology produced by Trend. When we first started, we were a specialist company dealing in energy management systems. As we have developed, our products have become the standard control systems in buildings, controlling everything in the building – heating, lighting, ventilation, lifts, fire alarms, the lot.
>
> We are extremely flexible. The intention is ultimately to be able to control, for example, entire office blocks with one system – all from one desk. We aim to produce something clever enough to know the difference between someone who's working legitimately on a Saturday morning, and therefore wants the ventilation and lighting on, and someone who is trying to burgle the place at midnight.

The team recognised, however, that their move away from the relatively small market for buildings energy management systems, to buildings systems control was going to put them on a collision course with their large competitors. While the latter might have turned a blind eye to them in a specialist market segment, this would not be the case as they branched out into the wider market. 'Whatever complacency the large companies might show to us is unlikely to continue in the new conditions with a potential transition from a market of £25 to £30 million to £150 million. When the side market threatens to take over their market, what do they do? Where are they going to get their orders from?'

A further aspect of the strategy was to shift away from the retrofitting of existing building to the installation of controls in new buildings. This meant establishing new customers and contacts which in turn increased selling costs.

5 SELL OUT

Since its inception, Trend Control had been hampered by cash restrictions. Apart from the high proportion of expenditure on

Table 5.2   Trend Control's financial performance after the buyout*

	Year ending 31 March (£000s)			
	1984	*1985*	*1986*	*1987*
Turnover	1585	2589	4251	6357
PBIT	(360)	122	197	557
PBT	(373)	86	127	483
Net assets	(145)	241	349	1534
R & D	150	264	433	509
ROS (%)		4.7	4.6	8.8
ROCE (%)		51	56	36
Current ratio	1.0	1.1	1.0	1.6
Acid test	0.6	0.6	0.8	1.4

Notes:
1. The figures for 1984 represent the accounts of the company from 1 March 1983 (the date it commenced to trade) and the results of the continuing activities of its subsidiary, Trend Control Systems, from 1 January 1983, the effective date of its acquisition.

   Net assets data and hence ROCE before and after 1982 are not strictly comparable as they are derived from different data sources. The differences are not sufficiently great, however, as to make them unsatisfactory for broad illustrative purposes.
2. Because most of Trend's bank loans and overdrafts are short-term falling due within one year, the gearing ratio (which includes only long-term debt) gives a misleading picture. We have, therefore, in this instance departed from the standard format used to describe the other buyouts in this book.
3. ROS and ROCE use the PBIT figure in the numerator.
* Accounts data for when Trend Control was a subsidiary of Holec are unavailable.

Source: Internal company information and Datastream.

Research and Development (see Table 5.2), plus all the associated costs of establishing themselves in a market dominated by corporate giants, the new strategy meant that Trend Control would need more cash if the business was to grow to a size commensurate with the same market share in the much larger market. (The management felt that if they lost market share, they would be in danger of being squeezed out through lack of a sufficiently visible market presence.) If they were going to compete successfully in the larger market, there was also the problem of external legitimacy. Often, Trend Control was not put on tender lists or lost tenders when competing for contracts against the corporate giants. Management felt that this was not because it wasn't the right product or the right price but because of the company's size.

Buyers said: 'Shall we give the contract to Trend, what are their current assets? £200 000: NO'! This problem increased as contracts moved out of the £20 000 to £50 000 range into contracts well in excess of £1 million.

In this environment, being part of a large group is a prerequisite to survival. We had the product, the contracts and the staff, but we needed the financial reserves. In fact, the need was less for the reserves themselves, than for what they symbolised: credibility.

It was not so much that we needed the money, it was that we needed the badge. So when anyone asked, 'what is the financial situation at Trend' we could just say that our parent company is worth £100 million and made a £20 million profit last year, and there is no problem at all.

The twin necessities of extra finance and external credibility led the team to consider changing the financial and ownership structure of Trend Control as a means to facilitate the next stage in the company's development. SUMIT were also looking to realise their investment and take their capital gain. The following comment from the managing director of SUMIT explains their motivation for wanting to exit.

One of our prime concerns is to support management to achieve a realisation. We made a heavy commitment in management time and resource to Trend and would have backed it further. However, further funding to the tune of Trend's requirements to enable it to achieve its objectives alone in the market place would have required substantial equity funding. Because there was a relatively large management team, though diminished by the departures of Messrs. Molony and Vickerstaff still retaining shareholdings, the management's equity position was not very large individually. . . . At that time, the UK equity market's interest in technology companies had waned on the back of a disappointing performance from America. Hence the rating that further venture capitalists would have required to come in to support development of Trend, at that time, in view of its financial performance would have meant substantial equity dilution for the management. We, therefore, recognised that the best opportunity for them to capitalise on their efforts and enable SUMIT to withdraw profitably was a third party sale.

The time was ripe for such consideration. Successful hi-tech companies have no shortage of suitors. By late 1986, Trend Control was relatively profitable, with 145 employees, exporting to the USA, Germany, Holland, Ireland, Denmark and Spain, and predicting growth of 45 per cent during 1987. Not surprisingly, the company was attracting a lot of attention from potential buyers. They had approaches from a dozen places and it seemed that every other week they were either receiving some discreet phone call or a letter from a merchant bank. For Casey, De'Ath and Rylatt, however, it had to be the right suitor. 'A number of major contractors tried to buy us, but we didn't want that because if you go in with major contractor A it makes it more difficult to sell our products to major contractor B. And none of the major contractors were major enough to guarantee, say, half the market. The same was true of large consortiums that were interested.'

Eventually, they were approached by MK Electric, 'the first company that came along that actually manufactured things and who we felt would actually know something about the engineering and technical context of our work'. MK Electric came up with a deal which was acceptable to the owner-managers and to SUMIT.

In November, 1986, MK Electric acquired 77.6 per cent of Trend for some £4.24 million. They paid £51.50 for the ordinary shares (and for the cumulative convertible preferred ordinary shares) which had been subscribed for £1 at the time of the buyout. They bought up SUMIT's shares completely: 'SUMIT were very pleased because they made a lot of money out of the deal, a very good return on their investment. They were prepared to come in and take a risk where it could have gone wrong. I think it turned out to be more of a risk than they expected – but then they made more money than they expected.'

MK Electric also bought half of Casey, De'Ath and Rylatt's holding and all of Molony's and Prestwich's holding. Casey and De'Ath each received £445 000, Rylatt received £228 000 and Molony and Prestwich each received £435 000. The other half of Casey, De'Ath and Rylatt's shares would be required over a four-year period beginning in June 1989 – an arrangement intended to lock-in and motivate in much the same way as the original buyout deal. As De'Ath put it, 'on the mercenary side we still have half our hand left'.

6 The March Concrete Story

1 INTRODUCTION

In early 1983, the concrete pipe manufacturing company, Cawoods Concrete Products Ltd, was being threatened with closure. Its parent company, Cawoods Holdings, had just merged with Redland and there was a conflict of interest with a Redland subsidiary. The Cawoods subsidiary had been put up for sale but there were no takers – the company was only just moving back into the black after a number of poor years.

On 11 July 1983, Tom Moore, the general manager who had been brought in by Cawoods to turn their subsidiary around or close it down, successfully concluded a management buyout. He and four of his managers, Messrs Daisley, Doyle, Paxton and Wilson, took a 32 per cent stake in the new company. They had had to raise £100 000 to fund the purchase of the assets of the company and a further £200 000 for long-term finance and working capital.

To strengthen their hand with the financial institutions backing the deal (ICFC and Lloyds Bank), Tom Moore had called in local MP, Clement Freud. Sixty jobs in Freud's constituency were being threatened by the closure. Freud had sufficient faith in the company that he was prepared to invest some £9000 of his own money and take a 13 per cent stake in the buyout. The new company was christened March Concrete Ltd, after the town in Cambridgeshire where it was located. There was much relief that the company, the fourth largest employer in March, had been saved.

For the first couple of years, the management buyout prospered as the new owners revitalised production, finance and sales. The culture of despondency and oppression which had characterised the company prior to the buyout was transformed as March Concrete was given a new lease of life by its owner-manager. The immediate outcome, improved profitability in 1984 and 1985, seemed to augur well for the renewal of a company long neglected and starved of funds by its corporate overlords. Three years out from the buyout, disaster struck. Technical difficulties and a market slump in the demand for March's core products severely dented profitability. Because of high gearing and a high proportion of short-term to long-term debt, a cash flow crisis ensued.

In 1987, the buyout team was forced to take the only action that would safeguard their original equity investment: the sale of the company's assets and land to a major rival, Amey Roadstone. Nevertheless, the buyout was not a total failure. Management, workforce and outside shareholders all benefitted – and the March plant, though under new ownership, had become more profitable, and produced better quality pipes, than for many years.

The story of March Concrete underlines the fact that irrespective of positive improvements in culture and structure, a management buyout is no guarantee of economic success.

2 BACKGROUND

In the 1960s, March Concrete had many product lines, ranging from fencing panels to concrete blocks. The core product was porous concrete pipes. The construction boom created a great deal of work – some 800 tons of product would be sent out on a good day (compared with barely half that amount on the busiest day in 1984.)

Decline

By the mid-1970s the market began to tail off, with the increasing use of other materials, notably plastic, as substitutes for concrete building products. Companies faced reduced margins with too many pipe manufacturers chasing too few contracts. As market conditions deteriorated, March became loss-making, just obtaining enough orders to survive. They responded by cutting the number of product lines but the unattractive nature of the heavy physical work involved in producing certain products pushed wage costs up. At the same time, March lost competitiveness as more and more of its products became obsolete. Modernisation was a vital, but very costly process. Citing the lacklustre performance, the parent company was unwilling to sanction the significant new investment needed by March to regain its former position in the market place. The company was caught in a 'Catch 22' situation. Without the investment, March could not succeed but new investment was not allowed because the company was doing badly.

March had little option but to cut back and specialise in its most profitable products. As new designs came in, or subsidies on certain products (e.g. concrete drainage) were withdrawn, March gradually streamlined its operations.

By the end of the 1970s, March manufactured only three lines: pipes, concrete blocks and paving slabs – with pipe sales comprising nearly 90 per cent of the company's much reduced total output. Even so, its product range included over 150 types of pipe of different size and strength – the most popular being porous concrete pipes for drainage, flexible-jointed pipes and Ogee-jointed pipes. It had also developed, in conjunction with a Belgian producer, a steel-fibre strengthened pipe, called Dramix. Over 80 per cent of the company's pipes were used in local authority projects, purchased mainly by the large building contractors – Fairclough, McAlpine, Wimpey, Laing, Bovis, etc. The remainder were sold to builders and for land drainage on farms.

Turnaround

In late 1979, Cawoods, the parent company, appointed Tom Moore as general manager of the March Concrete operations. Moore had previously closed down two other Cawoods' factories, at Greenwich and Belvedere, that had fallen foul of the excess capacity in the concrete industry. His brief with March was 'to either make it go, or to shut it down within two years'.

On arrival, Moore was surprised to discover how far March had deteriorated. Morale was low, a stark division existing between management and workers. Plant was antiquated: there had been very little investment in the development of either the basic products or of manufacturing processes. Apart from the occasional minor refinement, neither product nor process had changed in years.

Moore acted quickly to remedy this situation. He organised a stock auction and disposed of 5000 tons of produce. The six-lorry 'transport fleet' was sold – saving £25 000 p.a. More importantly, overmanning was tackled. Despite the fall in turnover, the workforce had not been significantly reduced from the levels of the 1960s heyday. Moore reduced the workforce from 90 to 35, and management from 24 to 17. These redundancies included the two company salesmen who were superfluous in a business based on 'contacts' rather than 'door-knocking'. (The concrete piping business is characterised by personal contact, sales take place through sealed tenders, generated through friendly contacts with buyers.)

Improving the climate

In contrast to the previous managing director who had been a
financial controller, Moore became involved in the works and technical aspects of operations. A strong believer in the value of good
relationships, he broke down the existing worker/manager hierarchy
and created an environment in which 'everybody mucks in'. He was a
good motivater and fought to save the company. Company morale
improved rapidly as both workers and management sensed the
commitment to March Concrete.

Moore's aim was to produce a better product, more efficiently.
There was a great deal of 'dumping' (selling at a loss) in the volume
segment of the market. Order values varied significantly but often ran
to well over £100 000 and involved 3000 tons for large motorway
projects. Moore made the firm more cost-conscious, and set the limits
beyond which they would not go in tendering for contracts. Each
contract was evaluated separately, taking into account location,
contractor, length of contract, competition, and so on. The manufacturing process, in particular, was subjected to close scrutiny. On the
selling side there was a rigorous attempt to obtain the highest possible
price for every contract. The firm also became far more customer
responsive, making sure that they saw the right people at the right
time (essential in the contracting business).

By late 1980, March had become financially viable although the
future remained uncertain. It was earning sufficient profits to prevent
closure, yet not enough to persuade the parent to commit investment
funds. Nor was it doing well enough to attract a buyer, despite almost
constant rumours of impending takeover, notably by Amey Roadstone, the Consolidated Goldfields subsidiary.

3   THE BUYOUT

The deadweight hand

The relationship between March and Cawoods, the parent company,
was reported to be beset with difficulties throughout the period.
These problems arose partly from poor corporate fit but mainly, in
the opinion of the March management, from the personalities of the
people involved.

Cawoods had always been run by its founder, Arthur Holmes, in a
fairly centralised manner, with clear-cut hierarchical divisions and

specific managerial roles. When Binks took over from Holmes, he further centralised decision-making within Cawoods. Though Moore was responsible for the day-to-day running of the March site, his decisions – be they giving a pay rise to a secretary, buying a new typewriter or hiring an office cleaner – had to be approved by the managing director, who was based at the group headquarters in Harrogate. This hierarchic and geographic distance generated mis-perceptions and frustration.

Coordinated decision-making remained particularly difficult in two key areas: investment and stock control. Between 1979 and 1983 there was virtually no new investment in March. According to senior March management, the Cawoods head office was distant from developments in the industry and appeared to have little idea of what actually took place day to day at the March site. Communications were lengthy and drawn out. When plans were submitted, debated and some investments approved – the decision was perceived to be 'too little and too late'.

The March management were also unable to do more than temper slightly, the effects of what they considered to be an overly aggre-gated regime of stock control.

HQ would point out that there was sufficient stock for three months' orders.' They would forbid further production unless it was for specific orders for which no stock was available. Such an approach is totally unsuited to the concrete piping industry. Each individual job requires different classes of pipe according to depth and specific requirements for pressure, etc. It takes some 28 days to manufacture and set a pipe – and there is a limit to the number of sizes of pipe that can be produced at any one time – so the building up of stocks is essential. Also contractors do most of their business between April and October, and it is therefore essential to produce in the winter for these months. Our current stock control policy means that many customers, with their specific and immediate requirements, take their business elsewhere. Central management feels we are bad salesmen to be unable to persuade customers to wait four weeks for their orders to be produced.

March's problems were further complicated when in late 1982, Cawoods merged with Redland (effectively an amicable takeover by Redland). Redland had previously closed down several of its concrete pipe-making operations, including those in Catterick, Wimborne and Poole, and sold the remainder to Amey Roadstone. As part of this deal, the latter had received assurances that Redland would not go back into concrete pipe manufacture. By acquiring March, Redland appeared to have contravened this agreement. They could resolve this situation by selling or closing the March pipe-works.

Motivation for the buyout

Moore wanted neither to close March down, nor have it taken over by another company. He also felt that the promise of a job elsewhere in the company (made before he joined March) was now in doubt. In his own words, he 'was up the creek without a paddle'. At this point he began to consider an MBO. He approached David Willetts, a chartered accountant whose father was chief engineer at March, and Clement Freud, the local MP. Moore asked a friend at head office to sound out whether a buyout would be favourably received. At first, the response was non-committal but on raising the possibility a second time, he was given the go ahead.

Moore also approached his colleagues at March to see if they wanted to join in the buyout. All those approached felt that despite the economic recession, the company had a future. Leo Doyle, sales manager, saw little risk in a buyout – even in an industry with substantial excess capacity. 'Somebody has to go to the wall. There are five companies, and it isn't going to be us.' Works manager John Daisley (who only stayed with the company in 1979 because he thought that closure was imminent, and wanted the redundancy pay) disagreed, considering the buyout a gamble – but a gamble worth taking. 'I could't possibly have gone out and started up a company with the amount of money I had, and with the potential returns that we have here.' He knew he had to be part of the team. 'I would hate to be working as hard as everyone else, but with them getting more than me.'

The entire March management were prepared to demonstrate their confidence in the company by putting up their own money. Even the office and administrative manager, Jill Winterton reported she would have put money in had she been given the opportunity.

The final buyout team consisted of: Moore, Doyle, Daisley, Wilson (company secretary) and Paxton (technical manager) for the company, plus Clement Freud, David Willetts, and three others brought in by Willetts.

Negotiating the deal

At first, the team could raise little interest from financial institutions because of the small size of the deal. Nevertheless Willetts and Moore persevered. Willetts analysed the company, and calculated that despite a turnover of £2 million, the business was only worth £100 000 – the price an outsider would be prepared to pay. In addition, another £100 000 in medium- and long-term finance would be needed for running the business. When the negotiations began with Cawoods, the buyout team immediately encountered resistance from Head Office management. Eventually the latter suggested a deal whereby the team would pay the value of the net assets. Willetts takes up the story:

> I said, give me three weeks and we will see at which price we can finance this deal. I told X it was worth £100 000 and he nearly choked. At this point, I went off to Pegasus and they also came up with the figure £100 000. I went straight to David Lyons, managing director at Redland.
>
> Having shaken hands with Lyons, I set off to try and raise working capital from Lloyds Bank and equity capital from ICFC (later 3i). Moore then came down to prepare a business plan with a beautiful set of financial projections. We came away with the ICFC money.

Moore later emphasised that one major benefit of ICFC involvement in the financing was that 'its name on the share register gave us respectability'.

The difficult process of 'translating the agreement into the details of the contract' then began. Clement Freud played an important part: 'Without him we could not have got the deal through.'

Another key factor, according to Willetts, was the possibility of the management team calling the deal off. 'I don't believe you can have a successful management buyout without a potential management walkout.' The buyout was finally completed on 11 July 1983.

Given Freud's Liberal Party commitment to employee share ownership, it is interesting that March did not use this type of participation – 'Freud raised the idea, but did not push it.' Moore had 'no philosophical objection' and indicated that the company operated a bonus scheme. However, 'when we looked into the principle of employee share ownership we could not see how we could make it work in this

Table 6.1 The financial structure of the March Concrete buyout

1. *Share capital*	*Authorised*	*Issued*	*Ownership/subscriber*
a) Ordinary shares £1		£21 000	Subscribed at £1 each by the buyout team in December 1983
b) Cumulative convertible participating preferred ordinary shares shares £1		£44 000	Subscribed at £1 in December 1983 by team and by ICFC
Total share capital		£65 000	
2. *Loan capital*		£40 000	Investors in Industry
		£26 270	Finance Leasing Agreements
Total loan capital		£66 270	
Overdraft (at 31 May 1984)		£57 096	Lloyds Bank
Total funding		£188 366	

Source: Company information.

instance'. In particular, employees were thought to prefer rewards related to personal rather than collective performance.

4   POST-BUYOUT

Autonomy

The buyout freed up the March management to take many decisions which they had previously been prevented from taking. No one measure was particularly significant but together the changes were perceived to create more effective management practice and a greater sense of responsibility for the fate of the company. Having the freedom to implement change also encouraged the team to search out areas for improvement.

For example, they were able to buy cement at a better rate than previously. Whereas cement used to be provided under a longstanding agreement between Cawoods head office and the Hall group, after the buyout March were able to search for the cheapest supplier.

Another crucial area was debtors. Previously, customers would order special items, and often more than was actually needed. They would then cancel which would result in substantial losses for March. Subsequently, the company required orders to be paid for in advance, and cancellations virtually disappeared.

Investment decisions were taken with more speed, issues that had taken 18 months to resolve were completed in a matter of days. This required streamlined accounting systems and much less, but more pertinent, information. Instead of the complex, six-monthly statement, a new monthly financial statement was produced alongside the monthly trading account: 'The high speed of decision making meant that finance data had to be at the board's fingertips' (Alan Wilson).

The company moved into merchanting – arranging packages for sizes of pipes that they did not manufacture. Doyle explained this development:

> Previously we were reluctant to become involved with other companies – but contractors prefer to invoice through one company. The advantage to us is that we increase our own turnover and we get a commission on all we sell. You can get a better bargain between companies than between a manufacturer and a contractor.

Not all the changes were in pursuit of efficiency. For instance, cars used by the directors and sales force were upgraded to a standard more in keeping with their positions. This had long been a sore point with Cawoods.

A changed culture

Morale improved markedly in line with the greater freedom afforded by the separation from Cawoods. Jill Winterton described a marked improvement in the atmosphere at March:

> Things are much better now – people are much happier and get on with each other better. There is more of a family feeling now, different from being part of a large group. Old privileges have been taken away. Managers don't seem to have the pressures and worries that they had before. If they have problems, they can talk

about them together. In the past the HQ did not understand us or
view the building products division sympathetically.

For the management, the key to greater happiness was the greater
involvement. Doyle and Moore – the only two representatives of the
management to sit on the board – went out into the field operations
much more than the senior management did before. They found time
to pay the odd visit, for example, to the contractors' site to talk to the
drainage engineer, the man on the ground, because 'he is the chap
who will pick up the pieces when things go wrong'.

Wilson had a similar view. 'Now I attend board meetings and help
to make decisions, whereas before I didn't do any more work than
that of an accountant. My wife says I am happier, and I enjoy
coming to work now, whereas it was all aggravation before.'

The improvement in morale was not restricted to management.
Daisley observed that:

'the workmen are much happier working in the buyout environment
than when they were part of a big company. The immediate threat
of closure has been removed, there is closer contact with the
people actually responsible for running and controlling the site –
rather than with "puppets that are controlled from afar", and
finally, they know that if we are profitable, they will be rewarded.
Even the Union was enthusiastic about the buyout – everybody's
seniority was carried through with no loss of rights.

An indication of this improved morale was afforded by the
wholehearted participation of the workforce in the concrete canoe
races at Thorpe Park in June 1984. Moore was able to write in the
1984 Annual Report that the enthusiasm of the workforce at this
event was so noticeable 'that it was the subject of comment by many
of the customers who joined us there'.

Performance

In the two years following the buyout operating profits increased
crom £135 000 in 1984 to £160 000 in 1985. The improvement was
almost entirely the result of increased margins. The manufacturing
process had become more efficient, whilst prices had gradually been
pushed up. Turnover had remained fairly constant in a largely stable
market. Some limited financial performance data is shown in Table 6.2.

Table 6.2   March Concrete's financial performance after the buyout

| | Year Ending 31 May | | |
	1983	1984	1985
Turnover (£000s)	1700	1848	1820
PBIT (£000s)	80	136	160
Net Assets (£m)	na	179	431
ROS (%)	na	7	9
ROCE (%)	na	76	37
Gearing	na	24	119

Note:
1. Gearing calculated as loans/debt falling due after more than one year divided by net assets.

Source: Annual Reports and Textline for the 1983 figures.

By early 1985, the company looked to the future with confidence. March planned to diversify into new products and to acquire companies with closely related products. There was, however, a more pressing need: to invest in new technology.

New investment

At the time of the buyout, March was dependent upon 'ancient machinery', which, they recognised, would need to be replaced in the longer term: In the Annual Review to May 1981, Moore stated:

> When we negotiated the 'management buyout' in 1983/84 it was well known that some of the machinery had passed its peak performance which inhibited marketing of products to water authorities and the foul sewerage market – a significant disadvantage given the traditional cyclical and fluctuating demands in the road and agricultural markets.
> During 1984/85 we made an in-depth study of pipe machinery in the USA and continental Europe – there are no UK manufacturers of pipe machinery – to ascertain the optimum plant and equipment for our future needs.

For some time government departments (water authorities, local government), whose purchases comprised 80 per cent of the concrete piping market, had been demanding pipes that, in addition to meeting the British Standard, carried the BSA 'kite mark' of quality. In 1985, what had been a gradual trend acquired new momentum, such that kite marks became a basic requirement. March found that there was no possibility of their existing 'big pipe' machine producing to the kite mark standard.

In February 1985 March took the plunge and invested in a new German machine, costing £0.75 million. Once up and running, the new technology would give March a distinct competitive advantage in terms of the quality of its pipes. The machine was planned to be installed and working by August of that year. There would be no margin for error. The investment was to be financed through debt and interest payments were to begin in June. Cash flows generated by production from the new machine would be needed to service the debt. Financing the investment had caused March's gearing to rise considerably, even after a revaluation surplus of £155 000 was added to reserves.

Disaster strikes

In the event, due to technical difficulties, the machine did not finally come on stream until May/June 1986. Anticipating that the new machine would be in operation by August 1985, stocks of the moulds used in the old machines had been allowed to run down and were eventually exhausted. There was a period when neither new nor old machinery was in regular production which, according to Moore, 'cost us about six months business'. Facing increased liabilities whilst suffering reduced sales revenues led to a severe cash-flow problem.

To make matters worse, this setback coincided with a major downturn in the UK piping market in mid-1986. Industry-wide falling prices and margins meant that March were only just able to break even in 1986 and faced a considerable loss in 1987.

5 TAKEOVER

The deteriorating trading position caused March's financial backers to 'begin to get jumpy'. They required financial data with greater frequency ('when things were going well they weren't interested'), and it became clear to Moore that he must search for another company 'to go in with, or be taken over by'. 3i became involved in this search, whilst Geoff Thomas, a chartered accountant known to David

Willetts, was brought onto the board as finance director. His task was to find a suitable buyer or partner.

At times March's position appeared perilous, with closure a real possibility (an outcome that would obviously have lost the buyout team everything). Fortunately, Thomas skillfully negotiated a deal with Amey Roadstone (ARC), March's major competitor.

ARC bought March's assets and land for £2 million but did not want the company's name. March was thus able to continue as an independent trading company under Thomas, with Moore as consultant. The much-reduced company took responsibility for outstanding debtors and creditors, and for the management of the March retaining/acoustic wall system (which in September 1987 had a turnover of approximately £17 000 p.a.).

ARC retained March's entire production workforce, and also made some temporary posts permanent. The sales and accounts departments, however, were considered superfluous. ARC already had its own effective centralised accounts and sales facilities. These reductions were an obvious economy, restoring the plant to profitability (aided, no doubt, by the greater margins earned by ARC, a company now with ten pipeworks and over 40 per cent market share).

As a result of the deal, the original buyout team resigned, Geoff Thomas taking up an option to buy all shares in the company. Moore, Doyle, Daisley, Wilson and Paxton each received generous golden handshakes. There was no ill-feeling. Indeed, the outgoing directors considered this a more than satisfactory solution, 'without Geoff, we might have lost all we'd put in'.

With hindsight, Moore considered that the buyout was 'underfunded'

For the first two years everything looked rosy, but when the downturn came there was no insulation. If we hadn't invested in the new machine, however, we would have gradually gone into decline and quietly faded away. If the new machine had been working on time, we might have weathered the initial storm, but it still would have been very hard going.

Despite the buyout not working out as originally hoped, Moore had no regrets. He felt that without the buyout, the pipeworks wouldn't have survived and that men who might not have worked again, continued in employment.

   The disappointment of seeing the buyout fail after all the high
hopes was made less bitter by the fact that the team all received
redundancy payments, and none of them lost any money. As for the
outside shareholders, they also got their money back, plus a small
profit.

7 The John Collier Story

1   INTRODUCTION

In September 1983, John Collier Menswear was bought out from its parent company, United Drapery Stores (which had itself been taken over two months previously by Hanson Trust), for £47.5 million. The purchasers were four of John Collier's senior management and a consortium of institutional investors. In competition with a bid from the Burton group, an arch rival in the menswear clothing market, the management succeeded in pulling off one of the largest buyouts to date.

However, the infant was not to reach maturity. In August 1985, following boardroom disputes over marketing strategy and with trading losses likely to exceed £5.7 million for the preceding fourteen months, the institutional investors withdrew their support from the management and forced a sale to Burton. Ironically, Burton had itself been the subject of an agreed takeover bid from UDS back in the late 1960s but the bid had been turned down by the Monopolies Commission on the grounds that the takeover would seriously impair competition.

Thus in the space of a little under two years, John Collier went from being a subsidiary to an independent company and back to a subsidiary, with four changes in ownership: UDS, Hanson Trust, the buyout and Burton. In the process, another chapter was closed on a saga that dates back to the 1930s and the rivalry between Montague Burton of Burton's, Moses Jacobsen of Jackson the Tailor, Samuel Lyons of Alexandre, and Henry Price of Fifty Shilling Tailors.

The story of John Collier prior to the buyout reveals a company captured by its history, organisation structure, leadership, management skills and culture; a company which failed to change its strategic direction and adjust its marketing strategy to changes in fashion. John Collier was unable to abandon fully its traditional tailoring image and move into the more lucrative leisure market. What changes were made were in defence of the overall concept of a tailored product rather than a shift to an alternative one.

John Collier's competitors suffered similar problems of adjustment but had greater pressure for change exerted upon them. Indeed a major selling point for the buyout was that it would release the company from the clutches of its parent. The management would then be able to change strategic direction and turn the company around. Yet after the buyout, John Collier was unable to escape the debilitating effects of its former servitude. A combination of cultural, political, managerial and financial factors conspired to thwart the buyout team's attempt to turn the business around within the limited time available.

The story of John Collier highlights many of the difficulties which buyouts may experience in implementing revenue enhancement strategies. The high gearing, the need to meet targets which have been set to please potential backers, and problems of tight (and divergent as between different stakeholders) time profiles, are perhaps more suited to cost reduction strategies. That John Collier failed may have more to do with its ownership and organisation structure than with the intrinsic merit of its chosen strategy.

2 PRE-BUYOUT

Ancestral beginnings

The story of John Collier dates back to the 1920s and a Leeds tailor called Henry Price. Price ran a small clothing business special-ising in men's outerwear. In a relatively short period of time, Price's Tailors became a leading local and national concern: their trading name of 'Fifty Shilling Tailors' is still remembered in Leeds today. The early history of the company is obscure, but in 1954 Price's were bought out by the United Drapery Stores group (UDS). The UDS chairman, Joseph Collier, lent his name to the product trade mark and his flowing script signature became the company logo.

UDS had bought Richard Shops, a chain of women's wear fashion shops some five years earlier. The acquisition of Price's Tailors was prompted by a desire to strengthen the group's position in clothing and to obtain a valuable retail property portfolio. The acquisition signalled the beginning of a period of considerable expansion and diversification by UDS of its retail clothing activities during the 1950s and early 1960s.

On acquiring Price's Tailors, UDS found that the company was short of top management. In the following year, it purchased another menswear clothing company, Alexandre, principally to acquire its top management, headed by Bernard Lyons. For the next twenty years it was the Lyons dynasty which was to rule UDS: Bernard Lyons who became Chairman of UDS in 1971, his brother Sir Jack Lyons, and his two sons Stuart and Robert Lyons.

UDS and menswear retailing

At the end of the 1960s, UDS was one of the largest retailing groups in the UK. It was also relatively successful with pre-tax profits of nearly £15 million, a return on capital employed above 16 per cent and a higher pre-tax profit to turnover ratio than Marks and Spencer. Its activities spanned a wide range of retailing activities and its strategy of acquiring freehold sites wherever possible in prime retailing sites had given it a valuable property portfolio. In fact, UDS (and likewise its competitors Burton and Hepworth) was viewed by many as a property company which happened to trade.

UDS was organised around five divisions: men's tailoring, women's wear, household supplies, department stores and duty-free trading. By 1968, the first of these, men's tailoring, accounted for about 35 per cent of group profits and just under 600 of the 1000 shops in the UDS group. The major part of this division's turnover was sold through the John Collier and Alexandre shops: John Collier, with 340 branches, being particularly strong at the lower end of the market, and Alexandre, with 130 branches focusing on the higher end. They both had their own factories, 13 in all employing 10000 people.

Following a change of managing director at the beginning of the 1970s a major rationalisation was instigated to get rid of excess capacity and rationalise production. This coincided with similar moves by the menswear division of the Burton group. The UDS rationalisation involved bringing together the John Collier and Alexandre factories under a single management. This allowed greater specialisation within factories and significant cost savings through cutbacks in duplicated areas such as buying, pattern selection, transport and administration. However, production and retailing were still geared overwhelmingly to tailored suits. This is not surprising, given that in 1971 the market for formal menswear was still growing and the UDS menswear division produced and sold 12 per cent of all men's suits sold in the UK. Of these, just under half were sold off-the-peg.

The tailoring culture

Any discussion of John Collier (or of any of the menswear specialist retailers who had their origins in bespoke tailoring) is illuminated by considering the symbolic importance of 'tailoring'. It was not by chance that the menswear division of UDS was incorporated as UDS Tailoring Ltd. Tailoring provided the conceptual underpinning for John Collier's trading strategy well into the 1970s, notwithstanding attempts to move out of manufacturing into casual wear.

Tailoring connotes made-to-measure and customised formal clothing. Although the customer is accorded individual attention, the culture of tailoring, as with most crafts, is production-oriented. It is the skill of the tailor which is paramount and manufacturing which has pride of place in the corporate culture. The following advertisement, taken from the script of a radio advertisement, reflects this culture.

> Hello there. This is Brian Mathews, it's Saturday night, the zippiest night of the week. It's the night when you can leave the worries of work far behind, go out on the town and live it up a little. It's for occasions like this when you want to look your very best that John Collier gives you the Saturday night suit. From the first skilful cut of the shears by a craftsman who took six years to learn how, to the last loving stitch, you get superb styling. John Collier Saturday night suit prices start at ten pounds nineteen and six. No other tailor in the country can match John Collier at prices like this.

John Collier's culture, honed in the 1950s when made-to-measure was at its peak, was built around the key symbol of made-to-measure suits. While this accorded well with the state of demand in the 1950s and 1960s, the Carnaby Street/Kings Road fashion revolution of the 1960s was to undermine this orientation. Moreover, improvements in manufacturing efficiency and the rise of import penetration were to lead to severe excess capacity and heavy manufacturing losses. The essential problems facing John Collier (and its major competitors) stemmed from being a retailer tied into manufacturing. In the following sections we explore how the changing patterns of demand led to significant changes in the specialist menswear market and how the John Collier management buyout was, in part, a belated attempt to adjust to changes which had their origins a decade or so earlier.

Decline

The 1970s inaugurated a period of fundamental structural change in the menswear market. The change was brought about through national, sociocultural and economic change, and increasing import penetration. At the beginning of the period, the menswear sector was one of the strongest in the clothing industry. Although the fast growth in made-to-measure formal clothes had begun to tail off in the latter half of the 1960s with a strong shift towards casual and ready-to-wear clothes, the *Yorkshire Post* (22 November 1973) felt able to proclaim that 'The multiple tailor is unique to Britain, so this could well be one field in which support for British Companies will be great when we enter the Common Market'. By the end of the period, the position had changed dramatically, as Table 7.1 shows.

Table 7.1 Value and volume of sales of men's and boys' suits in the UK and their import penetration

	By value		By volume			By value	
	All suits index	All suits import pen. (%)	All suits index	Made-to-measure suits index	All suits import pen. (%)	Outer-wear index @ 1980 prices	Outer-wear import pen. (%)
1974	48			300			
1975	57			275			
1976	88	26	128	183	34		
1977	96	31	122	150	36	77	26.2
1978	104	32	117	133	39	87	25.0
1979	110	39	117	125	47	101	26.2
1980	£139	41	4.6m	1.2m	52		
1981	92	48	93	83	63		
1982	87	51			66		
1983	99	49			64		

Source: Data from: Annual Abstract of Statistics, 1985, Mintel 1983, Department of Industry.

The market

There were three major changes during the late 1970s and early 1980s. First, there was a steady decline in the real sales value of mens' clothing sold by specialist menswear retailers. This coincided with a 30 per cent fall in the proportion of disposable income spent on men's clothes between 1976 and 1982. This decline compared with a modest increase in the (inflation-adjusted) sales of womenswear; growth in real expenditure on all items of clothing; and a growing proportion of all expenditure spent on clothing. The menswear market was generally regarded as a particularly unglamorous sector of the total clothing market.

Second, the market for made-to-measure suits collapsed and there was also a steep decline in men's formal outerwear. At the beginning of the 1970s, these garments formed the backbone of the menswear specialists' manufacturing and retailing operations. In just over six years the number of made-to-measure suits fell by two thirds from some 3.6 million in 1974 to 1.2 million in 1980. Sales of jackets fell by almost 90 per cent, while off-the-peg suits and woven trousers fell by a more modest 12 per cent.

Third, there was increasing import penetration, up to about 50 per cent of all mens' outerwear by the end of the period. Import penetration grew particularly strongly in the suit market. Although the absolute number of imported suits fell by a little under 30 per cent mens' outerwear between 1976 and 1982, this was much less than the decline in sales volumes experiences by UK manufacturers. Allied to the declining home demand, this increasing import penetration led to severe problems of overcapacity in UK menswear manufacturing.

The reasons for the changes in fashion are complex. Certainly, the post-1974 and 1979 increases in unemployment reduced the need, and the ability to pay, for men's clothes. This does not account, however, for the relatively greater decline in men's formal outerwear. The decline of the tailored suit in favour of casual wear traces back to the social revolution of the 1960s. This period saw the beginnings of a fundamental shift in attitudes as to what constituted acceptable social and work wear. Flower power and the emancipation of youth created a vast market for clothes symbolising youth's independence and their initiation into social groupings not based on kinship. The social importance for men of being 'formally well dressed' diminished through default, and consumption patterns shifted into those products which signified the new social order.

Although the multiple menswear specialists were aware of these trends they did not fully appreciate their depth or their significance. The people in charge of production, merchandising and sales were members of the 'old order'. Many of them could not imagine that clothes embodying values tracing back to Victorian times were fast becoming redundant. The new fashions were seen as a threat to established patterns of social interaction, and needed to be resisted rather than encouraged. A further constraint to change was that skills, techniques, and equipment suitable for bespoke tailoring did not easily lend themselves to the manufacture and retailing of ready-to-wear, fashionable clothes. Not surprisingly, as the decline in the importance of formal menswear gathered momentum, all the menswear specialist retailers suffered.

Their plight was worsened by the decision of Marks and Spencer (M&S) to introduce all-wool suits targeted at the executive middle classes. Owing to its buying power and economies of scope, M&S could offer product at very competitive prices. Ironically, John Collier had early on been approached to manufacture suits for M&S but had declined on the grounds that they did not want to supply a competitor. With hindsight, this was a key strategic mistake born of a failure to recognise changes in distribution channels and to perceive the distinctive competitive pressures operating at manufacturing and retailing levels.

Decline

John Collier suffered more than its competitors from these changes, although at first it managed to buck the trend. At its peak in 1973/4, the John Collier chain was making trading profits of £5.0 million derived from 13 factories, 500 shops and over 9000 employees. From that point on, there was a slow but remorseless downhill slide.

The changes in the menswear market outlined above led the menswear specialist retailers to chase dwindling sales through price reductions and product diversification into casual wear. Those retailers such as John Collier who had significant manufacturing capability were forced to rationalise production facilities. John Collier closed three factories in 1975 and 1976.

John Collier was not alone in its trouble. In fact, it was doing better than its major competitor Burton, the largest tailoring and menswear operation in Britain. In November 1976, the *Financial Times* reported that Burton was at the low point in a long decline. Burton's strategy of diversifying out of menswear had gone seriously wrong. Its attempts to make major changes in suit designs and patterns and move to casual wear in order to lift the group out of the volume, price-cutting suit market were unsuccessful. Burton lost market share to John Collier and their other major competitor, Hepworth.

In the latter half of the 1970s, all three companies followed similar approaches to manufacturing, radically pruning their production

Table 7.2 Comparison of John Collier, Hepworth, and Burton trading performance

	1976	1977	1978	1979	1980	1981	1982	1983	1984
Net margin on menswear operations on all sales (%)									
John Collier	5.2	2.9	1.4	3.1	2.3	(9.6)	(12.6)	(6.0)	(4.0)
Burton	1.8	(0.7)	7.8	13.0	16.0	14.7	14.8	17.2	
Hepworth	9.8	10.3	12.3	12.9	9.2	5.4	4.7	8.7	12.6
Turnover (excluding VAT) on menswear retailing (£m)									
John Collier	44.1	40.1	44.0	49.2	52.2	45.2	37.3	33.6	37.7
Burton	78.1	84.6	76.9	74.4	76.9	88.5	105.7	135.0	
Hepworth	28.6	34.5	42.6	51.3	61.9	75.7	83.4	98.6	108.3
Number of menswear stores									
John Collier	400	360	360	353	352	352			
Burton	537	452	349	347	348	249			
Hepworth	345	352	349	345	506	583			
Sales per store (£000)									
John Collier	110	111	122	140	148	128			
Burton	145	187	220	214	220	249			
Hepworth	83	98	122	149	122	130			

Notes:
1. Financial year for John Collier is to January, and with Burton and Hepworth to August.
2. Net margin defined as pre-tax trading profit divided by turnover exclusive of VAT.

Source: Annual Reports and the Centre for Business Research at the Manchester Business School: *UK Menswear Retailing*, October 1982.

operations to cut losses and sever the link between manufacture and retail. John Collier, however, failed to match its competitors in adjusting its trading formula to the structural changes in menswear retailing. Despite the introduction of a limited range of casual wear, John Collier was slow to modernise its stores, embrace casual, fashionable clothes, and tightly segment and merchandise its markets.

Although Burton and Hepworth hiccoughed their way into the 1980s as reorganisation and slimming-down manufacturing operations bit into profits, both benefited markedly from radical changes instigated by new leadership. Table 7.2 shows how John Collier slipped behind its competitors. Burton and Hepworth diversified away from men's clothes into the more resilient womenswear market and then applied the lessons they learned there to their menswear businesses. Operating in new markets undermined adherence to old beliefs about how best to merchandise and sell fashionable clothes.

The reasons for John Collier's failure to adapt are various, although retrospective accounts emphasize three factors: decline, but not fall, was anticipated; retailing was constrained by property and production strategies; and merchandising was not up to scratch because the buyers were locked into a subjective paradigm of what customers would buy.

According to Stuart Lyons, who was managing director of John Collier before leaving to become a UDS main board director in 1975, a strategic decision had been made by the main UDS board that menswear was not a good prospect for reinvestment. UDS were not prepared to match the resources that Burton had put into their networks in order to survive. They considered that, whereas Burton had to succeed in clothing or go under, UDS was a retailing conglomerate with a portfolio of businesses, and there were more attractive prospects for the limited investment funds at its disposal. After the event, the mistake was not to have divested John Collier:

It is a fair criticism of UDS that where John Collier was concerned, there was a strong belief by Bernard Lyons* that the existence of John Collier as a key part of UDS was given. Because of his own long involvement with the business which he had built up, it did not occur to him that one ought to consider closing it down or selling it. The intent in the 1970s was to get the business right without providing additional resources but making better use of the resources already in the business (Stuart Lyons, 1986). (*Bernard Lyons came to UDS when his company Alexandre was acquired by UDS in 1954. He was Chairman of UDS from 1971 to 1980 and his brother Sir Jack Lyons and his two sons, Stuart and Robert Lyons, were also on the Board.)

The decision to suborn John Collier's strategic needs to those of the group constrained marketing strategy in two ways. First, many of John Collier's shops had originally been bought in the days when 80 per cent of the business was in made-to-measure. Stocking or displaying a wide range of product was thus unnecessary and the shops were very small. Ideally, many of them should have been closed down. But because most were freehold and subject to Group property disposal policy they were stuck with them.

Second, the presence of excess capacity in the manufacturing facility forced the retailing end to source internally. High overheads and dwindling production had led to high unit costs, which placed the retail outlets at a severe pricing disadvantage. The failure to rationalise manufacturing was a result in part of practical difficulties (redundancy costs, supply bottlenecks and the need to negotiate with the unions) but mainly to errors of judgement. Bernard Lyons believed that the fall-off in demand for suits had already reached its nadir. In the 1977 accounts, published in June 1978, Bernard Lyons reported that:

> Men's suit production is now in balance with requirements, our programme of factory closures now having been completed. Meanwhile we have carried out a substantial programme of shop modernization and have introduced an extended merchandise range. With the replacement demand and the effects of our own reorganization coming through we now look with confidence to an upturn in profits from our menswear chains.

Admittedly, the UDS board's attentions were directed elsewhere at the time, owing to problems with other parts of its business which had gone wrong. Yet the extent of the decline in John Collier's core business, shown in Table 7.3, suggests that this is not sufficient explanation for the failure to recognise the downward trend.

Eventually, recognising that the halcyon days of the made-to-measure suit were over, the board sanctioned radical pruning of manufacturing capacity. In 1980, they announced that John Collier's Middlesbrough factory, the flagship in terms of manufacturing output though not modernity, was to be closed. This factory had a capacity of 10 000 two-piece equivalents per week (compared with a total production capacity of 26 500 units per week for all the 13 factories in

Table 7.3 John Collier's market share of made-to-measure suits

	1974	1975	1976	1977	1978	1979	1980	1981
UK sales of made-to-measure suits (m)	3.6	3.3	2.2	1.8	1.6	1.5	1.2	1.0
John Collier's market share (%)	15.4	14.2	13.6	14.3	13.3	11.3	11.6	9.4

Source: John Collier.

1972). In its last year, Middlesbrough was producing less than 5500 units per week. The closure of Middlesbrough left a single factory in Hartlepool and some minor manufacturing capacity at the Kirkstall Road complex in Leeds.

Third, merchandising continued to be a problem. The UDS board felt that the John Collier management was targeting the wrong market segment, buying the wrong merchandise, and not being sufficiently tough on cost control. John Collier's managing director was felt to have failed in building up the buying skills of the business. This was essential, given the changing role of the buyer within the trade.

Originally, a buyer in John Collier was responsible for selecting cloth patterns and having them made up in the company's factories. Later, the buying expertise spread to buying suits from other West Riding factories, but there was limited experience in overseas sourcing. Coupled to this was a tendency to buy staid clothes and then spend heavily on advertising and display, rather than buy the right product to be displayed. 'The key to performance, Burton style, was all about buying. Season after season the buying team would bring in new ranges, often bought in from the Far East, that they thought would be successful, and they weren't because they were too staid. They bought products that they wanted to wear, rather than products that the market wanted to wear' (Stuart Lyons, 1986). It is probable that if there had been faster and deeper rationalization of manufacturing capacity, there would have been much greater flexibility to source externally and much greater pressure to develop buying skills.

UDS eventually decided that John Collier needed a change in direction. They chose not to bring in a heavyweight retailing expert from outside (as had happened with Burton and Hepworth) but replaced John Collier's managing director with an internal candidate, David Hall. A new management team was created from within the company. Part of the reason, as already indicated, was that UDS did not want a radical redevelopment of the John Collier business; rather it wanted to return the company to profitability in a holding operation.

However, this message was either not communicated to or not received by the new team, who set about producing a corporate plan to revitalise trading prospects. The first part stressed the need to rationalise the retail end of the menswear business (by closing 25 per cent of the shops). The second adumbrated a new marketing strategy. UDS accepted the rationalisation because it released some £30–40 million assets to reduce the group's burgeoning overdraft. However, the plan to use £5 million of this money to implement a new marketing strategy was never realised.

There were four parts to the strategy: improve Collier's High Street image; put more value back into the product; develop contract tailoring to businesses; and seek out export opportunities. The first of these was seen as the most crucial. The company was still too dependent on suits; a uniform which was not applicable to Collier customers. Instead the company needed to enter the growth market of casual clothes, target a younger and more affluent sector of the market, and move away from the down-market image created through a continuous round of raising prices to improve margins, followed by special promotions, with unsaleable stock being put away to be dusted off when trading conditions improved.

These plans met stiff resistance from the UDS board. Bernard Lyons, in particular, felt that John Collier should sell more suits until the management proved that they could make profits through selling other sorts of clothes. He felt that the shops were not performing well because the merchandising and the shop presentations were wrong. He was also unwilling to sacrifice property priorities for retailing ones until the management showed that they could trade successfully.

While Lyons felt that the fault lay with the management team, the team felt that the fault lay with Lyons:

> Bernard Lyons did not want casual wear in the windows of his shops. So in order to show him the problems this was causing us, we took him to our Peterborough shop. This was situated in the old High Street which had been overtaken by the development of the new Queen's Mead shopping centre. We took him around this centre and showed him the new shop layout of one of our competitors, explaining that this was typical of the image that successful retailers were portraying. His response was – that is all very good but we don't want to sell that trash in our shops. If we wanted to do better then we needed to put more suits and models in the window. Although the trend is to more open, less cluttered windows, his view was that space doesn't sell clothes (David Hall, 1984).

There was a 'Catch 22' situation: until John Collier's management showed that they could trade successfully they could not change the fundamentals of the business; but they could not become successful unless they first made the changes. In the end the impasse was temporarily solved by a change of ownership. Following the retirement of Bernard Lyons at the age of 70, UDS was taken over by Hanson Trust in April 1983. In October 1983, David Hall and his team bought out John Collier from Hanson Trust and started to implement their chosen strategy.

3   DIVESTMENT AND BUYOUT

UDS

Since the early 1980s, UDS experienced trading problems across all its many retailing activities (see Table 7.4), although its clothing businesses were more seriously affected than other parts of the business. Bernard Lyons's long-established policy of diversification, with acquisitions in furs, leather garments, department stores, mail order, footwear, furniture retailing, television rental and duty-free retailing at Heathrow Airport, had done much for the group's asset base, but little or nothing for UDS trading activities. Management attention had been dissipated over a wide range of very different retailing businesses and away from the core business, and borrowings had shot up to finance the acquisitions at a time of rising interest rates and inflation.

In order to boost profitability, UDS began selling loss-making activities. One business disposed of was credit operations, sold to Citibank. The loss of control affected John Collier quite badly: 35 per

Table 7.4   UDS performance, 1978–82

	Year to 31 January				
	1978	*1979*	*1980*	*1981*	*1982*
Return on sales[1] (%)	7.4	8.5	8.8	6.0	5.2
ROCE[2] (%)	10.4	9.0	7.4	6.1	4.9

Notes:
1. PBIT/sales.
2. PBIT/net assets.

Source: Company accounts.

cent of their business was on credit and this slumped to 16 per cent –
losing them some £5 million in turnover in the process.

1981 was a particularly difficult year for UDS: a cash balance of over
£16 million at the start of the year was transformed into a £7.8 million
overdraft by the end of the year. Trading losses combined with heavy
costs of withdrawal from loss-making businesses (many of which had
only been recently acquired) put increasing pressure on the dividend,
which was already being financed by property sales rather than by
profitable trading. When it was announced that the dividend would be
cut for the year to January 1982, the City was horrified, and UDS shares,
which were already very low, lost one third of their value.

Increasing pressure began to bear on UDS from the financial
institutions. In May 1982, amidst remours of an imminent takeover
bid, it was announced that Sir Robert Clark, chief executive of Hill
Samuel, UDS's merchant bankers, was to become deputy chairman
immediately and would replace Bernard Lyons as chairman from the
beginning of January 1983. Stuart Lyons was to continue as chief
executive of UDS (and chairman of John Collier). The official reason
for bringing in Clark was that Bernard Lyons was approaching 70,
and the time was appropriate for him to retire. The real reason was
that the institutional investors in UDS, especially the Prudential, were
dissatisfied with the way things were going and felt that Clark,
already an executive director of UDS and a veteran of many takeover
battles, was an ideal person to have at the helm in a bid battle. The
Daily Mail (22 May 1982) quoted one big investor in UDS as saying:
'The management has lost its nerve. There have got to be major
changes at the top – or a bid. And let's hope it's a bid.'

The bid finally came on 4 January 1983, just two days after Sir
Robert Clark took over. It came from Bassishaw – a consortium of
businessmen, public sector pension funds and investment trusts,
headed by Gerald Ronson of Heron International and Cyril Spencer,
the recently deposed chief executive of Burton. It was followed by a
bid from Hanson Trust. As part of the defence tactics to make UDS
less attractive to a potential bidder, Clark 'started' serious negotiations with Burton group for the sale of 217 Richard Shops (the
women's wear multiple) and 242 John Collier outlets.

In February, it was announced that UDS had agreed in principle (but
subject to shareholder approval) to the sale to Burton of the John
Collier and Richard Shops chains for £78 million. The deal was strongly
opposed by both Bassishaw and Hanson. There followed a period of
complicated, behind the scenes manoeuvring, with bid and counter-bid.

In April, the retailing faction on the UDS board decided by a 6 to 2 majority to back Bassishaw. The majority, led by Stuart Lyons, felt that notwithstanding a higher bid from Hanson, the prospects for the UDS businesses to continue as a major British retailing concern were far better assured under Bassishaw than under Hanson. The fear was that Hanson would break UDS up and subject the group to substantial disposals and closures. The minority comprised Clark, and David Jessel of Eagle Star, who were more concerned with obtaining the best financial deal for shareholders.

In a letter and press conference to shareholders, the directors (with the exception of Clark and Jessel), recommended the Bassishaw offer. They stated that Bassishaw had pledged to retain and develop Richard Shops and John Collier, including the Hartlepool factory, and that the 'social elements' were uppermost in their minds. (Whatever the outcome, they all intended to resign once the takeover had been completed.) This affirmation of the social over the economic was final obeisance to the UDS founder culture. Culture is about (shared webs of) meaning and meanings do not so readily cluster around hard-nosed financial analysis and an extra 3.5p per share, as they do around history, vision and people. Sir Robert Clark, a newcomer and financier, and David Jessel, also a financier, could not be expected to adopt the thinking and emotional attachment of those who had spent much of their working lives in the business.

However, the institutional shareholders were not to be swayed by such considerations. At the end of April, Hanson emerged as victors with 62.3 per cent of UDS shares. On 26 May the proposal to sell Richards Shops and John Collier to Burton was rejected for the time being. On 1 June, Stuart and Robert Lyons resigned from the Board of UDS. On 1 July Bassishaw sold its minority stake to Hanson, thereby giving Hanson 98.2 per cent of UDS.

Negotiating the buyout

It was widely expected that following its successful acquisition of the UDS Group, Hanson would sell the John Collier and Richard Shops chains to Burton, though for substantially more than the agreed £78 million. However, while the takeover battle for UDS had raged, David Hall and the senior management of John Collier had been exploring the possibility of an MBO. Back in February, David Hall, David Simons and Ian Fletcher had been summoned to Marble Arch House – the UDS headquarters – to be told that John Collier

Menswear was due to be sold to Burton. They were told that if they fought it or tried to mount a MBO they would be in breach of contract and fired.

Once Hanson Trust were victorious, the team approached Sir James Hanson, to ask for permission to try for a buyout. Although the Burton bandwagon was still rolling, Sir James Hanson was broadly sympathetic, providing an acceptable deal could be put together. The team then met with Laurie Millbank, the stockbrokers, and asked them to act as intermediary with the financial institutions.

A set of accounts was drawn up for the five-month period ended 2 July 1983. These showed a continuing loss on flat sales, and for the first time blame was laid on existing policies rather than on external events. In order to gain institutional backing, the buyout team had to explain why the poor performance had not been their fault and what they intended to do about it. They blamed the UDS corporate management for forcing them to adopt an inappropriate strategy and outlined new proposals. Particular emphasis was placed on the lack of significant change in the company's image and the freeze on investment and development of the shops. The major finding of an in-depth market research assessment, clandestinely commissioned pre-buyout, was that a major barrier to the return to profitability was the High Street image of John Collier: the company was wrongly positioned in the retail clothing market, lacked a modern definitive image in both merchandise and premises, and was too concerned with price.

The team argued that the significant investment needed to change John Collier's image could be funded out of sale and leaseback of the freehold property portfolio. (Sale and leaseback would also be required to reduce the gearing if the deal went through.) The deal was to prove fairly complicated. Capital gains tax liability from the proposed property sales had to be minimised. Also, because of the way UDS had set up the asset structure of John Collier and Richard shops, Hanson Trust specified that the buyout of John Collier could only go ahead if it was linked to a similar deal for Richard Shops.

There were many times when the deal almost floundered, and things looked particularly grim when the management of Richard Shops failed to raise the finance for a buyout. Fortunately, the timely appearance of Sir Terence Conran as a bidder for Richard Shops, coupled with Hanson's forbearance, allowed the John Collier buyout to go through. On 7 October 1983, Collier Holdings Ltd acquired from Hanson Trust Plc for £47.5 million, the share capital of John Collier Menswear Ltd plus those premises not already owned by it.

Midland Bank provided the bridging finance pending the sale and leaseback of a significant number of the properties. Four directors of John Collier, David Hall (the MD), David Simons (finance), Ian Fletcher (merchandising) and Sidney Lipman (production) subscribed for 8.7 per cent of the shares of the purchasing company. Hall, Simons and Fletcher each had 300000 shares at 10.2p, while Lipman had 50000. The only director not to join the buyout was the sales and marketing director. A further 18.8 per cent of the shares was earmarked for sale at a later date to employees. A consortium of financial institutions subscribed for the remainder of the shares at the time of the buyout. Details are shown in Table 7.5.

4 POST-BUYOUT

There was widespread relief across the company that the buyout had been successful and that Burton had failed to acquire John Collier. It was generally felt that Burton would have made major surgery and that John Collier would not have retained its independent identity. Some measure of the enthusiasm that had been generated throughout the company was given by the success of a sale of shares to staff a few months after the buyout in April 1984. The offer was oversubscribed by 40 per cent with over 50 per cent of the full-time staff, ranging from machine operators in the Hartlepool factory through to newly-appointed senior management, taking a stake in the company. 'People had been badly served by UDS. Despite the enormous adversity there was a terrific commitment to win. The shop stewards of the various unions overrode the official union view and backed the buyout wholeheartedly' (David Hall).

As for the team who had masterminded the buyout, there was great exhilaration. It was not the money but rather the challenge which excited them. The following comment from David Simons sums up the general feeling:

To actually take a company getting on for a couple of thousand people, a £60 million company, to have a stake in that company and implement all the ideas that you have for running that company, is an opportunity of once in a lifetime and it only comes to a minute section of the population. There is a closer identity with the company. When you are part of a large conglomerate such as UDS or Hanson, how can you identify with someone who is down in London? The fact that you have had the dead hand

Table 7.5 The financial structure of the John Collier buyout

1. Share of capital	Authorised	Issued	
a) A Shares of 10p each	6 000 000	£950 200	subscribed at 10.2p each by the buyout team in September 1983
		£3 000 000	subscribed at 10.2p each by institutions in September 1983
		£2 049 800	subscribed at 10.2p each by employees in March 1984
b) B Shares of £1 each	5 785 000	£4 900 000	subscribed at 10.2p by Institutions in September 1983
Total share capital		£5 500 000	
2. Loan Capital		£43 800 000	Midland Bank
		£1 000 000	Hanson Trust
Total loan capital		£44 800 000	
Total funding		£50 300 000	

Notes:
1. The rights attached to the A and B shares are as follows:
   a) Dividends: The B shares have priority entitlement to the first £578 000 of dividend ever paid; thereafter the A shares will be entitled to the next £60 000 and thereafter both A and B shares will rank *pari passu* as if they were one class irrespective of nominal value.
   b) Capital: On a winding up B shares have a priority up to the nominal value of the shares.
   c) All shares carry identical voting rights.
2. Midland Bank has an option to purchase an additional 885 000 B shares at a price of 10.2p per share until October 1984.
3. Interest-free loans of up to £500 were available to employees to assist them in the purchase of shares.
4. The loan from Midland Bank is repayable out of the proceeds sale and lease-back of properties and attracts interest at 1.25 per cent above LIBOR.
5. The loan from Hanson Trust is interest free and only becomes repayable in so far as profits exceed those projected in the prospectus.
Source: Collier Holdings.

removed creates a greater enthusiasm, a greater excitement, a greater joy of actually doing the job. That in itself creates part of the sharper cutting edge at the top of the organisation, not just at the board level, although that is paramount, but also amongst the senior executives as well.... Our major priority is making a success of the company and turning it round. Why do you climb mountains if not for the joy of actually doing it? Getting hold of a large company and making it successful, hopefully, is the turn on. The second turn on is achieving that and watching our 10p shares grow in value.

The new strategy

The team were convinced that getting the front-end of the business right, rather than further tightening the screw on operations, was the key to a quantum leap in profits.

The consensus was that because of continuing decline in the market for made-to-measure suits, the current range of casual wear did not present a sufficiently distinctive image. The buyout team set itself a number of immediate trading objectives. These were stated in its corporate plan as follows:

to retain its established strengths whilst improving its market position using co-ordinated separates with a common colour palette as the key merchandise line;

to re-target Collier shops at the 25 to 44 year age group which is less vulnerable to unemployment and spends more on menswear; and

to market this proposition under the 'Collier' name which will benefit from the recognised relationship which John Collier has with value as the 'Window to Watch' whilst creating a sufficiently dramatic change to the shopping environment to persuade customers to recognise that 'John Collier' has changed.

A number of other priorities were also established including the revamping of the customer credit arrangements. Changing the image was, however, the central plank of the new marketing strategy. It assumed quasi religious proportions, encapsulating the team's faith in itself and becoming the major symbol for signifying the rebirth of the company. The key operational requirements for re-creating the Collier image were restyling the shops, site-refurbishment and re-location. Some £7.2 million had been earmarked for this in the buyout package.

Two shops were quickly modernised and more than doubled their weekly turnover overnight, confirmation enough for the new strategy. The plan was to refurbish the majority of the 241 shops in the portfolio within a two-year period. Collier needed new outlets in areas where it was not currently represented and a number of outlets needed resiting. Property management, therefore, needed to be brought more into line with the requirements of the retail chain. Here the buyout conferred distinct advantages. David Simons, who was in charge of the property sale and leaseback, described these as follows:

Decisions are much easier and we can move that much more quickly. Within about a month of the buyout we found 30 per cent of the locations where we wanted alternative sites. We thought that judging by the experience of all the problems we had been told about by the UDS property company, it would take us two years. We have been able to do all sorts of things with our property sites; UDS would have hummed and haahed and said it is all very difficult.

In terms of short term funding, cash generation, initial profit and the better use of our property portfolio, the buyout is a key factor. We have just managed to sell and leaseback for £15 million what was valued at £12.5 million at the time of the deal. Previously we had no involvement whatsoever in control of property assets and even if it had been done, the money would have gone into the central kitty.

The team aimed to give the shops a new look 'to get some drama into the window' and give a distinctive look from Burton. Don Watts and Associates, who had been responsible for the two pilot shops, handled the restyling. They gave the shops a red and black fascia, with coordinated colour schemes inside. The idea was to create a shop environment that was distinctive, attractive and friendly, with plenty of light and space. Conventional store layout – all the suits in one area, the trousers in another, etc – was abandoned in favour of having the clothes arranged by colour: for example, all the blues together. The hope was that this would 'persuade people who came to buy a pair of trousers to buy matching shirts and even a whole wardrobe'.

The modernised shops were called simply 'Collier' and aimed at family men between the ages of 25 and 44. With the concentration on fashion and boutique shops for teenagers, this market was felt to have been neglected in the past.

As part of the market research we did once we were unshackled from Bernard Lyons, we found that the Collier name was affectionately regarded by most of our older customers, although generally regarded as a bit passé. We decided to go for the 25/44 segment so as not to lose our old customers and to aim for the C1 and C2 socioeconomic groupings which constitute the largest sector of the market. The basic perception of that market is that it is the family man who wants stylish clothes without being high fashion, so it is not a high risk area. At the same time, this enables us to use our tailoring expertise because we have found that we can easily transfer this skill to trousers. So we have not gone overboard into jeans. When people want to smarten up they invariably change from jeans to trousers. Because the sales of trousers are expanding rapidly, we have taken them as a central theme for coordinating matching casual and sports jackets and knitwear. The clothes are reasonably priced formal and casual wear, with an emphasis on colour coordinated ranges. We are also emphasising colour coordination in the presentation of our shops, windows and layouts (David Hall, 16 December 1983).

Changing the strategy

A few months into the buyout, the marketing strategy was modified. The colour-coordinated shop designs were abandoned because 'It was a nightmare to operate and impractical for customers as when they did not want a colour-coordinated outfit, they had to walk over to another part of the store to get the clothes they wanted' (David Hall, 1985). The sales staff had constantly to make sure that not only were there enough of each garment but there were enough of the right colour. The need to change the stock around periodically to give the semblance of high stock turnover further complicated the problem.

The second modification concerned the age profile. While the age range of 25–45-year-olds was still considered correct in terms of the ultimate target customer, it was too broad for merchandising the product. The buyers had interpreted the spectrum on the basis of a life style of someone aged about 40, which was no good for attracting people at the lower end of the age range. It was decided to aim for the 30-year-old: 'We had shifted over to casual wear, but we were too old: we had anoraks but they needed bells and whistles and lots of zips.'

The third modification was the extension of a discount chain with a separate trading philosophy to that of the Collier chain. Instead of selling clothes on the basis of image, sites in secondary areas with spartan fixtures and low overheads were set up as clothing supermarkets.

Although there was some disagreement among the executive directors as to the merit of these changes, the board felt that things were going more or less according to plan. Also the sale and leaseback programme was progressing well, and prices realised were substantially greater than the valuations made at the time of the buyout. In February 1984, in the run up to the sale of Collier shares to the staff of the company, a pretax loss of £2.13 million was forecast for the year to June 1984 (which was in line with estimates produced at the time of the buyout). For the subsequent two years, profits of £1.15 million and £3.75 million respectively were mooted as relatively conservative estimates of future performance.

However, the next few months were to cast doubt on these estimates. Around the middle of the year, at the time when the budgets for the June 1984/5 period were being drawn up, it became apparent that the expansion of sales in line with expectations, had been achieved only through lowering margins and the company was facing significant trading losses in the following year. Some voiced doubt about the feasibility of a dramatic recovery along the lines of the Burton or Hepworth turnarounds. It was also suggested that the original proposals had been overly optimistic in gauging the time that it would take to turn the business around: 'it had taken many years for the company's fortunes to dwindle, and a miracle could not be expected overnight.'

A major reason behind the delayed recovery was difficulty in finding the right merchandise to put in the shops. A number of factors contributed to this. First, because of a ban on buying new merchandise during the pre-buyout period (it was not known who would win control of Collier), Ian Fletcher and his buyers had in the latter part of 1983 to buy for three seasons at very short notice and with undue haste. Casual wear for the new shops was sourced out of the Far East. Much of the Far East capacity is arranged in August/September for delivery in late December/January. But the Collier buyers were having to buy in late Autumn for almost immediate delivery. There had been no trouble in buying clothes for the two pilot shops opened very quickly after the buyout, but the buyers came up against capacity constraints when they tried to do this on a much larger scale. The problem was exacerbated because Collier wanted to specify its own styling requirements and cloth so as to enhance its distinctive image.

Second, because of the undue haste and the difficulties in buying the desired merchandise, the buyers were put under a lot of pressure and had insufficient time to consider what was selling in the shops. As a result the management was not sufficiently attuned to the merchandise and did not take sufficient account of the change in shop profile – hence the need already mentioned to target merchandising at 30-year-olds. Delayed monitoring of sales against forecast did not help in alerting the management to what was going on in the shops, and stocks rose partly also due to a tight spring season which hit all menswear retailers.

Although sales in the shops that had been modernised achieved their targets, this was only achieved by lower margins than originally envisaged. In order to get rid of stocks, margins had been cut. Moreover, concession sales contributing a lower margin were ahead of budget but own-buy were considerably below (there being evidence to suggest that this reflected the respective quality of the merchandise). Concessions had been granted in many of the shops to manufacturers who provided their own staff, fittings and product. The concessions were in areas of higher-risk clothing and were intended to give broader depth to the range of Collier goods. This would utilise space not otherwise used and shift the risks of holding high-cost stocks onto those granted concessions. (This is why concessions pay a lower margin.) As for sales in the unmodernised shops, these were badly hit by tight trading conditions and by the increasing disadvantage conferred by the shops' unmodernised appearance.

Given the shortfall in sales and profit margins, costs had to be cut. Various options were considered, including moving the headquarters in Leeds to a less expensive site, closing small and unprofitable shops, and reducing and rationalising production capacity in Hartlepool. (At the time of the buyout, keeping Hartlepool, the last of the manufacturing operations, was a symbolic imperative after all the rationalisations of the late 1970s. The team had thought that an increase in export and contract business added to Collier's own requirements would be sufficient to keep the factory fully employed.)

The drawback to rationalisation is that it would have involved heavy reorganising costs financed through further property sales. This would have reduced the asset backing for the company's borrowings. History seemed to be repeating itself. Although the modernisation programme was yielding results, this was not sufficient

Table 7.6 John Collier's trading performance, 1973–84

	Year to January						Year to June		
	1973	*1975*	*1977*	*1979*	*1981*	*1982*	*1983*	*1984*	*1984*
Return on Sales[1] (%)	17.5	8.1	2.8	3.1	(9.6)	(12.7)	(7.2)	(12.3)	(4.3)
ROCE[2] (%)	25.0	18.3	5.3	8.5	(48)	(108)	(145)	(205)	(107)

Notes:
1. Trading profit before tax and extraordinary items/sales.
2. Trading profit before tax and extraordinary items/net assets.
Source: Company accounts.

to avoid the never ending process of rationalisation and closures
financed by property sales which had characterised the latter days of
the UDS reign. Table 7.6 shows how John Collier's trading performance continued its downward path after the buyout.

5 SELL OUT

The results of the buyout's first nine month's trading to 30 June 1984
were published in December 1984. Reading between the lines, there
were some mixed messages which did not augur well for future
prospects. On the positive side, it was announced that during this
period, some 70 shops were converted to the new Collier livery, with
sales up by nearly 40 per cent on a comparative basis. Also, trading
losses had been reduced to £579 806, which was in line with the loss
forecast at the time of the buyout and reaffirmed in February. This
was a marked improvement to the three-month period immediately
prior to the buyout, during which the trading loss was in excess of £1
million.

   On the negative side, it was admitted that the performance of the
old John Collier shops had been disappointing and so the pace of
modernisation was to be accelerated with a further 56 branches
refitted by November 1984 in time for the peak Christmas trading
period. (Fortunately for the team, prices realised for properties sold
were significantly greater than had been expected, so the extra money
could be used for this.) Second, trading prospects for the coming year
were not mentioned in the report although in a separate comment,
John Thomson, Collier's non-executive chairman, said that the
overall return to a trading profit might take longer than originally
forecast. Third, more attention was to be given to developing the

discount chain. Fourth, a review of retailing activities had identified the need to close a number of small and loss-making branches, the rationalisation to be completed early in 1985.

Finally, the report contained one highly significant bit of information. David Simons, the finance director, and one of the founding members of the buyout, had resigned on 4 October 1984. He had been paid £46 500 in settlement of all outstanding contractual claims against the company. Although not stated, the reasons for the resignation were a clash of personalities, disagreement over personal domains of influence, and disagreement over market strategy and prospects for the business.

Simons wanted to follow the original proposals put forward at the time of the buyout. He thought that more radical action was needed at the retail end to bring the company back into profitability within a very short period:

Although we still retained Don Watts as a consultant we had effectively moved away from his designs. What happens is you water down the ideas of the designer until eventually it doesn't reflect his design at all. I was strongly opposed to dropping the coordinated colour palette. I was also unhappy about focusing on the 25- to 30-year-old.

I argued that we were not developing our original strategy but, at the behest of somebody who had come from Burton after the buyout, we were ending up with a Burton look-alike. Because I wasn't the person at the sharp end, the only way I could argue it was by saying two things. First, it is a major change from what we have sold our buyout on, and that needs to be a conscious decision rather than a creeping one. The second thing is that the results aren't coming through. However, it was me on one side and the rest of the board led by the sales director on the other (David Simons 1985).

Simons felt that a more aggressive marketing strategy was needed in the modernised shops with more price discounting and hard selling of credit business. He also argued that concession trading should be closely examined because not only were margins low, but concessions needed storage immediately adjacent to the selling space, and that better use needed to be made of prime high street space. He had become increasingly gloomy about the prospects for the business and felt the current course of action was unacceptable and that major changes had to be made so that retail division could be operating at break even within a few months. The other members of the team were unhappy at having their retailing skills challenged by someone whose expertise lay in finance and felt that it was unrealistic to expect that trading could be transformed overnight. They recognised that they had been overly optimistic at the time of the buyout and should have planned on a three-year rather than two-year cycle for turning around the company. It was pointed out that the turnaround of Richard Shops under Sir Terence Conran, which had been in a similar position to that of Collier, was also taking longer than planned.

The clash between Simons and other members of the team eventually led to Simons being forced to resign. This did nothing to bolster institutional confidence in the team's ability to turn the business around. Indeed, some of the backers saw the departure as crucial, for 'investing in buyouts is all about backing people and backing a team'.

In March 1985, a report was issued to shareholders which showed that there had been some increase in turnover for the 30 weeks ended 26 January 1985 over the corresponding period the previous year, and that the pre-tax trading loss of £1.4 million was in line with expectations. Perhaps more significantly, the directors reported that they anticipated that the loss for the remainder of the trading period to the end of August 1984 would not exceed £1.4 million making a trading loss on ordinary activities for the 14 months to 31 August 1985, of some £2.6 million. This was more or less in line with budget.

However, by the second quarter 1985, it became apparent that trading was way off target, the trading loss for this period being more than double this amount. Since Simon's departure, the institutions had been looking warily at their investment. In contrast to Collier's mediocre performance, Burton's menswear division had increased its profits 49 per cent in the year ending August 1984. Ralph Halpern, chief executive of Burton, having been rebuffed twice in his attempt to incorporate John Collier within the expanding Burton empire, again appeared on the scene. Despite strenuous efforts on the part of the executive directors to retain their independence, the institutions agreed a bid with Burton over their heads and presented it to the board as a fait accompli. At the end of June 1985 it was announced that the boards of Burton and Collier had reached agreement for Burton to acquire the whole of the issued capital of Collier for around £16.5 million (at the then market price of 469p for Burton ordinary shares). The Burton offer had been accepted by institutions holding 54 per cent of Collier shares.

In the recommended offer document sent out to all the private investors and the remaining institutions, John Thomson stated that:

Your Board has considered carefully the approaches made by the Burton Group, one of the leading multiple retailers in the UK. Your Board believes that whilst Collier has good prospects as an independent Group, the resources and skills of the Burton Group would enable these to be realised at a much earlier date.

The bitter pill was perhaps sweetened by the fact that Burton was offering 98p for the Collier A shares for which the management and staff of Collier had paid 10.2 (Burton was offering 192p for the B shares held by the institutions). This represented a capital gain of some 864 per cent (and 89 per cent on the B shares) in a period in which the company had made significant trading losses. For those of the financial institutions, such as the Midland Bank, who had purchased many of the properties sold under the sale and leaseback scheme, there was an added bonus in that the covenants on properties would be much enhanced if occupied by Burton.

8 Ownership, Managerial Motivation and Cultural Change

1 INTRODUCTION

In Chapter 1, we discussed three factors – private ownership, the reconciliation of ownership and control, and capital structure – as being the key characteristics of MBOs likely to lead to changes in managerial motivation, corporate culture, and thence to strategy and performance after a buyout. A summary of the arguments made throughout Chapter 1 are represented in Figure 8.1 and Table 8.1 below. The fourteen propositions of Table 8.1 encapsulate most of the received wisdom on the subject. These have been drawn from empirical research; the higher journalism of such publications as *Business Week, Fortune*, the *Financial Times* and the *Wall Street Journal*; and the armchair speculation of other commentators, advisers and observers of the business scene.

In this and the final chapter, we abstract from the accounts presented in chapters 2 to 7 the shared understandings, perceptions and experiences of the owner-managers and their companies and compare them with the received wisdoms. In doing so we aim to shed light on the four central issues which MBOs raise, namely:

- Whether ownership is a more powerful ingredient for corporate renewal and regeneration than traditional incentives;
- Whether there are repeated and significant failings in the public corporate structures and practices from which MBOs emerge;
- The strategic and cultural effects of high leverage; and
- The long-term viability of MBOs as a stable organisational form.

First, we look at how owners and managers evaluate ownership as a force responsible for changing managerial motivation and the corporate cultures of the companies investigated. We show that it has been a consistently positive influence on them. In Chapter 9, we look at other consequences of the ownership change, in particular the effects of the capital structure on MBO business strategy and life cycle.

177

Figure 8.1 Phases in the MBO process

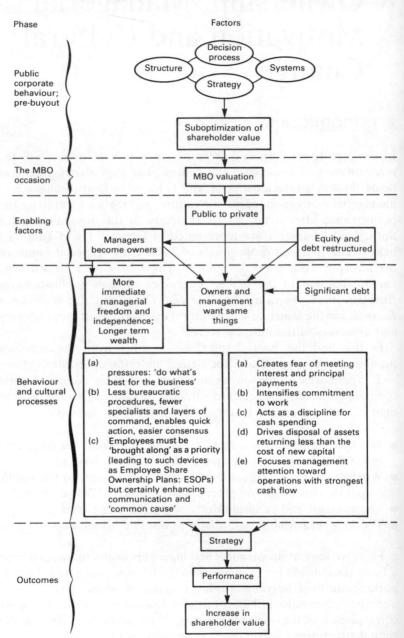

Table 8.1   Theoretical reflections on the MBO process

Phase	
I. Public corporate behaviour; pre-buyout	1. Managers can maximise personal status and political utilities more than shareholder value.
	2. Managers can be focused on misleading paper accounting goals; not shareholder wealth. Corporate compensation and evaluation systems can also reinforce this focus.
	3. Managers are risk-averse as to their corporate image and therefore tolerant of non-performance where change or correction contains risk to their status or image.
	4. Bureaucratic structure, procedures and attitudes extend and complicate decision processes, can debilitate managerial morale and dilute business focus.
	5. Overly fragmented organisational units and holding company structures prevent the capture of economic relatedness values between business units which together with, or exacerbated by, unintegrated acquisitions, can result in lowered shareholder value.
II. The MBO occasion	6. Public corporate management deficiencies create a substantial economic opportunity, understood (and therefore valued) differently by the managers involved as compared to their corporate directors.
III. Enabling factors	7. Owner-managers should be harder working, more committed, more focused on business opportunities and will relinquish personal perks.
	8. Private corporate form allows a more appropriate time frame for decision-taking
IV. Behaviour and cultural processes	9. Debt size focuses management attention on asset management of balance sheet and cash flows.
	10. Owner-managers should be more innovative and less risk-averse regarding business risks and opportunities.
	11. The firm's culture, strategy and management behaviour should be more appropriately geared to the needs of the business as opposed to quarterly earnings or other former corporate needs.
V. Outcomes	12. Decision-making should be faster, less bureaucratic and better aligned with shareholder interests.
	13. Shareholder value rises.
	14. New capital and ownership structure makes MBO an inherently unstable form.

2   OWNERSHIP

Classifying managerial perceptions

In searching for common patterns or themes across all the interviews, we find two separate principles underlying the way ownership affects owner-managers in MBOs. The first concerns the *type* of ownership effect. There are direct effects which derive from managers owning an equity slice of the business and indirect effects which derive from the organisational and financial implications of such ownership. The personal equity stake may be thought of as incentive effect and as a goal-sharing effect (it allies the objectives of owner-managers and investors toward increasing shareholder value). The indirect effects arise through ownership causing changes to the structure of the company in which the owner-managers now work: for example, from being a subsidiary to an independent company, a hive down in size, an increase in gearing.

The second principle concerns the primary *impact* of ownership. While recognising that the ultimate impact of ownership is always on the individual, we can distinguish between whether the primary impact of ownership is on the *individual* (e.g. working harder to increase profits in which one has a share) or on the individual as a member of a team (e.g. working harder because of social sanctions or a more supportive corporate culture.)

Combining these two principles gives rise to four complementary motivating factors. We have labelled them: Self-interest, Mutuality, Responsibility and Control.

Self-interest provides the rationale for referring to ownership as an incentive (in terms of agency theory; see Chapter 1). Ownership incentivises managers because personal remuneration is more closely tied to the creation of shareholder wealth. *Mutuality* operates through making people feel they are a part of a team and subjecting them to the social sanctions that group membership entails. *Control* operates (in the case of divested subsidiaries) through the buyout team members no longer being subject to parental control and collectively feeling more in charge of their destiny than previously. Finally, *Responsibility* operates through the enhanced personal visibility, responsibility and accountability which accompany the organisational structural changes in an MBO.

Mutuality, Responsibility and *Control* are essentially cultural processes which arise in a buyout as a result of the social and political

Figure 8.2 The social effect of ownership

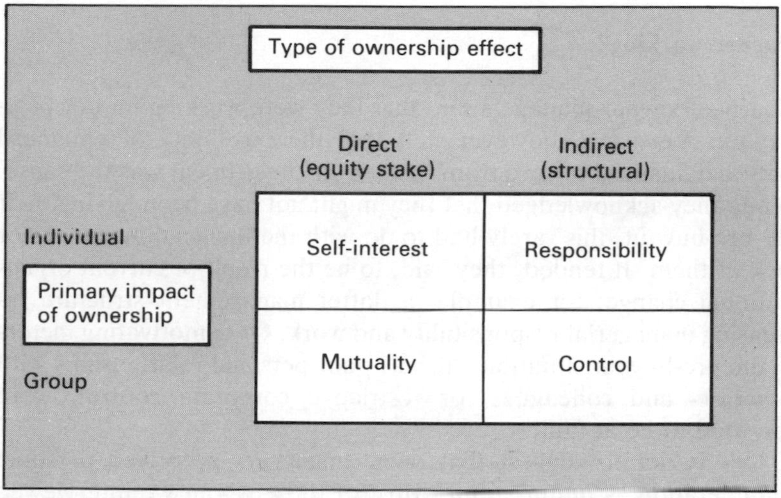

	Type of ownership effect	
	Direct (equity stake)	Indirect (structural)
Individual Primary impact of ownership **Group**	Self-interest Mutuality	Responsibility Control

changes enabled by ownership. Although their net effect may be to cause people to work harder in return for something (the esteem of others, group membership and acceptance, avoidance of social sanctions, status, personal fulfilment, etc.) they are not really incentives, although the word can be stretched to include them. The notion of incentive is best restricted to specific rewards, usually financial, which are designed to promote particular behaviours. (The psychological effectiveness of incentives is usually expressed as the size and utility of the reward times the probability of achieving it, (see Lawler, 1971).) The four resultant categories are shown in Figure 8.2.

We have resisted the temptation of presenting perceptions about these categories quantitatively in order to give a false semblance of objectivity. There is no good way of objectively measuring different views about complex, multidimensional issues or of measuring the strength of feeling which different people attach to their views.

We have also included material in this section from two other MBOs which were investigated (companies X and Y) and from people interviewed in parent companies and in financial institutions. Some of the owner-manager quotations have already been presented in the case histories. They are repeated below as illustrative of the shared experiences, views or beliefs that are more or less common to all the MBOs investigated. The only distinction here is that we place them in generic categories.

3 SELF-INTEREST

Harder working?

Nearly all owner-managers said that they were working harder post-buyout. Very few, however, felt that the possibility of enhanced personal financial reward from their equity investment was the cause. While they acknowledged that they might not have been 'giving their all' pre-buyout, this rarely had to do with the financial incentives or lack of them. It tended, they said, to be the result of current organisational change; for example, a flatter management structure increasing managerial responsibility and work. Or demotivating factors in the pre-buyout situation, such as poor personal relationships with superiors and colleagues, or restrictive corporate control, were reported to be at fault.

This is not to suggest that owner-managers perceived personal remuneration as unimportant. Most of those whom we interviewed were delighted at the prospect of making more money and highly motivated to do so.

> You can work for a company and earn high income but the only way of really achieving wealth is through capital accumulation, an equity share. When we went to Holec to start up Holec Energy UK [later Trend Control] we didn't manage to get an equity share out of the deal, although we tried; only a profit share. Had Holec stuck with us then so would we. Nevertheless the MBO gave us what we were really looking for, a share in the business (Trend Control executive).

> This [the MBO] gave me an opportunity to amass some disposable wealth rather than just have income. If I had gone to the States, I would probably have been better paid but I wouldn't have accumulated anything (Metsec executive).

The issue, however, is whether the prospect of enhanced material rewards gave people an incentive to work harder or more effectively. The shared perception was that the relation between material rewards and the work people were prepared to do was tenuous: 'Either you are committed to a business, or you are not, and having an ownership stake in it won't affect that. If you enjoy your job then you are going to give everything of yourself irrespective of whether your are working for yourself or for a corporation. Of course it is nice to see that we are better rewarded but I don't think that is a motivating factor' (Stone International executive).

In fact some people saw ownership as a negative incentive. Once they had become wealthy through the capital gains on their equity stakes, there was no reason to work quite so hard. 'The basic issue is that because we own a large chunk of the equity, we will earn a big reward in the end. In some ways that can be a demotivating factor because you start thinking, "do I need to work as hard as I do?" It does not stop you but as the day draws closer when you can see yourself cashing in, you start wondering whether it is time to take it easy and slow down' (Stone International executive).

In the case of Jacoa, a similar motivation followed a takeover bid. The potential for realising the capital gains from the equity stakes encouraged some of the owner-managers to give up their jobs, despite a lifetime's involvement in the business.

One way in which material reward did act as an incentive to work harder was through locking owner-managers into the company. This focused their effort on where they were rather than on employment opportunities elsewhere. A lock-in effect operated when the prospect of future capital gains in-house were more attractive than higher salaries elsewhere. This was equally important in companies such as Trend Control where much of the company's competitive advantage resided in the minds of a few key managers. These managers were a target for poaching by competitors. The buyout made moving to a competitor less attractive, even when stock options were offered.

Another factor, not so much encouraging owner-managers to work harder as allowing them to do so, was the attitudes of wives and other members of the family. Because of their ownership stake, wives were more tolerant towards their husbands working long hours and were more understanding of the pressures upon them. Whereas previously, devotion to corporate affairs had sometimes been viewed as misguided and interpreted as placing business life over family life, such objections were diluted by the prospect of ownership rewards.

Even so, it is worth pointing out that not all wives were so tolerant, fearful of failure or committed. At least three owner-managers were divorced within the first three years of a MBO and all cited the pressure of work as a significant contributory factor. But what is the cause and what the effect?

Vigilance?

There was generally an increase in vigilance (monitoring costs and market opportunities more closely) in all the MBOs. But this was not primarily or solely due to incentives. In the case of Jacoa and to a lesser extent March Concrete, it was the threat of collapse prior to the buyout which forced an onslaught on organisation slack. With Metsec, it was the survival of the company after the buyout, allied to the freedom to implement appropriate procedures which led to an attack on 'negligence and profusion' followed by a search for new market opportunities. With John Collier and Trend Control, a downturn after the buyout attracted external pressure and a reappraisal of opportunities for cutting costs. For Stone International, it was the individual impetus of the buyout, allied to structural changes, which fostered greater vigilance; although later events revealed that more needed doing. In addition, where leverage could not easily be reduced by asset sales, the capital structure contributed to the need to attack costs through cutting back wastage (rather than through technological change).

Nevertheless the incentive of personal ownership did exert an influence:

(Before the MBO) there was organisation slack, there was no motivation, it was really a company that had lost its way. Why didn't we implement many of the improvements before the buyout? Well, it comes back to the difference between being a manager in a company for someone else and managing it for yourself. I have asked myself long and hard the question and the fact is that it was somebody else's money. (Metsec executive).

I think the buyout has introduced a new element for us all who have money in it. Previously, I daresay that there were times when you sat back and said, well get on with it, because people seemed so involved. But when it's your own money it makes you take part. All right it's his responsibility but it's my money he's putting in and you have to be more attentive. (Trend Control executive).

There is more freedom now. When you have put money into a company, you are keener for it to do well than when you work for a large company (March Concrete executive).

Now people turn the lights off because they are paying for the electricity . . . it is the first time in any of our lives that we have had to put down our own money on a business decision. In the past, you played the game and often thought that as it wasn't one's own money, it didn't matter. But now, one is more careful. (company X executive)

We are a little less tolerant of non-performance. We have just fired two MDs who for three years had failed to meet their agreed targets. In the past, they might have been moved sideways. Now other senior executives come up and say, 'I see so and so hasn't performed well again.' (company Y executive).

In a number of MBOs, owner-managers were removed by colleagues. The latter frequently suggested that pre-buyout, they would probably have been more tolerant of incompetent colleagues. At one company, where the CEO was removed post-buyout, his colleagues stated that they would never have had the nerve to tell executives in the former parent company that the person running their (subsidiary) company should be replaced. Post-buyout, however, fear of loss led them to go to the outside equity investors to gain their approval for such a move.

Thus material reward, and *a fortiori* loss, did encourage owner-managers to greater vigilance. It was not, however, the sole factor, as we see below.

Perks?

According to the literature on the separation of ownership and control, salaried managers will be inclined to take perks as a way of supplementing their incomes in ways which are not apparent to shareholders. One would, therefore, expect owner-managers to take fewer perks after a buyout because they are robbing themselves rather than (or in addition to) the external owners. Given liquidity preference (and a tax neutral position as between income and perks), they should be unwilling according to motivational theory, to trade off income for perks.

Only one of the MBOs we studied, however, markedly cut the level of perks. Possibly the fact that the previous owner had been the government had encouraged excessive 'perking' pre-buyout.

If I go anywhere by train, I rarely bother now with a first-class ticket. If my company car is off the road, instead of hiring the largest car, I hire the smallest one I can get by on. After the buyout, we also hit one of the sacred cows of the organisation; company cars. Now personnel have to make a personal contribution to the cost of the cars. There was an enormous amount of hassle to get that through. There is a responsibility on me to set a good example to other members of the company (company X executive).

Apart from this, there was little change in the level of perks taken. What changes that there were, had little to do with 'rational calculations' of the trade-offs between perks and other forms of income. Perhaps the effects of joint ownership diluted the need for such calculation, although interviewees did not mention this. In one buyout, where the level of perks was increased, it was reported that this signified the liberated and enhanced status of the owner-managers.

Propensity to innovate or take risks

Views about the effects of the personal ownership stake on innovative behaviour/risk aversion were mixed. Many people felt that rather than ownership encouraging innovativeness, it was the other way round: mounting a buyout was highly entrepreneurial.

Is there a case that entrepreneurial managers will tend to move on to an ownership situation rather than stay in a professional management environment and that status-seeking managers will look for the security of the larger bureaucratic organisation where a significant employee shareholding would probably not be welcomed? (CEO Stone International).

When I took over the firm in 1977 it was worthless. The French shareholders wouldn't give the company a penny and the English shareholders wanted to get out. So I felt, along with the other executive board directors that because we had turned it around, we should own and control it (CEO Jacoa).

If this didn't work and the company actually failed and I found myself out of work tomorrow then I wouldn't be worried. I know that I am the kind of person who could go out and buy a ladder and clean windows (Metsec executive).

The buyout was a masterpiece for one man who was just not willing to take 'no' for an answer (company X executive).

Some people saw their collective decisions as more innovative but put this down to the removal of corporate control. Others saw their company as less innovative post-buyout but attributed this to the high gearing or the attitudes of outside investors. Also, the existence of outsider equity involvement meant that: 'This is not like owning 100 per cent of the business, you have to be careful because you are dealing with other people's money. I suppose my philosophy is that I take greater risks with my own money than I do with other people's (Stone International executive).

A few people said they were more cautious now that their own money was at stake. Such caution was not directed towards requiring a higher rate of return from capital projects but towards being more careful about assessing the quality of future cash flows from such projects. (This seems more of a vigilance and goal sharing effect than an innovative one.) No one mentioned the concentration in their risk as a factor leading them to 'Play it safe', be more risk-averse or raise their time preference of money. A possible reason why personal ownership was seen to have a marginal effect on innovative behaviour may be that any such effects were swamped, or diluted, by the need to reduce the high level of gearing. (See also the discussion below on capital structure.)

Institutional views on the self-interest effect

In contrast to the perceptions of owner-managers, many of the advisers and institutional backers to buyouts viewed the incentive of self-interest as the major factor explaining improvements in managerial performance post-buyout. The following views are fairly typical:

Conglomerates have the problem of motivating their senior management. The more it grows, the more share options in the quoted company become remote. Also they don't like giving away control so they are forced to give profit bonuses which don't lead to capital appreciation but lead to income tax (pension fund executive).

The main positive reason why performance improves is that a guy now has the opportunity of creating wealth on his own account. If he can see that, he is going to work very, very hard, often twice as hard as he worked before. In the majority of the buyouts we have done, this is certainly the case. It's the stick and the carrot. The carrot is the opportunity to make a lot of money, the stick is the personal guarantees, second mortgages and the worry that these may be called upon if the company doesn't succeed (merchant banker).

When I met X last week in London at 4 o'clock, I said 'I suppose you are staying the night.' He said 'No we don't do that anymore, it is our own money.' Expenses are not something which are tangible when you are part of a group (stockbroker).

One factor distorting outsider's perceptions is that owner-managers often feel obliged to convey a good impression to financial backers and shareholders. For example, we followed up the last comment with X. He said that the real reason he hadn't stayed the night was that he had to get back to his family in Leeds. The cost of a night in a hotel was immaterial but it didn't do any harm to show how conscientious and hard-working he was.

In talking to financiers we often detected an element of envy. A common complaint from financiers was that buyout teams wanted 'too much of the equity' (relative to what they were able or prepared to put up for it) and stood to make disproportionate capital gains for 'just doing their job properly'.

A salaried manager in a subsidiary doesn't do his job properly so the parent company decides to divest his subsidiary. Because of his position and perhaps privileged information, he can negotiate a good deal and end up with a hefty slice of equity for a minimal contribution. Then, with the incentive of profit to motivate him, he turns the company round and makes a killing. Why should he make more than a fund manager running a multi-million pound port-folio? (venture capitalist).

Some financial institutions backing buyouts felt that ownership should be spread down through a MBO so that all employees could be incentivised to work harder. They interpreted owner-managers' failure to do this as reflecting an overly proprietorial attitude and/or greed.

The evidence did not appear to bear this out. With the exception of one of our MBOs there was actually widespread support for spreading ownership down through the company. The problem was that legal and tax constraints often limited such action post-buyout. Those firms which had managed to find a way round these hurdles did extend ownership in recognition of the efforts of those who had contributed to the success of the buyout. It was not reported to have been done to encourage people to work harder. Many owner-managers felt that it was the financial institutions who were expropriating an excessive slice of the equity. The former pointed out that loans were well secured on the assets of the business, that it was the buyout team who really bore the risk if things went wrong, and finally that the success of the buyout depended on the team and the employees.

4 MUTUALITY

It was in terms of a common or shared interest deriving from joint ownership where some of the strongest positive motivational effects of ownership were reported. Joint ownership created a mutual dependency whereby individual owner-managers shared a common interest in working as a team and seeing the company made successful: 'The first and the prime interest is in making sure that Metsec is successful. Previously it was to make sure that the particular position one had responsibility for was being carried out successfully. This has led to less rivalry and a less political atmosphere at the top of the company. Before, in meetings, everyone used to point the finger, it was all political battles. Now we sink or swim together' (Metsec executive)

A 'better' culture?

If the sentiments expressed above were all that there is to mutuality, then it could be argued that mutuality is reducible to self-interest: it is in every one's self-interest to work together such that aggregate profits (or more correctly, shareholder wealth) are maximised. Whilst this is indeed true, the psychology of mutuality is more complex. Self-interest does not fully explain why people found working together and cooperating with each other so important post-buyout, unless one wishes to invoke de Rochefoucauld's maxim that 'toute vertue n'est qu'une vice deguisée'. Mutuality is based on reciprocity, a socioeconomic rather than economic principle. By strengthening social relationships within the team and by enveloping individual owner-managers within a web of reciprocal relations and obligations, mutuality transcends personal self interest.

In the case of MBOs, joint ownership seemed to encourage shared understandings about a whole range of organisational issues. A common theme raised by owner-managers was that they had to constitute a team. On occasion this was symbolically reinforced by the exclusion from the MBO of previous members, of the senior management team who, for reasons of personal enmity or 'not fitting in', were not invited to join the team attempting the buyout. Joint ownership affirmed team spirit and in some cases enhanced it.

Until the management buyout, I saw myself as heading up a team, but not being a team player. And I think that this is the biggest change in my thinking: I see myself much more as part of the team (Metsec executive).

The nice thing about the business is that it doesn't lead to conflict. There are differences of opinion about priorities and the like but there seems to be a tacit understanding that the reason we are arguing strongly is the same reason: the profitability and success of the company. We somehow feel we are talking in a common framework and we are not criticising someone but just discussing how the business can be better run. So far it has been a very constructive environment and a much nicer one (Stone International executive).

Everyone used to follow their own path and while we operated as a clique within the organisation, there was not the sense of shared purpose that now exists. We were members of a team but we weren't a team (company Y executive).

Before the buyout we weren't shareholders, but we thought and acted as though we were. It was just an oversight that we didn't have any shares. When the company was up for sale we felt that that undermined all the sacrifices we had made. It was not so much the monetary opportunity, it was the sense of identity that we had all developed with the company (CEO Jacoa).

Now I attend board meetings and participate in the decision-making process. My wife says I am happier and I enjoy coming to work whereas it was all aggravation before (March Concrete executive).

We are very much a team, leading a group of people. In all honesty, I would not like to pinpoint anything that we could not do before that we are now doing (company X executive).

Some of the above quotes indicate that joint ownership did not always create 'team spirit' (as writers Alchian and Demsetz 1972: 790, suggest) but was frequently an outcome of it. The team had already been formed some time prior to the buyout, often as a separate clique within the organisation. Joint ownership was a means of allowing the team to continue running the business. The sense of collective purpose tended to become even stronger after the buyout, (although factors apart from joint ownership contributed to that). One problem arising from this was maintaining continuity in the team when owner-managers retired or left. 'How can you introduce new people into a group which has developed as strongly as this?'

Not all aspects of joint ownership were seen as positive. The team spirit engendered by ownership was seen by one CEO (company Y) to compromise strong leadership: 'there is a danger of management by committee, of excessive consultation and discussion with colleagues'.

Another perceived drawback of ownership was that it was more difficult and potentially more dangerous (given concentration of ownership) to get rid of owner-managers who had been an integral part of the team taking the company into the buyout and beyond. This did not, however, stop the removal of owner-managers. In all but two of the MBOs, one or more owner-managers were removed by their colleagues within three years of the formation of the buyout. This emphasises the importance of creating a team approach to post-buyout management and clarity of accountability for each member of the team.

This team (group solidarity) aspect of joint ownership has by and large been ignored in the literature on MBOs. Yet the consistency and frequency of the comments of our MBO owner-managers indicate it is clearly a crucial part of the process whereby ownership affects managerial motivation and behaviour.

Outsiders' views

By and large, the advisers ignored the positive aspects of mutuality, and focused on the negative ones. Such factors as leadership by committee, 'my patch' problems and uncertainty over succession were mentioned but more as hypothetical problems than ones that had actually been encountered. To us this revealed much more about the motivational 'theories' of financial operators than about the actual motivation of those on whom they projected these theories. The factors that seemed important to the financiers were carrot and stick (largely financial) and they ignored what was not present in their own careers; teamwork, mutuality, ownership and the management of others. On the other hand, the focus on negative aspects is perhaps not surprising given that contact post-buyout tended to be minimal unless things were going wrong. In such circumstances, ownership tended to exacerbate tensions within the buyout team about which the outsider then became aware.

5 CONTROL

The buyout made us masters of our own destiny and that's what it is all about. That doesn't mean you become totally despotic and obsessed with control. We're a team and we are trying to develop other teams within the business (Metsec executive).

The ownership change in the MBOs out of divestment involves a series of structural (organisational and capital) changes. First, there is the separation out of the subsidiary from the group. Second, there is a reduction in the size of the bought-out company – the managers either can not afford or do not wish to take the full business they were managing through the buyout. Third, there is an increase in gearing. We have already considered some of the effects of these changes when assessing the impact of the self-interest effects of ownership. We, therefore, only mention here what has not yet been covered. And we defer discussion of the changes in capital structure until the next chapter.

More appropriate decision-making?

The overwhelming feeling among buyout teams was that they had been liberated from what they perceived as the 'deadweight hand of corporate control'. This took various forms: crucifying the subsidiary with excessive management charges and too much debt; being unwilling to write down overvalued assets and thereby allow a realistic appraisal of the business in question; starving the subsidiary of investment funds and other resources essential for strategic change; imposing a corporate culture and set of procedures which were inappropriate to the specific needs of the subsidiary; and stifling management with autocratic control.

Perhaps the most widespread complaint concerned the control of investment funds. Examples were numerous.

John Collier's management had long wanted to innovate in the area of shop design and the sorts of clothes sold in their shops. They reported feeling that they had been prevented from implementing such a strategy by the senior management in their parent company. As soon as the MBO was completed, they set about making these changes. 'To actually take a £60 million company and implement all the ideas that you have for running that company is an opportunity of once in a lifetime. The fact that you have had the dead hand removed, creates a greater enthusiasm, a greater joy of actually doing the job . . . that in itself creates part of the sharper cutting edge' (John Collier executive).

March Concrete had been controlled to the extent that the smallest expenditures had to go to head office for approval. Trend Control had been subjected to what were perceived to be totally inappropriate financial regimes.

> Holec just can't understand the business. They didn't understand that for a company like this, the trading losses over the first few years are actually development costs. It would have been OK if we were going to set up a factory to make motor cars. They would expect it to cost £50 million for plant, machinery and all the rest of it, and they would call that its capital and be quite happy with it. . . . There are not capital costs in our business because it is all software and services. Therefore, Holec assumed that we ought to make money on day one. They couldn't grasp the fact that trading losses due to development costs in actually writing the software, or costs experienced in getting further up the learning curve, or marketing costs of getting a higher market share and making it profitable, are all part of the start up costs and should be equated with capital costs (Trend Control executive).

Finally, Jacoa's parent company was more concerned about extracting the maximum dividend from the company than with developing the business over the long run.

Thus early on in most of the MBOs, one of the major benefits deriving from ownership was seen to be the freedom to approach external capital markets for funding rather than rely on the whims, portfolio trade-offs, current corporate strategy, or financial strength or weakness of the parent company.

A more appropriate culture?

A second aspect of the 'deadweight hand of corporate control' was the imposition of inappropriate procedures and culture. Instances of the former are too numerous to record here, as will be evident from even a cursory reading of the various case studies presented in this book. Suffice it to say that the most frequent complaints concerned inappropriate communications, management accounting and information systems. Witness, for example, the experience of Metsec with its monthly 65-page accounting information report, and its forced dependence (at an annual charge of roughly £100 000) on TI's central computer. TI's central software people were reported by Metsec managers to be too busy with more important work to develop software tailored to Metsec's specific needs. After the buyout, Metsec purchased a digital mini-computer for some £15 000 plus about £2000 for software. This provided the management with all the accounting information needed. Perhaps more importantly, it allowed them: 'To get real control into the situation, not just the paper control which appeared to be there in the TI days. That was a massive cost saving. Now the information that is churned out is relevant and accurate and we can make better decisions on this basis. Now we do not generate information unless we need it.'

Most owner-managers recognised that corporate HQs had to monitor subsidiaries, yet it was often *the way* in which control had been exercised and the unwieldy nature of corporate decision making which was frustrating to managers.

> There was a dramatic change of attitude after the buyout, not just by management but on the staff side as well. There is no question that people are more motivated now. Before it was management by imposition, now it is management by imposition after discussion. (CEO company Y).

> A MBO is an opportunity to think how a business is run. You get a much more appropriate form of control because very often the

controls in a large corporation are political controls, social controls. You don't tread on the MD's toes because he doesn't like such and such a thing (Jacoa non-executive director).

There used to be a very top heavy management structure such that it was almost impossible to reach decisions. The whole process was also fraught with politics. You had to go through umpteen administration levels and eventually you might be able to achieve a decision. But the length of time that it took was most debilitating whereas now we can decide things overnight and then act on it (Metsec executive).

What is the point of striving to find profitable opportunities when every time you put up a proposal, it is either ignored or turned down (March Concrete executive).

One of the things about a buyout is that it wipes the slate clean, you get rid of all your board and your advisers. One of the things about advisers is that sometimes they have been there for very many years and they are appointed by the parent company. After a buyout you choose your own advisers (merchant banker).

Perhaps one of the best expressions of the way in which corporate or group-wide procedures and culture may be inappropriate came from a senior manager in a parent company which had divested itself of a number of MBOs:

One of our less profitable branches was bought out by a divisional manager who had experience as a branch general manager. Ordinarily that would have been the last he would have seen of the branch except perhaps on a trouble-shooting assignment. Our career structure and status system prevented us from keeping him at the coalface even though he was the best person to run it. Although he wasn't very good as a divisional manager we couldn't then demote him back to the branch.

Our group personnel policy entailed high staff costs and prevented us from making employees redundant with a long service history. A LIFO approach to redundancy was reducing the quality and productivity of work staff. After the buyout they didn't have to worry about that. . . . Our reporting systems are inevitably more geared to head office needs than to the needs of individual branches and our trading formulae and corporate image do not allow the flexibility required for successful management in a highly competitive, fragmented business. Finally, we can't hope to generate the same commitment among our branch managers as you find in owner-managers.

6 RESPONSIBILITY

A corollary to the increased control by the MBO team was increased responsibility and a heightened sense of accountability for individual owner-managers. The hive down in assets and business frequently reduced the scope for specialisation and the need for hierarchy. Moreover, the change in the capital structure of the bought-out company prompted cost cutting and retrenchment strategies leading to the removal of one or more layers of managerial staff. The end result was that senior managers were brought nearer to operations and were held more accountable for their actions.

> Pre-buyout, the job was too divorced, the corporate structure with the divisions coming into head office made layers and layers of management barriers. You don't get close to operations that way.... It is no longer possible to pass the buck upstairs. We are no longer corporate executives striving for recognition and promotion. Our achievements and failures are self-evident. There can be no escape to other parts of the organisation if things go wrong (Stone International executive).

> Customers now feel that when the management take a decision, it is a personal commitment to the customer rather than just a corporate decision. They also know that the management will continue to be around at the end of the contract. In TI days this place was like a railway station waiting room, people in and people out, no continuity (Metsec executive).

> Many people in the organisation will have a wider responsibility because of the need to reduce overhead exposure and hence the degree of specialism that can be afforded.... The Board of Directors have also recognised the need for change and the requirement to climb down in the organisation will be given paramount importance (Metsec Buyout prospectus).

The enhanced responsibility and visibility were generally welcomed, being one of the major factors improving individual morale and enhancing job satisfaction. People were also more able to identify with the company now that it was hived off from a large Group.

> There is a closer identity with the company. When you are part of a large conglomerate such as UDS or Hanson, how can you identify with someone down in London? (John Collier executive).

> Things are much better now – people are much happier and get on with each other better. There is more of a family feeling now, different from being part of a large group. Old privileges have been taken away (March Concrete manager).

> X was traditionally a family company. When it was taken over by a public company, people became disillusioned by the remoteness of the parent company. They didn't like being part of a great big company, the new corporate culture just did not fit (company X executive).

7 CONCLUSION

Max Weber (1949) wrote that explanations of social phenomena have to be 'adequate on the level of meaning.' The meanings which managers attach to ownership appear to sit uneasily alongside armchair theorising about the impact of ownership on managerial motivation and action. Many managers, without prompting, contrasted their own perceptions about ownership with the 'commonly held' view that ownership causes managers to work harder through the prospects of increased material rewards. Many saw this as a slur to their professional status: they were professional managers first and owners second.

The incentive effects of ownership on managers are complex and not reducible to simple cause and effect statements about shirking, withholding commitment, taking perks, and encouraging innovation. Nevertheless, ownership was seen to exert strong positive influences on the firms. Some of these were: improved social relations among buyout team members; enhanced mutuality of interest among executives; the challenge of controlling a business unhampered by the culture or politics of a parent company; the freedom from autocratic policies geared to the whole rather than the specific needs of the subsidiary; the greatly increased visibility of managerial effort and skills; as well as increased vigilance and focus stimulated through self-interest and shared goals.

The incentive effects of ownership are, therefore, possibly less important than the control effects. By removing various corporate constraints, ownership *allows* managers to perform their tasks better. This is quite different to suggesting that ownership is as an incentive, a better carrot to dangle in front of managers, which induces them to become better managers. It is clear that a great deal of satisfaction was reported about the teamwork, shared responsibility and personal identification enjoyed after the buyout. Its lack in the prior situation seemed to introduce frustration in managers from which ownership and self-control provided a release.

Taking, then, the first two central issues concerning MBOs:

Is ownership an under-utilised ingredient for corporate renewal and regeneration?

Are there in our sample consistently similar and significant failings in the corporate structures from which MBOs emerge?

We can suggest a tentative yes to the ownership issue as far as motivation and culture are concerned. The line of cause and effect, however, is complex and not as simplistic as many financial investors and advisers seem to believe. Also, the alliance or goal-sharing effects of ownership appear to be powerful. First, owner-managers, through mutuality, comprise teams with the same shared values and goals. Second, owner-managers and outside investors share similar goals concerning shareholder value. The result in the firms studied seems to be a rather widespread congruence in the organisation about primary goals and a management focus on implementing them. The repetitive and consistent pattern of this effect attests to its power and its importance. (As we see in the final chapter, however, there are other aspects of ownership in MBOs which affect their potential as instruments for long term corporate growth.)

As to the second question, the frightening consistency in the failings of corporate management which led to the buyouts we examined is well evidenced in our case studies. The size of the economic prize left by this mismanagement seems hard to underplay. It allows for high debt service charges in the MBO company even after substantial reorganisation costs. The more pressing question may be whether the parent corporations we studied were too under-leveraged, particularly relative to the discipline and focus debt seems to create (see following chapter). There does seem to be, in corporate life, an unexamined, instinctive fear of debt that speaks to the dysfunctional gulf between financiers and business managers in the US and the UK.

Finally, on the basis of the evidence presented to us, it would seem reasonable to suggest that the scale of mis-management in the public corporations from which MBOs emerge not only helps to ensure buyout success, but also contributes to the sometimes extreme differences in valuation at the time of the MBO. The corporate management divesting the company is inherently (by the self-same character of the failings) unable to see beyond current asset values and historical trading prospects. In stark contrast operating management knows something of the likely scale of both the structural and business opportunities. What's more, they believe in their own ability, when unfettered by corporate overlords, to realise these opportunities. This seems to us a more likely explanation of an 'undervalued sale' than indignant accusations of 'cosy deals' or 'violations of fiduciary responsibility' or economists' explanation of 'asymmetric information'. As the English political bromide would have it: 'where you stand depends on where you sit.' Valuation differences are a result of managerial beliefs in what hopefully can be done, as compared to the default of corpocrats in creating shareholder value. The valuation spread appears to us as a systemic misperception of opportunity on the part of the large, public corporation – itself a prisoner of its 'trained incapacity' – not moral failure by operating management.

9 Structure, Strategy and the MBO Life Cycle

1 INTRODUCTION

The context of change

MBOs, through divestment, frequently attempt strategic and other business changes within the first few months of their existence. The need for a rapid turnaround; an increase in autonomy following the cut in the umbilical cord to an often ailing parent; the increase in gearing; the (hopefully) agreed preferences of institutional shareholders; the attitudes of employees, creditors and other stakeholders; the circumstances in which the buyout came into being; the hive down in assets or business taken through the buyout; and the motivating and incentive effects of personal ownership; all create a context for rationalisation (a change of degree), or a strategic redeployment of assets or redirection (a change of kind).

Disentangling cause and effect with respect to strategic choices and outcomes in these contexts is more than a little hazardous. Nevertheless, in the case of MBOs, *the process of change is indelibly marked by the ownership structure and the capital structure to which it gives rise.*

In the previous chapter we considered the extent to which the ownership stake enjoyed by owner-managers affected managerial motivation and social relations within the senior management team. We also considered how it encouraged vigilance and focus and improved processes of decision-making and the making of a new culture. All of these feed into the implementation decision-making process and colour implementation outcomes.

Having looked at the first two central propositions concerning MBOs (the corporate failings of the parent company structure, and the positive motivational aspects of ownership) it remains, therefore, for us to review the strategic limitations of high leverage and the long term viability of MBOs as a stable organisational form. We look at how capital structure, the pattern of external shareholder control (which is related to the capital structure), and external events shaped both intentions and outcomes in the MBOs investigated (see Figure 9.1 overleaf).

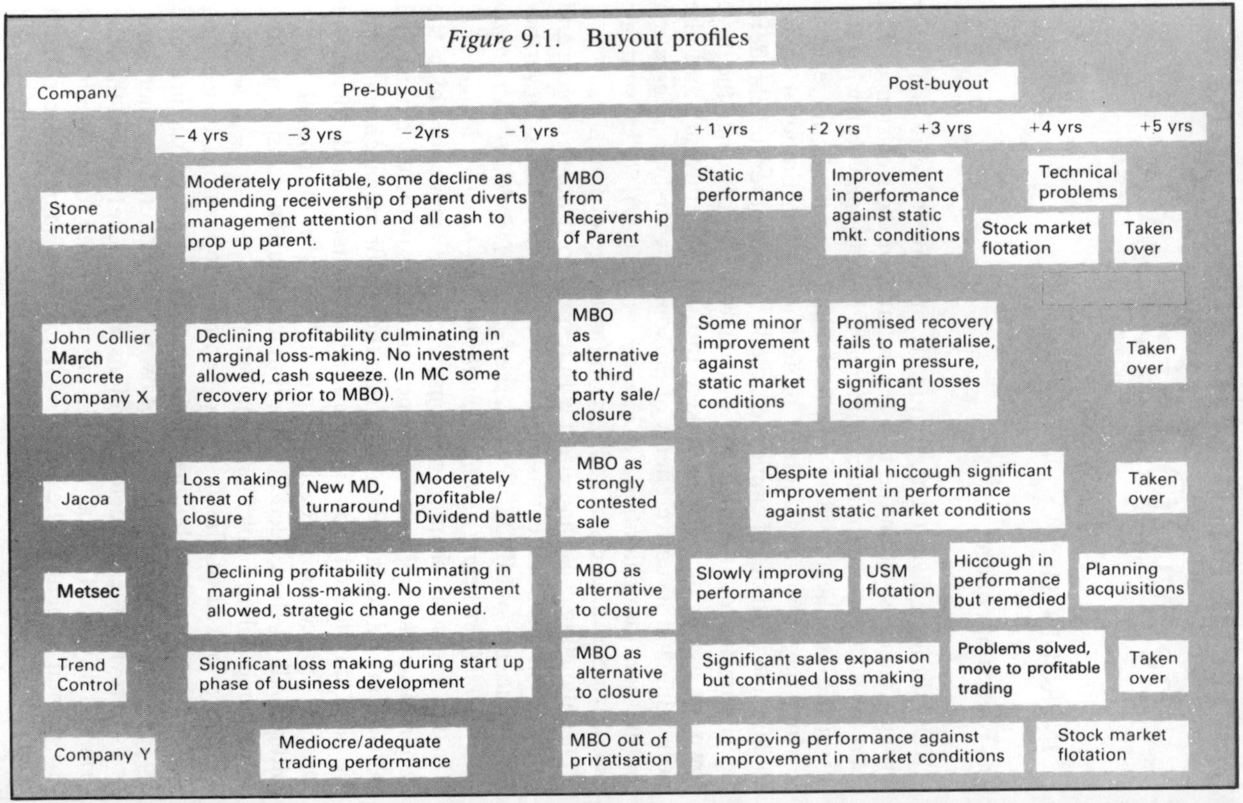

Figure 9.1. Buyout profiles

Company	Pre-buyout					Post-buyout				
	−4 yrs	−3 yrs	−2yrs	−1 yrs		+1 yrs	+2 yrs	+3 yrs	+4 yrs	+5 yrs
Stone International	Moderately profitable, some decline as impending receivership of parent diverts management attention and all cash to prop up parent.				MBO from Receivership of Parent	Static performance	Improvement in performance against static mkt. conditions		Technical problems / Stock market flotation	Taken over
John Collier March Concrete Company X	Declining profitability culminating in marginal loss-making. No investment allowed, cash squeeze. (In MC some recovery prior to MBO).				MBO as alternative to third party sale/ closure	Some minor improvement against static market conditions	Promised recovery fails to materialise, margin pressure, significant losses looming			Taken over
Jacoa	Loss making threat of closure	New MD, turnaround	Moderately profitable/ Dividend battle		MBO as strongly contested sale	Despite initial hiccough significant improvement in performance against static market conditions				Taken over
Metsec	Declining profitability culminating in marginal loss-making. No investment allowed, strategic change denied.				MBO as alternative to closure	Slowly improving performance	USM flotation	Hiccough in performance but remedied	Planning acquisitions	
Trend Control	Significant loss making during start up phase of business development				MBO as alternative to closure	Significant sales expansion but continued loss making		Problems solved, move to profitable trading	Taken over	
Company Y	Mediocre/adequate trading performance				MBO out of privatisation	Improving performance against improvement in market conditions			Stock market flotation	

We consider these issues in the context of the relevant propositions described in Figure 8.1. Following on from this we then construct a picture of the MBO life cycle which we observed. This incorporates the various changes, organisation processes and external events that underpin the life cycle.

2   CAPITAL STRUCTURE

MBOs are financed at the outset with high levels of debt to equity. In Chapter 1, we described the typical capital structure of MBOs and suggested why it might be important. As we show below, this is confirmed by the experience of our MBOs. Leverage has major implications for post-buyout strategy, in part because of the concentration of ownership among the institutional shareholders who subscribe *both* debt and equity to the financial package. For this reason, it makes little sense to consider capital structure separate from the attitudes of the institutional shareholders towards leverage. A highly-leveraged capital structure increases the riskiness of the firm's earnings stream and concentrates this risk on shareholders. Accordingly, the latter have to be compensated for this extra risk by a higher expected rate of return. One of the central issues for financiers in MBOs is to understand the business risks associated with the firm's business plans (i.e. those risks which are inherent in the business even if it used no debt) so that the proportions of debt and equity can be structured in such a way that the financial risk (the additional risk resulting from the use of debt) is not beyond the bounds of prudence. (For a detailed exposition of the impact of leverage on risk and shareholder values see Weston and Brigham 1987; and Rappaport, 1986).

Traditional views as to what constitutes prudence (in capital structure) are being shaken by the experience of LBOs. The evidence of the past fifteen years in the US, where LBOs are even more highly geared than in the UK, has been favourable with very few bankruptcies (Jensen, 1989). Although the high interest rates in 1990 and 'excessive' purchase prices have led to some well-publicised failures and re-financings, there have not – at least at the time of writing – been sufficient to justify the doom merchants' views of high leverage. There are a number of factors which help investigators manage the risks of high leverage in MBOs:

● Many buyouts protect themselves from sharp increases in interest rates by purchasing 'caps' that limit any increases or by using swaps that convert the floating-rate debt to fixed rates.

● Financiers typically like to keep business risk low so that even if the company gets into difficulty with debt payments, there is still enough residual value left in the company to encourage a financial reorganisation rather than bankruptcy.

● Investors use 'strip financing' (each party holds approximately equal proportions of all financial instruments used to fund the deal) and thereby reduce conflicts between different classes of claimants.

● Debt holders can be compensated for riskier propositions by a higher fixed rate of return.

● Investors can move swiftly to replace management or sell the company if the projections made at the time of the buy are not fulfilled.

These kinds of activity mark a change in the traditonal role of financial institutions. Normally they are advisory to principals, bearing only a risk for unsuccessfully striking a deal. The MBO makes investors principals.

This is more like the German system (under so-called 'universal banking', where banks can be both clearing and merchant, investor and adviser) and the old Japanese 'Zaibatsu' system (where major companies are, effectively, derivative from and frequently controlled by the major banks that were the original Zaibatsu houses).

The possibilities of genuine partnerships under these types of financial and business arrangements seem to us to:

1. enable a better balancing of financial and business risk: and
2. enable learning and understanding (and therefore identification) to occur between financiers and businessmen. In our language, mutualisation rather than just self-interest.

Let us now look at how our MBO companies did with their new financial partners.

Reducing debt

Four of our MBOs (Jacoa, Stone International, Metsec and company X) acknowledged that in the immediate post-buyout period, the need to reduce the debt to equity levels within as short a time frame as possible was *the* prime consideration. Other matters had to be put on the back-burner until this had been accomplished. The interest payment requirements, institutional insistence that leverage be reduced, and owner-managers' own preferences led these four companies to try to maximise cash flow to service and pay off debt. Cost savings through productivity increases, streamlined management levels, improved inventory and debtor control; extended credit facilities from suppliers; and asset sales and/or sale and leaseback, were the norm. In all these companies, leverage was reduced to acceptable levels within three years of the buyout.

Four companies, John Collier, March Concrete, company Y and Trend Control, did not slavishly follow the objective of reducing leverage. The first three of these came to a sticky end. In the cases of John Collier and company Y, the outside investors pulled the rug from under the incumbent management. A downturn in sales cast doubt on their ability to meet strategic objectives within the time period originally envisaged. In the case of March Concrete, the company invested in new technology which failed to come on stream as quickly as planned. In view of the high leverage and debt repayment schedule, it was only through being taken over by a third party that the company was saved from disaster. The exception was Trend Control. Trend was fortunate that its financial backers recognised the developmental nature of the business and were prepared to refinance the company once they had made sure that tighter management controls were installed. Despite trading successfully, however, and partly because of the need to avoid the restrictions imposed by its capital structure, Trend Control's management eventually decided to seek refuge under the umbrella of a large company.

Short-term horizons

In view of the high leverage, one might expect that management would seek to skimp on market development expenses, in particular marketing and advertising; on new capital investment; and even on capital maintenance and replacement. That way they would be able to squeeze every last pence out of operations to pay off debt; even if this meant sacrificing market share some years down the road. Like a farmer who doesn't fertilise his land but extracts maximum crops, such a strategy is all right for the short term but disastrous for the long term. That is why leverage has often been criticised – for encouraging disinvestment.

We found only limited evidence of such behaviour, (although leverage did discourage certain types of investment). On the contrary, our MBOs generally increased marketing expenses – in three cases quite significantly – post-buyout. Moreover, capital expenditure increased in all cases. Looking across all the companies, uprating manufacturing plant for those involved in manufacturing, and improving retail outlets for those involved in retailing, were favoured over other investment options. Projects were typically self-funding or financed out of asset sales. As one CEO put it: 'if you can't get money from anywhere else then you have to make it yourself'. Except in the cases of Jacoa and John Collier which we consider below, investment was directed at allowing management to do better what it was already doing. Cost reduction strategies aimed at squeezing out organisation slack, improving productivity and providing quick and sure returns were clearly preferred to *new* market development or diversification strategies with more uncertain payback.

This meant that typically there was relatively little change in either the customer or the product base after the buyout. Marketing strategy was overwhelmingly geared to existing customers and basic production technology remained unchanged. Only in the case of Jacoa was the company successful in expanding its retailing base substantially after the buyout; although the general strategic direction had been set some years earlier. (Also, while the major investment in EPOS was, from the standpoint of the industry, innovative, this did not involve a change in the fundamentals of the business.)

External control

In the other case where management attempted to do something radically different post-buyout, the change ended in disaster as results failed to materialise as quickly as planned. The institutional backers forced a sale to a competitor over the heads of the incumbent management. It is worth revisiting briefly the experience of John Collier, as it highlights the role of the institutional investors and the risk of attempting fundamental strategic redirection after a MBO. For while the management must take most of the blame for the failure, the capital structure and the role of the outside shareholders exacerbated the situation.

John Collier's demise was due to its failure to implement successfully a strategy aimed at changing its market position. It embarked on a radically different marketing strategy which involved significant investment targeted at a *new* customer segment. The strategy may have been the wrong one; or all strategies may have failed because Collier's market position was too weak for it to catch up. The strategy may have been the right one for the long run but the wrong one to serve Collier's institutional shareholders in the short term. The buyout members themselves disagree as to which of these three explanations best accounts for what happened.

There were a number of positive factors encouraging the change process. The stymying effects of the former autocratic corporate control had been removed; the investment denied for so long had been allowed; new skills had been introduced onto the board; good advice had been sought; managerial motivation to succeed was never higher; the external environment was no more hostile than usual; and the need for change had been clearly perceived. Yet despite these good intentions and a favourable context, the change process either did not progress quickly enough nor was it sufficiently radical to transform trading prospects. Why?

First, the team did not fully appreciate the difficulty of turning the business around or the need to show fairly quickly, some hard evidence of recovery in financial performance. Possibly the euphoria of succeeding in the buyout negotiations and their advocacy of the new marketing strategy led them to be overly optimistic. They succumbed to the belief that by seeking specialist advice or following a lead set by successful competitors, success would be ensured. It is the case in all service businesses that servicing a new customer segment is a major diversification that increases strategic risk.

Second, they did not critically assess their own part in the company's downfall, partly because the corporate centre had been too easy a scapegoat. The team lacked the merchandising and retailing skills needed to push through the new strategy and reassure the institutions that, despite initial hiccoughs, exciting positive changes were underway. (Their competitors, by contrast, achieved a turn-around through bringing on board outsiders with widely admired retailing flair.)

Third, they allowed internal conflict to degenerate into rivalry when problems appeared. Rather than creating a shared mutual interest overriding sectional interests, ownership exacerbated conflict. The three founding members each had the same equity stake. This was allied to different roles taken in the setting up of the MBO which undermined strong leadership, blurred individual competencies and encouraged an offensive/defensive ambience rather than a collective, consensual one. The board of Collier seemed to under-estimate the impact that the forced resignation of the financial director would have on the institutional shareholders, especially if his warn-ings of impending trading disaster came to pass (as they in fact did).

But whatever the problems that the buyout team experienced in their endeavour to restore Collier to its former level of commercial success, some of the responsibility must attach to the capital structure and to the attitudes of the financial institutions. The need to reduce the gearing quickly meant that the team did not have adequate time to pilot test their marketing changes to assess whether they had the trading formula right. It also meant that an improvement in trading performance had to happen virtually overnight, something which none of Collier's competitors had managed to achieve. Also, by funding the investment programme out of the sale and leaseback programme, the strategic redirection of the company cut into the strong asset backing, thereby reducing free cash flow and effectively increasing rather than reducing leverage on the remaining assets.

As for the institutional shareholders, they sought to extricate themselves in the easiest way when things did not go as well as planned. They had too short a time horizon for seeing a return on their investment and were not prepared to allow management the additional time needed to test the long-term viability of the new strategy. The position of the Midland Bank, as the owner of many of the properties that were sold by and then leased back to Collier, gave them an additional reason apart from their shareholding for selling out to Burton. Their properties would become more valuable if leased to the market leader.

Arguably, a more positive approach would have contributed much to the buyout's chances of success as an independent entity. One drawback of the ownership structure of buyouts is that in exchanging control by a parent company for (ultimate) control by a financial institution, the irksome tyranny of an over-domineering parent may well be exchanged for an equally irksome opportunism of an institu-tional shareholder.

The story of John Collier highlights many of the difficulties which buyouts may experience in implementing revenue enhancement strategies. The high gearing, the need to meet targets which have been set to please potential backers, and problems of tight (and divergent as between different stakeholder) time profiles, are perhaps more suited to operating improvement or cost reduction strategies. The most brilliant strategy is worse than useless if it can't be implemented. The failure of John Collier's strategy may have had as much to do with its ownership and capital structure constraining implementation as with its intrinsic merit. However, it should be borne in mind that a high debt load may prevent a company from pursuing a flawed strategy.

Another example of high leverage undermining management's ability to withstand the pressure of a set back is given by the case of March Concrete. The company introduced a new production technology in response to pressure from customers for better quality product. Teething problems with the new technology, allied to a cyclical downturn in demand, put cash flow under pressure and, as with John Collier, there was a forced sellout to a competitor.

A similar train of events was averted at two MBOs which became involved in new product development but pulled out as soon as this looked like becoming a serious short-term cash drain. In both cases much had already been done to improve productivity and reduce costs, so the consequences were not overly damaging. The only exception where a developmental strategy was not threatened by a downturn in performance was Trend Control. And as all the players there suggest, Trend was not a typical MBO in that the financial backers were prepared to regard the long-term debt as development rather than bridging finance.

Finally, a number of the buyouts wanted to make acquisitions in order to strengthen their market position. Yet as the following comment from the CEO of Jacoa indicates, while the capital structure did not constrain this, the time span in which the institutional backers wanted to realise something of their gain mitigated against acquisition:

We managed to reduce our gearing very quickly. This was mainly through a very tight dividend policy and profitable trading – not through asset sales and sale and leaseback. Yet it was essential to grow the business through a sizeable acquisition. The main obstacle, however, was the attitude of the institutional backers. They weren't very keen on us diversifying because of the risks involved and because they didn't want to jeopardise the spectacular capital appreciation they had obtained on their investment in us. Nor did they want to lock in their investment for the time required to apply our turnaround recipe to another company. Their caution meant we had to adopt excessively strict criteria towards potential acquisitions. Their caution also had a psychological knock-on effect on the other members of my team. The Banks would say, Do you realise that you are risking your own millions in going for a takeover?

In the event, this company, which was very successful, was itself taken over by a competitor. The CEO attributed this in large measure to his inability to find a suitable takeover target. The same was true in the other buyouts. Notwithstanding much senior management attention to potential acquisitions, none of the companies investigated were successful in completing sizeable acquisitions while they were a MBO. The experience of the MBOs we have looked at suggest a number of general lessons concerning leverage and post-buyout strategy.

First, one of the strong lessons learned from buyout experience on both sides of the Atlantic is the need for clear agreement between owners and investors as to strategic business plans. It is only through this process that investors can value the business. It is only through this step that two of the major opportunities of the buyout process can be effectively realised: the focused nature of the goal setting, and the harmonisation of investor and owner/manager goals around increasing shareholder value (and how and when to measure the achievement of these goals). A third lesson is that building growth of market share into sales projections as a planned source of cash to service high debt loads is very risky. Morgan Stanley, for example, states that in their buyouts they seek neither turnaround situations nor companies that *might* achieve technological breakthroughs. For them, the key is 'strong market shares in stable industries'. One of their directors states: 'we need to improve operating performance because we can't guarantee a rescue from a rising stock market' (*Business Week*, 20 June 1988, p. 122).

Lastly, it is well to remember that debt providers look for security to the underlying (and therefore alternative use of) assets. The value of the assets in Collier was a function of the use to which management were able to put them. If a banker loses confidence in management, this changes the perceived security value of the assets. It is then that 'alternative use' becomes an issue for the lender. Confidence in management is maintained if agreed performance plans are, or look about to be achieved and if the financial and business risks appear balanced. Alternatively, the debt holders in the financial structure of the buyout can (for riskier propositions) be compensated by a higher fixed return. A managing director at Salomon Brothers observed: 'People tend to see equity as a warm, fuzzy pillow and debt as a knife in the back. But if you are paying me an extra three percentage points for the high-yield debt, I'm willing to be understanding if you get into trouble and I think you have a chance to pull through. We can negotiate new terms until the slump is over. I'm not doing it gratuitously, but because of the extra interest' (*Fortune*, 2 January 1989, p. 49).

Either way, the essential business risk of the strategic plans for the buyout company must be jointly agreed at the time of the buyout itself and the appropriate instruments and rates applied. Our sense is that in both Collier and March this didn't happen. In the end, it meant refinancing via takeover for both of them. This was in contrast to Trend Control where either the inherent business risk was better evaluated or more flexible instruments or attitudes applied. In all these takeover cases, it is worth noting that the MBO was not a failure as such; but the initial financial vehicle was. The comments of SEC Commissioner, Joseph Grundfest, are pertinent: 'Bankrupt LBOs are not fire-bombed. Their productive capacity does not disappear from the economy. They continue to do business, often with operating profits, as their capital structures are renegotiated.' For example, in the US Revco case (the largest MBO to go bankrupt thus far) not one store has yet been closed nor one employee fired (*Fortune*, 2 January 1989).

Finally, the failure by MBOs successfully to implement their preferred growth strategies does not imply leverage encourages firms to eat up their physical capital and sacrifice market share in favour of short-term gains. Rather it stresses that in high-leverage circumstances, the primary objective is improving efficiency while maintaining or marginally improving market position into the future. Once efficiency is achieved, by a combination of one-off changes in operating procedures plus improvements in process technology, and leverage reduced, then the next phase of revenue enhancement or market development can be embarked upon. This may require or coincide with a different ownership structure to that of the MBO. But that is not a function of high leverage per se but of capital structure in conjunction with the ownership structure which it reflects.

Corporate versus institutional control

It is also important to point out that while the highly leveraged capital structure and the attitudes of the financial backers may have limited strategic redefinition or innovation in the MBOs we investigated, the constraints were not considered nearly so onerous as what was seen to be the tight-fisted approach of corporate parents. A number of factors help explain this perception. The institutions left the buyout teams alone unless things started going seriously wrong. Then they pulled out quickly rather than nurture antagonism from the owner-managers. Second, the strategic direction of the buyout over the first few years was discussed and agreed at the time of the buyout. Thus the formula adopted was not felt to have been imposed by outsiders. Third, growing the business by introducing new products or by diversification, was, with the exception of John Collier, seen by owner-managers as secondary to putting the existing business on a better footing by better implementation of existing strategies. Fourth, even though increased debt payments were generally more onerous than the previous corporate charges, the former were seen as legitimate whereas the latter had been resented because they did not represent good value for money. Finally, as the Trend Control story attests, the institutional shareholders don't always pull out at the first sign of trouble.

3   LIFE CYCLE OF MBOs

Stock market flotation/takeover

In terms of the MBO life cycle, the ownership and capital structure leads to a cycle which is energy-creating, disciplined and invariably relatively short. It is energy-creating because of the euphoria of succeeding in the buyout, because of the improvements in corporate culture and individual motivation, and because of the potential capital gains if the MBO is successful. It is disciplined because, as we have seen, the high leverage and the rights and attitudes of institutional backers do not generally allow much leeway in the timely achievement of corporate objectives. It is short because various pressures quickly build up for a further structural transformation. On the basis of what we have observed, the MBO appears to be essentially a transitional state suited to recovery in shareholder value but not to long-term strategic redirection or significant growth. Stock market flotation or takeover, and in one case both, signaled the limitations of the MBO as an enduring organisation structure.

As far as flotation is concerned, the key push comes from institutional shareholders wanting to realise their capital gains and exit in search of future, high-return (40–100 per cent) investments. Principal shareholders in buyouts are effectively locked into their stake, unless there is a public flotation or a well-developed internal market for transferring shares. Even company Y, which had developed significant employee share ownership and a well-developed internal market for buying and selling shares, went public in the end. A third-party sale may be as profitable as, or more profitable than flotation but management do not favour the former, except as a last resort. (A possible exception was Trend Control.) Apart from institutional shareholders, owner-managers may themselves favour a flotation. They may want to reduce personal indebtedness taken on at the time of a buyout to fund personal equity stakes; introduce employee stock option schemes; raise more equity capital in order to fund investment or acquisitions. There is also a more subtle reason. Owner-managers may want the kudos of going through a process which signals their arrival or coming of age: 'We were concerned about the credibility of the company; it was important that we moved from the management buyout thing where everyone patted us on the head and said well done, to a higher profile' (Metsec executive).

One CEO (Jacoa) wanted his company to remain a private company because he considered that 'it would be more difficult if listed to make the essential sacrifices of short-term earnings in favour of future growth as are involved in the development phase of a company's life cycle'. Yet he was eventually 'forced' by the other principal shareholders to sell out to a publicly quoted competitor.

Interestingly, of the eight MBOs, only two (Metsec and company X) retained their independence either on the stock market or off it five years after a buyout. All the rest were taken over by other companies; in all but one case, competitors.

Shareholder value

Organisation futures
The final issue which needs to be addressed in terms of the MBO life cycle concerns economic performance. According to the received wisdom (proposition 13, Chapter 8) '(on average) the value of the firm will rise as a result of a MBO'. This is primarily due to the incentive of personal ownership reducing inefficiencies of management or agency costs.

Six of the MBOs experienced a significant increase, and none experienced a decline, in shareholder value during the period of the buyout. This was despite the fact that three companies suffered trading problems and a deterioration in financial performance (return on investment (ROI) and return on sales (ROS)), post-buyout (see Figure 9.1) In the five MBOs which improved financial performance, a significant appreciation in shareholder value was achieved. Some initial fillip to ROI was achieved in most cases through assets being sold or written down, or inventory being bought at a substantial discount and then not renewed. This was not nearly as significant, however, as an underlying improvement in the unit cost structure and in sales revenues.

We have already examined many of the internal organisational factors such as culture, motivation, decision-making, corporate procedures and so on which led to increased profits in the MBOs we looked at. We have also looked at the impact of the high leverage which has the effect of multiplying up the returns to shareholders for any level of profit. There is another factor that needs to be considered: the external economic climate which also affects both the value and the performance of the firm.

Recession

All our MBOs came to life during a recessionary period in the UK. Such conditions favour MBOs in a number of ways. First, by putting companies under pressure, recession encourages divestment, the main route through which UK MBOs emerge. Second, by depressing PE ratios, recession puts management in a better position to be able to afford to purchase their company, especially as they have to rely on debt which sets an upper limit to the price at which the deal is financeable. When the stock market is booming, incumbent management is at a disadvantage relative to third-party buyers because the latter can use their own inflated paper or balance sheet strength, or presumed synergies, to finance acquisitions. Third, the recessionary conditions and the general unemployment that it creates, foster a greater willingness among the workforce to accept change. 'A factor promoting receptivity to change was that only those members of the workforce who were the most productive, or who were willing to accept new practices, were taken through the buyout. There was a real sense of being one of the chosen few who had been kept on to see the company restored to its former glory. The result was much improved industrial relations, and a more relaxed and free dialogue between management and staff'.

Rising stock market

Some of the rise in shareholder value achieved by our MBOs was due to the changing nature of the market for companies and the rise in the stock market between the time they were bought out (1980/1/2) and the time they were sold (1985/6/7). The rise in the stock market increased PE ratios for MBOs, facilitated flotation of new issues, and encouraged a wave of acquisition activity. The fact that some of the MBOs experienced a deterioration in trading performance and conditions at the same time as an increase in value when sold out attests to the importance of these changes.

While commentators often point to asymetric information as the reason why incumbent management obtain their companies at a discount to net assets, the state of the market is an important influence. For example, in the case of both John Collier and to a lesser extent Stone International, a rise in property values led to revaluation surpluses even though the relevant assets had been professionally valued prior to the buyout. In the case of Metsec, the reverse process benefited the company. Metsec's management bought the company at a discount to net assets, largely because they were expecting to have to find and move to new premises within a couple of years. In the event, depressed property prices locally led the site owners (TI group) to sell to Metsec rather than develop the whole site. Thus Metsec were saved the expense and trouble of moving and obtained a discount in the bargain.

The massive gains in shareholder wealth experienced by some of our MBOs had little or nothing to do with insider information or management manipulating the value of the company in order to buy it cheaply. The fact that many owner-managers were made millionaires in a few short years is a function of the high leverage, management's faith in the business, management's relative freedom to manage the business as it sees fit, better asset utilisation, and a revaluation of assets associated with improved market conditions. Together these factors account for the rise in the value of the firm. Our study thus confirms the rise in value of the firm suggested by Adam Smith and agency theory although the process is far more complex than just the dynamics of 'personal self-interest'.

In terms of our MBO process model given on page 180, we have found that:

1. *Corporate behaviour pre-Buyout*
a. Shareholder value creation was substantially less for the pre-buyout business units than the post-buyout MBOs.

b. The managerial inefficiencies of large corporate holding companies helped to destroy shareholder value.
c. The pre-buyout political and social practices of those corporate managements described to us seemed excessive in their creation of frustration and antagonism at the subsidiary management level.
d. The energy released by the new MBO structure and its felt freedoms were extremely strong – not only in sustaining managers through the buyout process but also in driving managers to prove their managerial effectiveness.

2. *The MBO occasion*
a. The scale of corporate managerial dysfunctions in the situations we studied created the potential for large value increases and, therefore, enabled the buyout to be 'non-traditionally' financed.
b. The size of the potential increase in shareholder value appeared to account for a large part of the differences in asset valuation as perceived by corporate and subsidiary management.

3. *Enabling factors*
a. The control effects (autonomy) of ownerships were significant and consistent. While many factors contributed to increased performance, managers themselves attributed much of the power of the buyout to their new freedom. Less emphasis was placed on the incentive effect of potential wealth increases.
b. Privatisation, in the minds of managers, enabled a 'business needs' focus but did not appear to enhance it.

4. *Behavioural and cultural processes*
a. Large debt and the servicing of it was a clear and consistent disciplinarian for a cash and balance sheet focus on the part of buyout managers. When it wasn't, there were failures.
b. A cash and balance sheet focus also became part of the cultural values at levels of management *within* the firm.
c. New, improved social relationships and shared understandings were consistently and positively reported by managers. Also reported was a greater adaptation of systems and procedures to the true needs of the business. Identification with the business, hard work and feelings of responsibility were widely reported.
d. The alignment of owners and investors aims was mixed in our buyouts. But where there were clear, mutual understandings, the buyouts functioned best. What we can say, therefore, is that the

buyout provides an opportunity for more clearly matching business and financial risk to increase shareholder value.

The MBO transformation in Figure 9.2 captures much of the above. What we heard about and observed were significant social, cultural and behavioural changes which were described as positively associated with success in increasing shareholder value. While not wishing to underplay the role of fear or debt, or changes in market circumstances we think the core of the performance change is from this 'soft side' of the organisation. The MBO, in the achievement of its high energy culture, is not unlike results reported from a number of empirical studies of 'high involvement' or 'high commitment' organisations (see Lawler, 1978). The ultimate performance power of the structural changes are derived from the focus and quality of human energy released in new structures.

While these conclusions have been derived from the particular circumstances of the MBOs we investigated, we believe they have broader relevance to business processes in the UK.

4 THE WIDER IMPLICATIONS

It has been our intention through describing a succession of organisational stories to, in the words of Braudel (1986), 'try to classify, order and reduce this disparate material to the bold outlines and simplifications' of some model about the process of change in MBOs. From this, it remains to draw out the wider implications of what we have witnessed for other organisations for public policy and for the future.

But first let us deal with the limitations of so doing. We observed companies bought out because the parent companies could not make the business work to their satisfaction. Therefore these businesses are hardly 'typical'; their success and failures post-MBO speak in the first instance to that subset of (large multibusiness) companies that divest subsidiaries, either through strategic or forced circumstances. Neither are the managements of MBOs likely to be 'typical'; their revealed preference for a business life outside the confines of a large corporate structure may mark them off from 'typical' corporate executives. Finally, our sample of MBOs was highly selective, although our findings are consistent with (and expand) the findings of more broadly based studies of MBOs/LBOs in Europe and the US.

Despite these specific limitations, and the hazards of moving from the particular to the general, we believe that any study of one type of

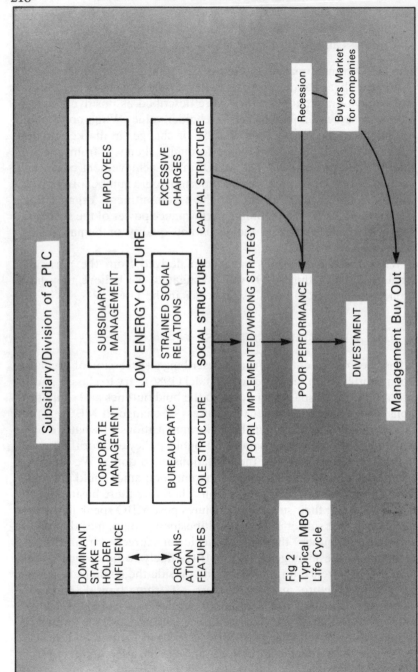

Subsidiary/Division of a PLC

LOW ENERGY CULTURE

DOMINANT STAKE-HOLDER INFLUENCE	CORPORATE MANAGEMENT	SUBSIDIARY MANAGEMENT	EMPLOYEES
ORGANIS-ATION FEATURES	BUREAUCRATIC	STRAINED SOCIAL RELATIONS	EXCESSIVE CHARGES
	ROLE STRUCTURE	SOCIAL STRUCTURE	CAPITAL STRUCTURE

POORLY IMPLEMENTED/WRONG STRATEGY → POOR PERFORMANCE → DIVESTMENT

Recession

Buyers Market for companies

Management Buy Out

Fig 2
Typical MBO
Life Cycle

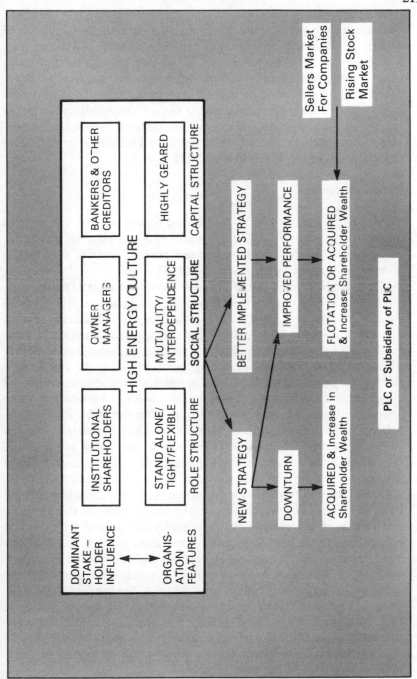

Figure 9.2 Corporate Transformation

business enterprise has the potential to help us to understand all others. Nevertheless, in seeking general lessons from MBOs, we take it as read that our comments refer in the first instance to companies experiencing the same sorts of organisational malaise as those described by the owner-managers and corporate executives whom we interviewed. How widespread this is we can only conjecture. From our own experience and the findings of numerous studies on corporate failure, we believe our study has broad relevance to corporate organisations in the UK and elsewhere.

Corporate control

There are general lessons to be learned concerning the way control ought to be exercised within organisations. It is possible that other organisations might benefit from the positive aspects of a MBO without necessarily going down the MBO route.

The experience of many of our MBOs prior to their nascence is an indictment of the ways some corporate headquarters management exercise control over their subsidiaries. One of the recurring themes that crops up again and again in the various cases presented in this book is the autocratic, frequently patronising attitude taken by senior managers towards subsidiary management, at least in the eyes of subsidiary managers. Another is the way outmoded procedures designed either for other purposes or geared to the needs of a corporate whole were forced on subsidiaries with little regard for their relevance, appropriateness or demotivating consequences. The 'deadweight hand of corporate control' is a serious indictment of the failure of those UK organisations to adjust, in their managerial practices and scale, to the competitive business market place of the late twentieth century.

One of the justifications for corporate control of subsidiaries is the broader perspective which the centre can bestow on the strategic orientation of the subsidiary. Another is the potential for greater efficiency in terms of making advice, specialist services, R&D know-how, cheaper borrowings, asset backing and group-wide synergies, available to subsidiary management at a much lower cost than the latter would sustain if they had to go it alone. Yet the positive aspects of such a potentially supportive relationship were mostly absent in the cases we have looked at. Rather the relationship between subsidiary and corporate centre prior to a MBO was generally antagonistic rather than nurturing, demotivating rather than motivating, and wasteful rather than efficient.

The outcomes for some of the MBOs investigated suggest that in cases where there was disagreement about the strategic direction of the subsidiary, corporate headquarters management were not necessarily wrong in their appraisal of what their subsidiaries ought to be doing. But while the content might have been right, the process they used was wrong. They certainly did very little to bring about an environment of trust or consensus or, at the very least, of understanding which might have allowed the subsidiary management to apply themselves with the same vigour that they displayed after the MBO. While it may be inevitable that corporate control entails some agency costs dictated by the need to ensure that subsidiary managers don't follow personal goals at the expense of maximising shareholder wealth, these agency costs were far higher than need have been the case. The failure to listen to subsidiary managers, to regard them as colleagues rather than underlings, to allow them to develop appropriate procedures which still allowed corporate control, and to support them to be more effective, negated the positive contribution that headquarters management might have made.

For their part, subsidiary managers were on occasion too quick to discount the advice from their corporate masters and to recognise their own weaknesses. Perhaps they also over-estimated the positive consequences that would emerge from their forceful aspirations, and discounted the harsh realities of the market place. The road to hell is paved with good intentions, and there is more to business success than an improved corporate culture and more motivated senior management.

This raises the whole question of the time dimension of strategy. From a theoretical standpoint both shareholder value analysis and other financial economic perspectives are deficient in arguments for shareholder wealth if they ignore competitive advantage over time. There are innumerable, but short term, ways of maximising shareholder wealth. Ultimately, however, shareholder value can only be obtained by creating sustainable competitive advantage in the market place. We have argued that our MBOs generally had a strategic perspective and were not simply short term, cash flow maximizers; that they looked toward the future and invested in it. Yet the robustness and clarity of the relatively short term objective and the forceful discipline of debt accompanying it must provide the lens through which the future is visualised by the MBO managements. The very fact of the relatively short life cycle of MBOs attest both to this central dilemma and the resolution of it.

Policy observations

Positive learning
In the five-year period covering our research the accumulated experience of MBO/LBOs has risen dramatically. The growth in successful buyouts (plus the growth of funds for MBO/LBOs) has generated:

1. More competitive pricing, more participants from wider sources (companies, pension funds, insurance companies, etc.) and a more responsive and experienced marketplace for this type of deal.
2. Larger deals and more deals.
3. A wider spread of industries involved.

When MBO/LBO financing is added to other asset restructuring and hostile takeovers, the total market is huge and growing worldwide. We expect many adjustments in both instruments and pricing arrangements. Financial techniques will get both better and keener. One negative result could be a bidding up of prices at which LBO/MBOs are negotiated such that debt servicing becomes extremely sensitive to interest rate rises and market changes. Also, bondholder lawsuits or a recession could sideline the movement. Assuming all the above, we still believe there is substantial growth ahead. In our view, there simply has not been the requisite variety and depth of adjustment in US and UK corporate managements to forestall corporate restructuring through MBO/LBOs. There is too much unrelated diversification, too many unsuccessful (or unsuccessfully integrated) acquisitions: there is widespread inability to manage *across* business units. And there is inadequate exploitation of motivational and cultural opportunities to unleash energy on productive performance. One way to regard the success of the MBO/LBO movement is as a social exercise in debureaucratisation. The UK holding company – in form and style – seems alarmingly Victorian in its pace of evolution. It is likely that in the decade ahead, new forms of corporate governance will be unleashed by the LBO/MBO movement.

Financial markets and public policy

The political reaction to MBO/LBOs is yet to come from the financially gored oxen. But one thing seems certain. The non-traditional use of large amounts of debt have surfaced the tax inequality of equity and debt. It seems to us that the current bias against dividends or returning cash to shareholders is counterproductive. It encourages, through double taxation, keeping cash within the company which, empirical evidence shows, is not spent wisely. Equity and the bearing of risk need to be made more attractive for internationally productive economies.

Shareholder value

More large, public corporations must move away from accounting numbers management to strategically focused shareholder value planning. The techniques are available with only tax issues and central functional staffs standing in the way. Executive compensation ought to become more pinned to shareholder value creation and a larger proportion of executive reward made available upon its achievement. This is the closest surrogate to ownership we have. But without it as our case studies show; the 'lock-in' effect plus vigilance over one's own money is the best answer. Perhaps more managers should be real owners as it is they who are ultimately at risk and who create value. But a rebalancing is only possible if managers actually are allowed, stimulated and encouraged to create value.

US LBO v. UK MBO

We prefer the UK model for three reasons:

1. An unseemly combination of immediate ego and greed seem to dominate Wall Street, while 'the city' in the UK appears more conservative, if not equally impatient and arrogant.
2. The UK deals are smaller, less 'hostile' and result in managers actually becoming owners as opposed to institutional servants.
3. All our research shows that in UK MBOs there is a significant increase of 'buy-in' and commitment from the real ownership involved.

One problem, however, is the inherent thinness of the UK equity and 'new venture' market compared to the US. Already US houses (eg Bankers Trust) have come to dominate many of the large UK deals as they provide the full financing 'in-house' – an attractive advantage in a market where confidentiality and timing count for so much.

Longer-term consequences

The strategic and external control consequences of high leverage need to be reconsidered. MBOs and *a fortiori* their American cousin the LBO, have changed the context in which both financial institutions and companies operate. MBOs have inaugurated a new era of debt financing and have fundamentally changed the ways companies will have to manage their financial assets in the future to maximise shareholder wealth. High leverage is indeed risky, but not, it would appear, as much as people previously thought. Nor perhaps as risky as failing to make use of unused borrowing capacity. Even if the ownership-as-incentive consequences of MBOs are discounted as anything but an intriguing aberration peculiar to a particular point in history, the broader financial implications of MBOs will live on. The issue of the power of the MBO experience has been clouded by the rise and lull, if not fall, of the 'junk' financing which evolved to grow the size of MBO deals. Many, if not most of the recent MBO deals seem driven more by financial engineers than by managers; and it shows. The magic which we believe exists in MBOs is primarily a managerial and behavioural phenomenon supported by finance; not financial sorcery manipulating managers and management. Yet we acknowledge the fact that the market for junk and the threat of raids has changed complacent management thinking in public corporations.

This leaves still, then, in a post-LBO/MBO, post-junk business world the problem we started with: namely, that business can be run for the benefits of its managers and that their interests can be dissimilar to those of shareholders in the company; and vice-versa. A recent spate of popular books (*Liars Poker*, Michael Lewis, Norton, N.Y. 1989; *Barbarians at the Gate*, Burrough and Helyar, J. Cope, London 1990) give shocking, live testimony to the problem and the exploitation of it by both financiers and managers. So there will continue to be future tilts at entrenched managers who are underperforming financially for their investors – proxy fights; the removal and replacement of blocking directors; more activism by institutional shareholders on management compensation schemes. All of this is part of the continuing evolution of the public corporation and its central owner/manager/investor dilemma.

We believe that our MBO learning sheds light on these conflicts which testify to the fact that interests can be better harmonised by new organisational and financial structures. As the securities firms lose pre-eminence in financial markets and yield to the increased power of commercial banks (who are becoming more like "universal banks") the ground may be being set for a better alignment of owner/ investor/manager goals. We believe that LBO/MBOs will increasingly return to being done by sponsors who pay down debt and improve operations rather than by financial firms who sell assets to pay interest or do deals solely to earn fees. LBO/MBOs will revive; particularly if the stockmarket declines, lowering P/E ratios and exposing underperforming companies. Global competiveness and industry consolidation will drive an emphasis on core businesses and "de-diversification'. This is the context in which LBO/MBOs are likely to flourish.

In the end, there is good magic, we believe, in MBOs. This derives from the powerful combination of:

1. The disciplinary effect of higher debt;
2. The alignment of owners' and managers' objectives;
3. The operational impact of clear, shared objectives;
4. The motive drive of ownership incentives;
5. The pulling power of true teamwork and social relationships, built on a clear mutuality of interest;
6. Enhanced managerial freedom and responsibility creating positive energy towards taking whole rather than partial decisions;
7. The transparency of skills and efforts in achieving success or failure;
8. Clear feedback and reward systems reinforcing efforts and achievement;
9. The liberating of commitment and vigilance through goal-sharing that is focused in time.

These facets and fundamentals of MBOs have been independently and generally known to teachers and practitioners of management for some time. Rarely have they been seen in such high impact and practical combination as in MBOs. Perhaps not powerful enough to overcome all eventualities, but sufficient to give managements some distinctive advantages in their attempts to make their businesses a success. Some of this magic must inevitably rub off on other types of organisation and other types of corporate governance and control. Even if the corporate scene eventually transforms MBOs into just another financial mechanism for facilitating the transfer of organisational resources between different owners, or for increasing shareholder gain; the MBO phenomenon has already planted an indelible flag for a new kind of 'entrepreneur'. The managerial learning from MBOs creates hope that *any* organisation could benefit from some of the same magic.

Bibliography

Alchian, A. A. and Demsetz, H. (1972) 'Production, information costs, and economic organisation', *American Economic Review*, LXII, 5: 777–95.

Amihud, Y. (1989) *Leveraged Management Buy Outs: causes and consequences* (Dow, Jones & Irwin).

Barton, S. and Gordon, P. (1987) 'Corporate strategy: useful perspectives for the study of capital structure', *Academy of Management Review*, vol. 12, no. 1, 67–75.

Baumol, W. J. (1959) *Business Behaviour, Value and Growth* (Macmillan).

Bettis, W. (1983) *Academy of Management Review*, vol. 8, no. 3.

Berle, A. A. Jr and Means, G. C. (1932) *The Modern Corporation and Private Property* (Macmillan).

Blair, R. D. and Kaserman, D. L. (1983) 'Ownership and control of the modern corporation – antitrust implications', *Journal of Business Research*, vol. 11: 333–43.

Braudel, F. (1986) *Perspective of the World*, vol. 3 of *Civilization and Capitalism, Fifteenth Century to Eighteenth Century* (Collins).

Burrell, G. and Morgan, G. (1979) *Sociological Paradigms and Organisational Analysis* (London, Heinemann).

Burrough, B. and Helyar, J. (1989) *Barbarians at the Gate* (Cape).

Cable, J. R. (1984) *Capital Market Information and Industrial Performance.* (EARIE Conference, Fontainebleau).

Channon, D. (1973) *The Strategy and Structure of British Enterprise* (Macmillan).

Child, J. (1974) 'Managerial and organisational factors associated with company performance', *Journal of Management Studies*.

Clutterbuck, D. and Devine, M. (1987) *Management Buyouts: success and failure away from the corporate apron strings* (Hutchinson).

Coase, R. H. (1937) 'The nature of the firm', *Economica*, new series, IV: 386–405. Reprinted in *Readings in Price Theory* (Irwin) 331–51.

Coyne, J. and Wright, M. (1986) Divestment and strategic change' *Lloyds Bank Review*, October 1982.

Cubbin, J. and Leech, D. (1983) 'The effect of shareholder dispersion on the degree of control in British companies: theory and measurement', *Economic Journal*, 93: 351–69.

Cuthbert, N. H. and Dobbins, R. (1980) 'Industrial democracy, economic democracy and ownership of British industry: scenarios for the 1980s, *International Journal of Social Economics*, 7: 5, 286–95.

Cyert, R. M. and March, J. G. (1963) *A Behavioural Theory of the Firm.* (Prentice-Hall).

Demsetz, H. (1983) 'The structure of ownership and the theory of the firm', *Journal of Law and Economics*, vol. XXVI (2).

Drucker, P. (1946) *Concept of the Corporation* (John Day).

Eisenhardt, K. (1989) 'Agency theory: an assessment and review', *Academy of Management Review*, 14: 57–74.

227

Etzioni, A. (1988) *The Moral Dimension: towards a new economics* (Collier-Macmillan).

Euromoney Seminar Transcripts (1987) *Management Buy-Outs*.

Fama, E. (1937) 'Agency problems and the theory of the firm', *Journal of Political Economy*, 88; no. 2, 288–307.

Fruhan, W. (1979) *Financial Strategy* (Richard D. Irwin).

Geertz, C. (1973) *The Interpretation of Cultures* (Basic Books).

Gouillart, F. and Wortzel, L. (1987) *Relatedness* (The MAC Group).

Green, S. and Willman, P. (1987) *The incidence of qualitative and quantitative research: a framework for classification*, Paper to the Academy of Management Conference, August 1987.

Hanney, J. (1986) 'The management buy-out – an offer you can't refuse', *Omega*, 14.

Hill, C. and Snell, S. (1989) 'Effects of ownership structure and control on corporate productivity', *Academy of Management Journal*, 32: 25–46.

Hobbs, R. (1986) 'The role of leverage', *Financial Times Mergers and Acquisitions*, XVI–XVII, April.

Jensen, M. and Meckling, W. (1976) 'Theory of the firm: managerial behaviour agency costs and ownership structure', *Journal of Finance and Economics*, 3: 305–60.

Jensen, M. (1986) 'Agency costs of free cash flow, corporate finance and takeovers', *American Economic Review*, Papers and Proceedings. vol. 76, no. 2: 323–9.

Jensen, M. and Warner, J. (1980) 'The distribution of power among corporate managers, shareholders, and directions', *Journal of Financial Economics*, 20: 3–24.

Jensen, M. C. (1989) 'Eclipse of the public corporation. *Harvard Business Review*: Sept–Oct, 61–74.

Jick, T. (1979) 'Mixing qualitative and quantitative methods: triangulation in action', *Administrative Science Quarterly*, 24: 602–10.

Kamerschen, D. (1968) 'The influence of ownership and control on profit rates', *American Economic Review*. 58: 437–77.

Kaplan, S. (1988) *Management Buyouts: efficiency gains or value transfers?* mimeo, University of Chicago, October.

Kensinger, J. and Martin, J. (1988) 'The quiet restructuring', *Journal of Applied Corporation Finance*, 1: 16–25.

Larner, R. J. (1970) *Management Control and the Large Organisation* (Dunellen).

Lawler, E. E. (1980) *High Involvement Management* (Jossey-Bass).

Lee, J. (1989) *Ireland: 1912–1985* (Cambridge University Press).

Lewis, M. (1989) *Liars poker* (Norton).

Lowenstein, L. (1986) 'No more cozy management buy outs', *Harvard Business Review*, Jan–Feb 147–56.

Margotta, D. (1989) 'The separation of ownership and responsibility in the modern corporation', *Business Horizons*, Feb, 32:1

Marris, R. (1964) *The Economic Theory of Managerial Capitalisation* (Free Press).

Miles, M. B. (1979) 'Qualitative data as an attractive nuisance: the problem of analysis', *Administrative Science Quarterly*, 24: 590–601.

Monsen, R. J., Chiu, J. S. and Cooley, D. E. (1968) 'The effect of separation of ownership from control on the performance of the large firm', *Quarterly Journal of Economics* 82 (3), 435–51.
Pettigrew, A. (1985) *The Awakening Giant: continuity and change in Imperial Chemicals* (Blackwell).
Porter, M. (1985) *Competitive Advantage* (Free Press).
Porter, M. (1987) 'From competitive advantage to corporate strategy', *Harvard Business Review*, May–June, 43–59.
Porter, L. W. and Lawler, E. E. (1968) *Management Attitudes and Performance* (Dorsey).
Radice, H. (1971) 'Control type, profitability and growth in large firms, *Economic Journal*, September.
Rappaport, A. (1986) *Creative Shareholder Value* (Free Press).
Rappaport, A. (1981) 'Selecting strategies that create shareholder value', *Harvard Business Review*, May–June 139–49.
Sandberg, C. and Lewellen, W. (1987). 'Financial strategy: planning and managing the corporate leverage position', *Strategic Management Journal*, 8: 15–24.
Simon, H. A. (1959) 'Theories of decision making in economics and behavioural science', *American Economic Review*, June, 253–83.
Sloan, A. (1963) *My Years at General Motors* (Doubleday).
Smith, A. (1937) *The Wealth of Nations*, Cannan edition (Modern Library).
Steer, P. and Cable, J. (1978) 'Internal organisation and profit: an empirical analysis of large UK companies', *Journal of Industrial Economics*.
Stigler, G. and Friedland, C. (1983) 'The literature of economics: the case of Berle and Means', *Journal of Law and Economics*, June 1983, 237–69.
Trostel, A. D. and Nichols, M. L. (1982) 'Privately-held and publicly-held companies: a comparison of strategic choices and management processes, *Academy of Management Journal*, March, 25: 1, 47–62.
Van Maanen, J. (1979) 'Reclaiming qualitative methods for organizational research: a preface', *Administrative Science Quarterly*, 24: 520–26.
Weber, M. (1949). *The Methodology of the Social Sciences* (Free Press).
Welch, J. B. and Pantalone, C. C. (1987) *The Magazine for Industrial Executives*, vol. 3, issue 4.
Weston, J. and Brigham, E. (1987) *Essentials of Managerial Finance* (Dryden).
Williamson, O. E. (1964) *The Economics of Discretionary Behaviour: managerial objectives in a theory of the firm* (Prentice-Hall).
Williamson, O. E. (1975) *Markets and Hierarchies: analysis and antitrust implications* (Free Press).
Wilson, H. (1980) *Report of the Committee to review the Functioning of Financial Institutions* (HMSO).
Wright, M. and Coyne, J. (1985) *Management Buy-outs in British Industry* (Croom Helm).

Index

Page numbers in *italic* denote tables or figures.